THE CONDITION, ELEVATION, EMIGRATION, AND DESTINY OF THE COLORED PEOPLE OF THE UNITED STATES *and* OFFICIAL REPORT OF THE NIGER VALLEY EXPLORING PARTY

CLASSICS IN BLACK STUDIES

THE CONDITION, ELEVATION, EMIGRATION, AND DESTINY OF THE COLORED PEOPLE OF THE UNITED STATES *and* OFFICIAL REPORT OF THE NIGER VALLEY EXPLORING PARTY

———————

Martin R. Delany

WITH AN INTRODUCTION BY

Toyin Falola

Humanity Books

an imprint of Prometheus Books
59 John Glenn Drive, Amherst, New York 14228-2197

Cover images: Courtesy of the Massachusetts Commandery of the Military Order of the Loyal Legion of the United States (MOLLUS) and the U.S. Army Military History Institute

Published 2004 by Humanity Books, an imprint of Prometheus Books

Inquiries should be addressed to
Humanity Books, 59 John Glenn Drive, Amherst, New York 14228–2197
VOICE: 716–691–0133, ext. 207; FAX: 716–564–2711
WWW.PROMETHEUSBOOKS.COM

08 07 06 05 04   5 4 3 2 1

The Condition, Elevation, Emigration, and Destiny of the Colored People of the United States originally published: Philadelphia: By the author, 1852. *Official Report of the Niger Valley Exploring Party* originally published: New York: T. Hamilton, 1861.

Cataloging-in-Publication Data on file at
the Library of Congress
ISBN 1–59102–159–6

Printed in the United States of America on acid-free paper

MARTIN ROBISON DELANY was born in Charles Town, Virginia (now West Virginia), on May 6, 1812, the son of a slave father and a free Black woman. In 1823 his father purchased the family's freedom and relocated them to Pennsylvania. Delany was educated both privately and at the Bethel Church School in Pittsburgh, and later apprenticed himself to a doctor. In 1843 he married Catherine Richards, whose family were members of the Pittsburgh Black elite. In 1850 he was admitted to Harvard Medical School for formal medical training, but eventually withdrew because White classmates protested.

Delany founded a Black weekly magazine, *Mystery* (1847–49), and then helped Frederick Douglass publish the *North Star* (1847–49). A Black abolitionist, Delany campaigned against the Fugitive Slave Act. In 1852 he advocated emigration as a new start for American Blacks, and traveled to West Africa in 1859 seeking lands for resettlement.

During the Civil War Delany recruited African Americans to serve in the Union army, and he himself served as a surgeon with the famous Fifty-fourth Massachusetts Volunteer Infantry. In 1865 he was commissioned as a major, the highest-ranking African American officer in the army. After the war, he became an official in the Freedmen's Bureau for three years; served as a customs house inspector in Charleston, South Carolina; and in 1874 was nominated for lieutenant governor of South Carolina on the Independent Republican ticket, but lost. In the late 1870s he again turned his attention to Liberian emigration.

Among his published works are *The Condition, Elevation, Emigration, and Destiny of the Colored People of the United States, Politically Considered* (1852); *Blake, or, The Huts of*

5

America (1859); *Official Report of the Niger Valley Exploring Party* (1861); and *Principia of Ethnology* (1879).

Delany moved to Xenia, Ohio, where he died on January 24, 1885.

INTRODUCTION

As a preeminent African American abolitionist, author, public intellectual, physician, the highest-ranking Black officer during the Civil War, radical nationalist, and notable activist for the emigration of Blacks to Africa, Martin Robison Delany's legacy has endured in his writings, the power of his ideas, and his political activism. If many of his contemporaries were armchair thinkers and analysts, Delany went to Africa to see things for himself. So influential was he during the nineteenth century that a number of people now refer to him as the "Father of Black Nationalism," based on his ideas on creating a powerful Black and African identity, and his goal of seeking Black emancipation and freedom through practical projects undertaken by African Americans returning to Africa, an opportunity for a new beginning within the context of political freedom and a society devoid of racism. The two books presented are *The Condition, Elevation, Emigration, and Destiny of the Colored People of the United States*, which presents Delany's separatist views, and *Official Report of the Niger Valley Exploring Party*, which provides information about selected sites in which to live in West Africa. These are two of the most important books on Black emigration written during the nineteenth century.

Martin Delany belonged to a group that created, during the nineteenth century, what is now known as the African Consciousness Movement. Together with the notable leaders of the era, Frederick Douglass, William Lloyd Garrison, and John Brown, he not only spoke about the plight of African Americans, but he sought concrete means to change their situation.[1] He coedited with Frederick Douglass the *Rochester North Star*, a popular antislavery magazine, established in 1847 and primarily devoted to Black issues. There was an eagerness to understand the self and overcome the negative consequences of slavery. Delany and his contemporaries wanted to reject negative images about Black people and solve the problems of alienation created by slavery and the enforced removal from Africa. In the first half of the nineteenth century, when Delany was growing up, protests against slavery were on the rise. In the second half of the nineteenth century, a crop of Black radical activists and intellectuals had emerged, and Delany was among them.

Delany's history was marked by shifting ideas, moments of greatness, and setbacks, not all of which are captured in the two books presented here. Delany's conversion to separatist views, the basis of his fame, also alienated his allies and others, especially those who believed in Black integration to mainstream society, in which Delany himself had previously put his faith. Frederick Douglass, a contemporary of Delany's who became more famous, remained an integrationist—starting as friends, he and Delany ultimately became opponents because of their divergent responses to the plight of Blacks in a White-dominated country. Nevertheless, Delany's idea of separation and Douglass's idea of integration survived both of them and drew admirers and critics right through the twentieth century and beyond.

Delany was born on May 6, 1812, in Charles Town (now Charleston), West Virginia, to a slave father and a free mother who, by law, made it possible for Delany to enjoy free status as well. Early in life his family moved to Chambersburg, Pennsylvania. Delany was privileged to receive a good education in Pittsburgh where he had moved in 1830 and where he lived for twenty-five years. He received private education from Molliston M. Clarke, the future editor of the *Christian Recorder*, and from the school established by the African Methodist Episcopal Church. In addition, a White doctor trained him in medicine, and by 1836 he had set himself up as a bleeder, leecher, and cupper.

His career was both varied and impressive. He began his medical practice in 1843 (also the year he married Catherine Richards, who bore seven children, each of whom was named after a famous Black person). In later years Delany entered politics and dealt in real estate. He was an officer during the Civil War, the first African American to serve as a field commander, and as a major the highest-ranking Black officer. After the war he joined the Freedmen's Bureau in South Carolina and held political office during the Reconstruction era. He wrote several pamphlets and books, including the two discussed here, a novel,[2] and antislavery essays, and he edited newspapers,[3] all mainly concerned with Black issues.[4]

His principles were clearly reflected in his books, lectures, newspaper articles, and even lifestyle. He was a man of great versatility and a gifted writer who was able to lecture on many issues and subjects. He had a burning desire to use his skill and talent to uplift the Black race not only in the United States but in Africa as well. Delany was proud of his color, his African (Mandingo) ancestry, and critical of slavery and racism. He was a strong promoter of Black self-reliance, while preaching the importance of Black civilization and history. In the 1840s he assisted escaping slaves seeking refuge and freedom. Reflecting on his lectures and lifestyle in the 1840s, Frederick Douglass regarded Delany as so passionate about Black concerns that he preached them as a doctrine, much as Whites of the time advocated the doctrine of White supremacy. The first biography of him, written by a contemporary, stressed Delany's passion for affirming his African origins, his connections with African royalty, and his pride that God created him a Black man.[5] To Douglass, Delany was "the intensest embodiment of black Nationality to be met with outside the valley of the Niger."[6]

Delany gradually grew to become one of the most famous Black leaders and thinkers of his era, not only as a physician and scientist, but also as a spokesperson and explorer. As he was growing up into adulthood, he became a staunch abolitionist—that is, an advocate for the end of the slave trade and the emancipation of all Blacks from conditions of slavery. His political involvement began with the Black community and political associations in Pittsburgh of the 1830s. He must have gained respect very quickly, as a member of moral, literary, and temperance societies; an officer of the Pittsburgh Anti-Slavery Society; and an active member of the Philanthropic Society, a highly organized fugitive slave association. By the late 1830s he had become a community leader. He played an active role in the protest movements that followed the abolition of the right of free Blacks to vote in Pennsylvania.

Delany's stature began to grow from the 1840s onward, with his involvement in debates on slavery and improving the conditions of freed slaves. During the early 1840s, he was a reformer who criticized the American Colonization Society and others who called for the emigration of Blacks to Liberia, which Delany interpreted as forcible exile. In 1843 he established the *Mystery*, a weekly newspaper published in Pittsburgh, and when it ceased publication in 1847 he joined Douglass as coeditor of the *North Star*. As an editor he traveled in the Midwest, seeking news and subscribers. His letters published in the newspaper became a popular feature, while he often gave three public lectures in a day. He experienced hardship from his travels and lectures, and escaped being lynched on one occasion. He sought an end to slavery through political action, attacking the alternative but widespread view that slavery should be brought to an end through moral persuasion. As he traveled, he began to complain more deeply about American society and to express concerns about the future and prospects of Blacks, and his radicalism became firmly established. In 1850 he was admitted to Harvard Medical School to seek further training, but he was only able to stay for a semester due in part to protest by White students against his presence. He went ahead, however, to assume the title of doctor— licensing requirements did not exist at this time—and returned to Pittsburgh to practice. But politics remained important to him, and he entered his most radical phase in the 1850s. In 1851 he visited Canada for the first time to attend the North American Convention led by Henry Bibb, a major political figure among Black emigrants. In Pittsburgh he organized a series of protests against the Fugitive Slave Act. By 1852 he had finally concluded that for Blacks to overcome their worsening conditions, they had to leave the United States.

His changed position on emigration became, to him, a defining moment, which he reflected upon in the two books presented in this volume. By 1849 he was clearly moving away from reform and from his previous ideas of

forging alliances with White reformers and moving toward
advocating greater Black self-reliance and radicalism. He
grew frustrated with many Black leaders and was angered by
the increasing implementation of the federal Fugitive Slave
Laws, which prevented the emancipation of many slaves. He
was active in the "great debate" that followed the passage of
the Fugitive Slave Act of 1850. As a leading spokesperson,
he criticized the society for its racism and various acts of
injustice toward Blacks. He called for the teaching of
African civilization and culture among African Americans
so that they could fully understand their roots and develop
a strong identity, the promotion of the ethics of hard work,
and respect for Blacks and their contributions to society.
Rather than seeking integration, Delany began to call on
Blacks to seek an alternative solution in emigration.

Separatist Views:
The Emigration Agenda and Project

Delany's book, *Condition, Elevation, Emigration, and Destiny,*
was shaped by slavery, the race politics of mid-nineteenth-
century America, and the search for solutions to the problems of Blacks, both slaves and free. To many scholars of
African American political thought, this book marks the
origin of Black nationalism in print. Published in 1852,
Condition was the first book-length study to present an
account of the economic and political status of Blacks in the
United States. The book's sources and coverage are rather
broad, as Delany drew from contemporary history, the Bible,
geography, European class structure, and current abolitionist
views to talk about a wide variety of issues relating to
Blacks. Divided into three parts by themes and subjects, the

first part is a critical analysis of the status of Blacks and how they were treated by Whites. With solid data, he reached a rather depressing conclusion about the lives of those in slavery and even struggling free Blacks. In the second part, he restored race pride by documenting the achievements of Blacks in various occupations and endeavors. In the last section, he offered as a solution emigration to Central America.

The book is now one of the most frequently cited on the early manifestations of Black nationalism, and it contains Delany's strong conversion to the idea of emigration from the United States as a solution to the problems of racism and slavery. It was written against the background of the worsening political and economic conditions for Blacks in the 1850s. It is abundantly clear from the tone and contents that Delany was frustrated and desperate for a solution. Four years after the book appeared, he temporarily migrated to Chatham (modern-day Ontario) in Canada and attended the gathering convened by John Brown, who announced the formation of a rebel army and Black state in exile. The crises of the 1850s drove him and about ten thousand others to Canada to escape possible reenslavement and the widespread harassment of Black people. As he outlined in *Condition*, emigration of Blacks outside of the United States to live or "colonize" new areas was becoming a major option.

Emigration and colonization were not new ideas, but Delany devoted both his intellectual prowess and physical energy to them and their implementation. Many African Americans of Delany's generation strongly believed that a return to Africa was the best solution to the lingering problems of slavery and race relations. As early as 1788, the Negro Union of Rhode Island had proposed that all free Blacks should undertake a mass exodus to Africa.[7] In later years, the idea of going "back to Africa" remained strong, although there were those who argued against it. In the mid-nineteenth century, the issue of emigration to Africa dominated many discussions and was on the agenda of a number of conventions. Delany took a strong stand on the issue, not just calling for emigration as some before him had done, but actually presenting in *Condition* a justification and "blueprint" for pursuing it. In *Condition* he suggested migration to Central and South America, areas close to the United States, and he mentioned in the appendix Africa as yet another possibility. After a first visit to Africa, he began to promote emigration to the Niger Valley in West Africa.

Delany and those who were persuaded by the separatist ideology of emigration had a number of reasons. To start with, it would reduce conflicts in race relations. More importantly, it would empower Blacks by allowing them to create new states that they could govern. Indeed, many anticipated a powerful Black nation that would be able to compete with others, even selling products far cheaper than those produced by American slaves. A successful and independent Black nation would uplift the entire Black race by being able to fight for the freedom of those in bondage in America, Canada, and Africa; stop the trade in slaves; and contribute to the development of the African continent. As Delany expressed in *Condition* and other lectures, emigration is about creating an autonomous Black nation; showing the capacity of Blacks to raise money, lead, and organize; inspiring the free Blacks to work for those in bondage; creating projects independent of White men; using the majority power in their new land to create a superior civilization; and obeying the will of God to work for freedom.

To be sure, not all Blacks of the era believed in the idea of emigration, and controversies about how to solve the problems of Blacks often divided them, as in the case of the publicized disagreement between the two former friends Delany and Douglass. There were Black leaders opposed to emigration who continued to urge that changes within the United States could come through reforms or revolutionary struggles. Not only did many point to the difficulties of relocation, including possible high death rates, they also believed that those who were already free should stay in America to work for the emancipation of those still in slavery, and that they were entitled to all the rights and privileges of American citizenship and free birth. Indeed, a number of other prominent leaders, such as Douglass, simply ignored Delany and his book challenging their quest for Black equality in America, but his ideas struck a chord in a Black community clearly disillusioned with living in the United States and becoming more militant.

As clearly articulated in *Condition*, Delany also believed in Black cooperation, the idea that Blacks in specific settings and across different regions must collaborate to establish economic projects, political territories, and collective actions in various ways. At a time when not all Blacks were yet free, Delany argued that those who had the privilege of freedom and education must lead the way by formulating antislavery principles and leading struggles to liberate those still in bondage. The idea of Black consciousness and Black cooperation merged in the project of emigration that Delany strongly advocated. He was very active in the emigration conferences of 1854, 1856, and 1858. It was at the August 1854 Cleveland (Ohio) National Emigration Convention that Delany offered his most persuasive support for emigration in a well-circulated pamphlet titled *The Political Destiny of the Colored Race*, which was well received at the convention. It argued that Blacks lacked citizenship in America, and developed the point that freedom could only come to a race if it constituted the majority in a country. Political freedom, argued Delany, would not come easily and might have to be seized by force. He aggressively made his case for Black emigration. The editor of a newspaper, the *Colombian,* praised Delany's gospel of self-determination and emigration even before the convention adopted it, describing it as a "gallant faith" and the very first step for Blacks to show that they could "develop a higher order of civilization and Christianity than the world has yet seen."[8] The convention established a board, with Delany as its head, to find a new homeland for Blacks. Delany began to pursue emigration vigorously, raising funds from only Black sources and recruiting the members of his team, comprising Blacks born in the United States.

By 1858 ideas about emigration were now put to the test, with a visit to Africa and a major, well-publicized report. In late 1858 Delany accepted the leadership of the first exploratory mission to Africa with considerable passion and enthusiasm. Contrary to allegations by his critics, Delany did not intend a mass exodus to Africa. Rather, he envisaged a number of small colonies in various parts, to be settled by carefully selected African Americans with good character and morals. In addition, the settlers would be skilled in agriculture, commerce, and crafts in order to create a new and competitive economy. Not only would their influence end slavery on the African side, their success in the production of cotton and other crops would compete with those products of the American South, thereby helping to free Blacks still in slavery.

Shortly before Delany departed, a former associate previously recruited to be part of his team, Robert Campbell, a science teacher at the Institute for Colored Youth in Philadelphia, was on his way to Africa with a similar motive, sponsored by another organization with better funding.[9] Although they met in Africa, shared experiences, and actually returned together, they wrote separate reports,[10] which made them both the most successful in the search for new settlements in Africa for African Americans and Black Caribbeans to live and begin a new life. Delany, now designated the Chief Commissioner to Africa, set sail for West Africa in May 1859, primarily to investigate the possibility of a colony for Blacks in the Niger Valley. The journey lasted till April 1860, and on the return journey he and Campbell went to Great Britain to seek support and resources for their ideas before finally arriving home in December to a hero's welcome. Delany's *Official Report* was published in New York and London in the following year, the first of its kind in tone and focus.

The exploration was appropriately described as a pilgrimage to the homeland. *Official Report* contains his schedules, treaties, observations, and findings. The expedition took Delany and his team to West Africa, stopping in July 1859 in Liberia where a meeting was held with Alexander Crummell, the famous leader, abolitionist, and emigrationist. The team traveled westward to Nigeria, reaching the port city of Lagos in September. Delany signed a treaty with the king of Lagos for a tract measuring 335 square feet. Thereafter he proceeded to Abeokuta, where some missionaries had previously settled, and again he signed a treaty with the Alake (king) to create a settlement for educated African Americans and the establishment of a cotton production company that would use free African labor. He then traveled in the Yoruba heartland, an impressive feat that saw him visit most of the major cities of the Yoruba, including Ijaye, Ogbomoso, Oyo, Iwo, and Ibadan. With the skill of an explorer and an eye for detail, he recorded various aspects of life and economy that would be valuable to Black emigrants. In addition, he signed some treaties with African rulers to obtain land to settle the emigrants. Delany was accorded respect in many of the places he visited: certainly in Abeokuta his blackness was an advantage, compared with a number of previous White missionaries and visitors who were treated as total strangers and outsiders.

Official Report clearly presents the conditions in West Africa and what immigrants would encounter on arrival. Delany was able to present his position in West Africa, and he reported favorable responses. His report provides clear information on the way of life, diseases and their treatment, climate, soil, animals, plants, and people to show that resources existed to develop settlements and economies. He also provided an impressive amount of data on how to improve agriculture, land, ventilation, and housing in Africa so that the emigrants would have higher living standards. He talked about religion, expressing an anti-Catholic sentiment and asserting the relevance of Black missionaries in spreading the right type of Christianity in Africa. Moreover, he paid attention to the economy, with information on how to promote commerce, crops, and transportation. To Delany, resources and opportunities were so abundant that emigrants would be able to compete with the economy of the American South.

When *Conditions* and *Official Report* are read together, the focus is clear: the creation of a Black nation. In the process of the creation, Blacks must plan and finance all aspects, Blacks must lead, they must imbibe the ideology of race pride, they must see themselves as the solutions to their own problems, they must reject the notion of White superiority, and they must work hard toward social and economic equality with the rest of the world. The proud history presented by Delany is designed to motivate emigrants to work for a brighter future. One-third of *Official Report* states the reasons for the separatist views and emigration, thus linking it with the earlier book, *Conditions*. The literary style of both could perhaps benefit from greater refinement, but the contents are clear, and the positive and passionate character of Delany is unmistakable. Both books reflect the dreams for a greater future, the genius of Blacks to shape their lives, and their impressive contributions to development and civilization. Delany presents Blacks as intelligent and moral beings, victims of slavery and exploitation who must now struggle on their own terms to become free. Both books present the nobility of the Black race and Delany's belief that there were a sufficient number to transform the others in America and Africa.

On their way back home, while in London, Delany presented his findings to many receptive groups and audiences. A number of English businessmen promised to invest in the cotton industry. The attention and applause he received at the meeting of the International Statistical Congress in July 1860 offended the American ambassador in the audience, and the American delegation walked out in protest. In Canada and the United States, Delany embarked on speaking engagements to sell his ideas, and he set up an office in Brooklyn to coordinate his efforts on emigration.

Then came the American Civil War and the legal emancipation of slaves, which changed the political landscape and the terms of the debate about the options of Blacks in American society. The war prevented the emigration of the first group of settlers and disrupted all other emigration activities and plans by Delany and his associates. Delany's own career was similarly altered.

The Civil War Years and After

Initially, the government of President Lincoln was actually in support of Delany's view; indeed a congressional committee published in 1862 Delany's *Political Destiny of the Colored Races* in order to justify its position on emigration. However, a year later Lincoln changed his mind in favor of the abolition of slavery, and the Emancipation Proclamation of 1863 made him popular among Blacks who also now began to support the war effort. Seizing advantage of the small change in the political climate, Delany relocated his family to Wilberforce, Ohio, in 1864. At the same time, he called for the recruitment of Blacks into the army, led by Black officers who would fight in the slaveholding South. He was even privileged enough to present his ideas to President Lincoln in person, at a meeting on February 8, 1865.

When the War Department changed its policy to admit Black volunteers into the Union Army, many joined, including Delany and his son. Delany himself worked as a full-time recruiting officer of Black soldiers for the Commonwealth of Massachusetts, and served as a surgeon with the Fifty-fourth Massachusetts Volunteer Infanty. He was commissioned as a major in the Union Army in 1865, making him the highest-ranking Black officer of the war years.

There followed various amendments to the Constitution, especially the Thirteenth and Fourteenth, which began the process of integrating Blacks into American society. The changes led to a belief among many that Blacks were now in America forever. Many were to be disappointed, as they did not enjoy the citizenship and dignity they had expected after the Civil War and emancipation. Frustration and disappointment led to the various revivals of Delany's idea of emigration after the war. In different ways and words, many began to agree with Delany that for Blacks to obtain justice and freedom, they must leave their minority status and seek areas where they would use their majority number and power to uplift themselves.

Meanwhile, Delany's career after the Civil War initially moved him away from the pursuit of emigration to West Africa, to politics and business. When the war ended, he was in the South Carolina Low Country where he took a job with the Bureau of Refugees, Freedmen, and Abandoned Land (Freedmen's Bureau) until 1868. In the immediate postwar years, Delany was a major public figure, a leader who represented both blackness and freedom. He gave a series of lectures, identified with the Republican Party, which was pro-Black and pro-poor, and became a real-estate investor.

Delany's radicalism of the 1850s began to give way to more conservative views in the 1870s. In 1875 Delany returned to medical practice; edited another newspaper, the *Charleston Independent*; and served for a while as a judge. His political fortune began to decline after 1874, when he unsuccessfully ran for the office of lieutenant-governor on the ticket of the Independent Republicans, a coalition of moderate Democrats and conservative Republicans. In 1876 he supported Wade Hampton III, the richest slaveholder in the South in the pre–Civil War years, a Democratic candidate, for governor. Hampton won, and Delany's support for him proved to be a mistake: within two years Hampton had removed all Black officeholders, including Delany himself.

Although disillusioned by politics and his failed business, he did not retreat into obscurity. As if to return to his roots, Delany in his last years returned to the issue of emigration, calling for many to return to Liberia. In 1878 he revived his old ideas in a series of lectures that found favor

with many southern Blacks. He participated in the unsuc-
cessful Liberian Exodus Joint-Stock Steamship Company—
after seven shiploads of emigrants to Liberia, the company
went bankrupt. He wrote his last book in 1879, extolling
the virtues of the Black race and the contributions of
Ethiopia and Egypt to world civilization.[11]

Conclusion

Delany's ideas did not die with him in 1885 at Wilberforce,
Ohio. Delany died just when the scramble for Africa was
about to begin, ushering in the age of imperialism that
would never have allowed his ideas to be realized. Forces
were already in place in Europe to sabotage efforts at creating Black colonies, and in Africa itself the kings and chiefs
had reneged on the kind of treaties signed with Delany.

Nevertheless, the belief in emigration to Africa was still
strong in the minds of many African Americans well into
the twentieth century. Leaders such as the Reverend
Alexander Crummell and Bishop Turner continued to
speak about the need to return to Africa. In the years that
followed, productive interactions were promoted between
the United States and Africa by way of sending African
American missionaries to Africa, and sponsoring Africans to
attend schools in the United States. By the end of the nineteenth century, many Black leaders began to talk about steps
to unite all of Africa and the Blacks in the diaspora. When
H. Sylvester Williams, the Trinidadian lawyer, organized the
first Pan-African Conference in London in 1900, the ideas
of Delany and others before him had encouraged the emergence of Pan-Africanism, a vision that defined Black struggles in the first half of the twentieth century.[12] With the rise

of Marcus Garvey from 1915 to 1925, the ideas of Delany were not only revived, but they acquired a revolutionary flavor. W. E. B. Du Bois invested more energy and intellectual power in the development of Pan-Africanism during the twentieth century, borrowing some ideas from Delany. Emigration lost its appeal, but not Delany's ideas of "Africa for Africans," Black redemption, regeneration and emancipation, and other key elements associated with the rise of Black nationalist thought and political struggles. Delany's successors are more confident, and they have penetrated all occupations and walks of life to such a degree that their contributions can no longer be ignored.

A century after his death, intellectual interest in him remains strong. In addition to recent biographies,[13] he is mentioned in all the major studies on Black leadership and nationalism during the nineteenth century.[14] Delany is regularly listed among the most revered Black intellectuals and activists for his ideas on Black consciousness, Black cooperation, and emigration to Africa.[15]

Toyin Falola
Frances Higginbothom Nalle
Centennial Professor in History

Notes

1. On Black leaders of this era, see August Meier and Leon Litwack, eds., *Black Leaders of the Nineteenth Century* (Urbana: University of Illinois Press, 1988); and Howard Brotz, ed., *African American Social and Political Thought, 1850–1920* (New Brunswick, NJ: Transaction, 1992).

2. *Blake, or The Huts of America; A Tale of the Mississippi Valley, the Southern United States and Cuba*, published serially from 1859

by the *Anglo-African Magazine*, and in 1861 and 1862 by the *Weekly Anglo-African Magazine*. For a recent edition, see Martin R. Delany, *Blake; or, The Huts of America*, ed. Floyd J. Miller (Boston: Beacon Press, 1970).

3. His *Mystery*, a newspaper published between 1843 and 1847, was the first Black-owned one west of the Alleghenies; he was coeditor of the *Rochester North Star* from 1843 to 1849, which allowed him to make many comments on antebellum free Blacks, and publisher of the *Anglo-African Magazine* in 1859.

4. For comments on all his publications, see, for instance, Victor Ullman, *Martin R. Delany: The Beginnings of Black Nationalism* (Boston: Beacon Press, 1971).

5. Frank A. Rolling (Frances Rollins Whipper), *Life and Public Services of Martin R. Delany* (Boston: Lee and Shepard, 1868).

6. *Douglass' Monthly*, August, 1862, p. 695.

7. Floyd J. Miller, *The Search for a Black Nationality: Black Emigration and Colonization, 1787–1863* (Urbana: University of Illinois Press, 1975).

8. The *Colombian*, January 4, 1854, quoted in Bernard Makhosezwe Magubane, *The Ties That Bind: African-American Consciousness of Africa* (Trenton, NJ: Africa World Press, 1987).

9. Campbell's trip was sponsored by the African Civilization Society (ACS), established in Philadelphia in 1858, with substantial support from Whites who also believed in the idea of emigration. When raising funds for his trip, Delany refused to take money from Whites or associations with which they identified. Campbell, on the other hand, did not accept this view, and he accepted money from the ACS. Delany regarded this as a betrayal.

10. For the one by Campbell, see Robert Campbell, *A Pilgrimage to My Motherland: An Account of a Journey among the Egbas and Yorubas of Central Africa, in 1859–60* (New York: T. Hamilton, 1861).

11. *The Principia of Ethnology: The Origin of Races and Color, with an Archaeological Compendium of Ethiopian and Egyptian Civilization, from Years of Careful Examination and Enquiry* (Philadelphia: Harper and Bros., 1879).

12. For details, see Cyril E. Griffith, *The African Dream: Martin R. Delany and the Emergence of Pan-African Thought* (University Park: Pennsylvania State University Press, 1975).

13. See, for instance, Ullman, *Martin R. Delany: The Beginnings of Black Nationalism*; and Dorothy Sterling, *The Making of an Afro-American: Martin Robison Delany, 1812–1885* (Garden City, NY: Doubleday, 1971).

14. See, for instance, Rayford W. Logan and Michael R. Winston, eds., *Dictionary of American Negro Biography* (New York: Norton, 1982); Litwack and Meier, eds., *Black Leaders of the Nineteenth Century*; Blyden Jackson, *A History of Afro-American Literature*, vol. 1 (Baton Rouge: Louisiana State University Press, 1989); and Griffith, *The African Dream: Martin R. Delany and the Emergence of Pan-African Thought*.

15. See, for instance, Magubane, *The Ties That Bind: African-American Consciousness of Africa*; and John Henrik Clarke, *Africans at the Crossroads: Notes for an African World Revolution* (Trenton, NJ: Africa World Press, 1991).

CONTENTS

The Condition, Elevation, Emigration, and Destiny of the Colored People of the United States

Preface   35

Chapter I.   Condition of Many Classes in
             Europe Considered   41

Chapter II. Comparative Condition of the
             Colored People of the United States   44

Chapter III. American Colonization   58

Chapter IV. Our Elevation in the United States   63

Chapter V.   Means of Elevation   67

Chapter VI. The United States Our Country   74

Chapter VII. Claims of Colored Men as Citizens
             of the United States   75

Chapter VIII. Colored American Warriors   91

Chapter IX. Capacity of Colored Men and Women
             as Citizen Members of Community   106

Chapter X.   Practical Utility of Colored People

of the Present Day as Members
of Society—Business Men
and Mechanics   113

Chapter XI. Literary and Professional
Colored Men and Women   128

Chapter XII. Students of Various Professions   148

Chapter XIII. A Scan at Past Things   151

Chapter XIV. Late Men of Literary, Professional
and Artistic Note   155

Chapter XV. Farmers and Herdsmen   158

Chapter XVI. National Disfranchisement
of Colored People   161

Chapter XVII. Emigration of the Colored People
of the United States   175

Chapter XVIII. "Republic of Liberia"   177

Chapter XIX. The Canadas   189

Chapter XX. Central and South America
and the West Indies   193

Chapter XXI. Nicaragua and New Grenada   202

Chapter XXII. Things as They Are   204

Chapter XXIII. A Glance at Ourselves—Conclusion   211

Appendix. A Project for an Expedition of Adventure, to the Eastern Coast of Africa   221

Official Report of the
Niger Valley Exploring Party

Section I. Political Movements 229

Section II. Succeeding Conventions 234

Section III. History of the Project 236

Section IV. Arrival and Reception in Liberia 254

Section V. Liberia—Climate, Soil, Productions, etc. 263

Section VI. Diseases—Cause—Remedy 278

Section VII. The Interior—Yoruba 284

Section VIII. Topography, Climate, etc. 288

Section IX. Diseases of This Part of Africa, Treatment, Hygiene, Aliment 312

Section X. Missionary Influence 332

Section XI. What Africa Now Requires 338

Section XII. To Direct Legitimate Commerce 345

Section XIII. Cotton Staple 351

Section XIV. Success in Great Britain 361

Section XV. Commercial Relations in Scotland 379

Section XVI. The Time to Go to Africa 387

Section XVII. Concluding Suggestions 391

THE CONDITION,
ELEVATION,
EMIGRATION,
AND DESTINY
OF THE
COLORED PEOPLE
OF THE
UNITED STATES

Sincerely dedicated to the American People,
North and South.

By Their Most Devout, and Patriotic Fellow Citizen,
the Author

PREFACE

THE author of this little volume has no other apology for offering it to the public, than the hurried manner in which it has been composed. Being detained in the city of New York on business, he seized the opportunity of a tedious delay, and wrote the work in the inside of one month, attending to other business through the day, and lecturing on physiology sometimes in the evening. The reader will therefore not entertain an idea of elegance of language and terseness of style, such as should rule the sentences of every composition, by whomsoever written.

His sole object has been, to place before the public in general, and the colored people of the United States in particular, great truths concerning this class of citizens, which appears to have been heretofore avoided, as well by friends as enemies to their elevation. By opponents, to conceal information, that they are well aware would stimulate and impel them on to bold and adventurous deeds of manly daring; and by friends, who seem to have acted on the principle of the zealous orthodox, who would prefer losing the object of his pursuit to changing his policy.

There are also a great many colored people in the United States, who have independence of spirit, who desire to, and do, think for themselves; but for the want of general information, and in consequence of a prevailing opinion that has obtained, that no thoughts nor opinions must be expressed, even though it would eventuate in their elevation, except it emanate from some old, orthodox, stereotyped doctrine concerning them; therefore, such a work as this, which is but a mere introduction to what will henceforth emanate from the pen of colored men and women, appeared to be in most anxious demand, in order to settle their minds entirely, and concentrate them upon an effective and specific course of procedure. We have never conformed with that class of philosophers who would keep the people in ignorance, lest they might change their opinion from former predilections. This we shall never do, except pressing necessity demands it, and then only as a measure to prevent bad consequences, for the time.

The colored peole of to-day are not the colored people of a quarter of a century ago, and require very different means and measures to satisfy their wants and demands, and to effect their advancement. No wise statesman presumes the same measures for the satisfaction of the American people now, that may have been with propriety adopted twenty-five years ago; neither is it wisdom to presume, that the privileges which satisfied colored people twenty years ago, they will be reconciled with now. That with which the father of the writer may have been satisfied, even up to the present day, the writer cannot be content with; the one lived in times antecedent to the birth of the other; that which answered then, does not answer now: so is it with the whole class of colored people in the United States. Their feelings, tastes, predilections, wants, demands, and sympathies, are identical, and homogeneous with those of all other Americans.

"Fleecy locks and black complexions,
   Cannot alter nature's claim;
Skins may differ, but affections,
   Dwell in black and white the same."

Many of the distinguished characters referred to in this work, who lived in former days, for which there is no credit given, have been obtained from various sources—as fragments of history, pamphlets, files of newspapers, obsolete American history, and some from Mrs. Child's Collection. Those of modern date, are living facts known to the writer in his travels through the United States, having been from Canada and Maine to Arkansas and Texas. The origin of the breast-works of cotton bales on Chalmet Plains, at the battle of New Orleans, the writer learned in that city, from old colored men in 1840, and subsequently, from other sources; as well as much useful information concerning that battle, from *Julien Bennoit*, spoken of in the work. He has before referred to it some five or six years ago, through the columns of a paper, of which he was then editor, and not until subsequently to his narrating the same facts in these columns, was he aware that it was ever mentioned in print, when he saw, on the 3d day of March, on looking over the contributions of the "Liberty Bell," a beautiful annual of Boston, the circumstances referred to by DAVID LEE CHILD, Esq., the particulars of which will be found in our version.

The original intention was to make this a pamphlet of a few pages, the writer commencing with that view; but finding that he could not thus justify the design of the work, will fully explain the cause of its present volume. The subject of this work is one that the writer has given thought for years, and the only regret that he has now in placing it before the public is, that his circumstances and engagements

have not afforded him such time and opportunity as to do
justice to it. But, should he succeed in turning the attention
of the colored people, in general, in this direction—he shall
have been amply compensated for the labor bestowed. An
appendix will be found giving the plan of the author, laid
out at twenty-four years of age, but subsequently improved
on, for the elevation of the colored race. That plan of course,
as this work will fully show, has been abandoned for a far
more glorious one; albeit, we as a race, still lay claim to the
project, which one day must be added to our dashing strides
in national advancement, successful adventure, and unsur-
passed enterprise.

One part of the American people, though living in near
proximity and together, are quite unacquainted with the
other; and one of the great objects of the author is, to make
each acquainted. Except the character of an individual is
known, there can be no just appreciation of his worth; and
as with individuals, so is it with classes.

The colored people are not yet known, even to their
most professed friends among the white Americans; for the
reason, that politicians, religionists, colonizationists, and abolitionists, have each and all, at different times, presumed to
think for, dictate to, and *know* better what suited colored
people, than they knew for themselves; and consequently,
there has been no other knowledge of them obtained, than
that which has been obtained through these mediums. Their
history—past, present, and future, has been written by them,
who, for reasons well known, which are named in this
volume, are not their representatives, and, therefore, do not
properly nor fairly present their wants and claims among
their fellows. Of these impressions, we design disabusing the
public mind, and correcting the false impressions of all
classes upon this great subject. A moral and mental, is as

obnoxious as a physical servitude, and not to be tolerated; as the one may, eventually, lead to the other. Of these we feel the direful effects.

> "If I'm designed your lordling's slave,
>   By nature's law designed;
> Why was an independent wish
>   E'er planted in my mind!"

I | CONDITION OF MANY CLASSES IN EUROPE CONSIDERED

THAT there have been in all ages and in all countries, in every quarter of the habitable globe, especially among those nations laying the greatest claim to civilization and enlightenment, classes of people who have been deprived of equal privileges, political, religious and social, cannot be denied, and that this deprivation on the part of the ruling classes is cruel and unjust, is also equally true. Such classes have even been looked upon as inferior to their oppressors, and have ever been mainly the domestics and menials of society, doing the low offices and drudgery of those among whom they lived, moving about and existing by mere sufferance, having no rights nor privileges but those conceded by the common consent of their political superiors. These are historical facts that cannot be controverted, and therefore proclaim in tones more eloquently than thunder, the listful attention of every oppressed man, woman, and child under the government of the people of the United States of America.

In past ages there were many such classes, as the Israelites in Egypt, the Gladiators in Rome, and similar classes in Greece; and in the present age, the Gipsies in Italy and Greece, the Cossacs in Russia and Turkey, the Sclaves and Croats in the Germanic States, and the Welsh and Irish among the British, to say nothing of various other classes among other nations.

That there have in all ages, in almost every nation, existed a nation within a nation—a people who although forming a part and parcel of the population, yet were from force of circumstances, known by the peculiar position they occupied, forming in fact, by the deprivation of political equality with others, no part, and if any, but a restricted part of the body politic of such nations, is also true.

Such then are the Poles in Russia, the Hungarians in Austria, the Scotch, Irish, and Welsh in the United Kingdom, and such also are the Jews, scattered throughout not only the length and breadth of Europe, but almost the habitable globe, maintaining their national characteristics, and looking forward in high hopes of seeing the day when they may return to their former national position of self-government and independence, let that be in whatever part of the habitable world it may. This is the lot of these various classes of people in Europe, and it is not our intention here, to discuss the justice or injustice of the causes that have contributed to their degradation, but simply to set forth the undeniable facts, which are as glaring as the rays of a noonday's sun, thereby to impress them indelibly on the mind of every reader of this pamphlet.

It is not enough, that these people are deprived of equal privileges by their rulers, but, the more effectually to succeed, the equality of these classes must be denied, and their inferiority by nature as distinct races, actually asserted. This policy is necessary to appease the opposition that might be interposed in their behalf. Wherever there is arbitrary rule, there must be necessity, on the part of the dominant classes, superiority be assumed. To assume superiority, is to deny the equality of others, and to deny their equality, is to premise their incapacity for self-government. Let this once be conceded, and there will be little or no sympathy for the oppressed, the oppressor being left to prescribe whatever terms at discretion for their government, suits his own purpose.

Such then is the condition of various classes in Europe; yes, nations, for centuries within nations, even without the hope of redemption among those who oppress them. And however unfavorable their condition, there is none more so than that of the colored people of the United States.

II | COMPARATIVE CONDITION OF THE COLORED PEOPLE OF THE UNITED STATES

T HE United States, untrue to her trust and unfaithful to her professed principles of republican equality, has also pursued a policy of political degradation to a large portion of her native born countrymen, and that class is the Colored People. Denied an equality not only of political but of natural rights, in common with the rest of our fellow citizens, there is no species of degradation to which we are not subject.

Reduced to abject slavery is not enough, the very thought of which should awaken every sensibility of our common nature; but those of their descendants who are freemen even in the non-slaveholding States, occupy the very same position politically, religiously, civilly and socially, (with but few exceptions,) as the bondman occupies in the slave States.

In those States, the bondman is disfranchised, and for the most part so are we. He is denied all civil, religious, and social privileges, except such as he gets by mere sufferance, and so are we. They have no part nor lot in the government of the country, neither have we. They are ruled and governed without representation, existing as mere nonentities among the citizens, and excrescences on the body politic— a mere dreg in community, and so are we. Where then is our political superiority to the enslaved? none, neither are we superior in any other relation to society, except that we are defacto masters of ourselves and joint rulers of our own domestic household, while the bondman's self is claimed by another, and his relation to his family denied him. What the unfortunate classes are in Europe, such are we in the United States, which is folly to deny, insanity not to understand, blindness not to see, and surely now full time that our eyes were opened to these startling truths, which for ages have stared us full in the face.

It is time that we had become politicians, we mean, to understand the political economy and domestic policy of nations; that we had become as well as moral theorists, also the practical demonstrators of equal rights and self-government. Except we do, it is idle to talk about rights, it is mere chattering for the sake of being seen and heard—like the slave, saying something because his so called "master" said it, and saying just what he told him to say. Have we not now sufficient intelligence among us to understand our true position, to realise our actual condition, and determine for ourselves what is best to be done? If we have not now, we never shall have, and should at once cease prating about our equality, capacity, and all that.

Twenty years ago, when the writer was a youth, his young and yet uncultivated mind was aroused, and his tender heart made to leap with anxiety in anticipation of the promises then held out by the prime movers in the cause of our elevation.

In 1830 the most intelligent and leading spirits among the colored men in the United States, such as James Forten, Robert Douglass, I. Bowers, A. D. Shadd, John Peck, Joseph Cassey, and John B. Vashon of Pennsylvania; John T. Hilton, Nathaniel and Thomas Paul, and James G. Barbodoes of Massachusetts; Henry Sipkins, Thomas Hamilton, Thomas L. Jennings, Thomas Downing, Samuel E. Cornish, and others of New York; R. Cooley and others of Maryland, and representatives from other States which cannot now be recollected, the data not being at hand, assembled in the city of Philadelphia, in the capacity of a National Convention, to "devise ways and means for the bettering of our condition." These Conventions determined to assemble annually, much talent, ability, and energy of character being displayed; when in 1831 at a sitting of the Convention in September, from their previous pamphlet reports, much interest having been created throughout the country, they were favored by the presence of a number of whites, some of whom were able and distinguished men, such as Rev. R. R. Gurley, Arthur Tappan, Elliot Cresson, John Rankin, Simeon Jocelyn and others, among them William Lloyd Garrison, then quite a young man, all of whom were staunch and ardent Colonizationists, young Garrison at that time, doing his mightiest in his favorite work.

Among other great projects of interest brought before the convention at a previous sitting, was that of the expediency of a general emigration, as far as it was practicable, of the colored people to the British Provinces of North America. Another was that of raising sufficient means for the establishment and erection of a College for the proper education of the colored youth. These gentlemen long accustomed to observation and reflection on the condition of their people saw at once, that there must necessarily be means used adequate to the end to be attained—that end being an unqualified equality with the ruling class of their fellow citizens. He saw that as a class, the colored people of the country were ignorant, degraded and oppressed, by far the greater portion of them being abject slaves in the South, the very condition of whom was almost enough, under the circumstances, to blast the remotest hope of success, and those who were freemen, whether in the

South or North, occupied a subservient, servile, and menial position, considering it a favor to get into the service of the whites, and do their degrading offices. That the difference between the whites and themselves, consisted in the superior advantages of the one over the other, in point of attainments. That if a knowledge of the arts and sciences, the mechanical occupations, the industrial occupations, as farming, commerce, and all the various business enterprises, and learned professions were necessary for the superior position occupied by their rulers, it was also necessary for them. And very reasonably too, the first suggestion which occurred to them was, the advantages of a location, then the necessity of a qualification. They reasoned with themselves, that all distinctive differences made among men on account of their origin, is wicked, unrighteous, and cruel, and never shall receive countenance in any shape from us, therefore, the first acts of the measure entered into by them, was to protest, solemnly protest, against every unjust measure and policy in the country, having for its object the proscription of the colored people, whether state, national, munipical, social, civil, or religious.

But being far-sighted, reflecting, discerning men, they took a political view of the subject, and determined for the good of their people to be governed in their policy according to the facts as they presented themselves. In taking a glance at Europe, they discovered there, however unjustly, as we have shown in another part of this pamphlet, that there are and have been numerous classes proscribed and oppressed, and it was not for them to cut short their wise deliberations, and arrest their proceedings in contention, as to the cause, whether on account of language, the color of eyes, hair, skin, or their origin of country—because all this is contrary to reason, a contradiction to common sense, at war with nature herself, and at variance with facts as they stare us every day in the face, among all nations, in every country—this being made the pretext as a matter of *policy* alone—a fact worthy of observation, that wherever the objects of oppression are the most easily distinguished by any peculiar or general characteristics, these people are the more easily oppressed, because the war of oppression is the more easily waged against them. This is the case with the modern Jews and many other people who have strongly-marked, peculiar, or distinguishing characteristics. This arises in this wise. The policy of all those who proscribe any people, induces them to select as the objects of proscription, those who differed as much as possible, in some particulars, from themselves. This is to ensure the greater success, because it engenders the greater prejudice, or in other words, elicits less interest on the part of the oppressing class, in their favor. This fact is well understood in national conflicts, as the soldier or civilian, who is distinguished by his dress, mustache, or any other peculiar appendage, would certainly prove himself a madman, if he did not take the precaution to change his dress, remove his mustache, and conceal as much as possible his peculiar characteristics, to give him access among the repelling party. This is mere policy, nature having nothing to do with it. Still, it is a fact, a great truth well worthy of remark, and as such as adduce it for the benefit of those of our readers, unaccustomed to an enquiry into the policy of nations.

In view of these truths, our fathers and leaders in our elevation, discovered that as a policy, we the colored people were selected as the subordinate class in this country, not on account of any actual or supposed inferiority on their part, but simply because, in view of all the circumstances of the case, they were the very best class that could be selected.

They would have as readily had any other class as subordinates in the country, as the colored people, but the condition of society *at the time*, would not admit of it. In the struggle for American Independence, there were among those who performed the most distinguished parts, the most common-place peasantry of the Provinces. English, Danish, Irish, Scotch, and others, were among those whose names blazoned forth as heroes in the American Revolution. But a single reflection will convince us, that no course of policy could have induced the proscription of the parentage and relatives of such men as Benjamin Franklin the printer, Roger Sherman the cobbler, the tinkers, and others of the signers of the Declaration of Independence. But as they were determined to have a subservient class, it will readily be conceived, that according to the state of society at the time, the better policy on their part was, to select some class, who from their political position—however much they may have contributed their aid as we certainly did, in the general struggle for liberty by force of arms—who had the least claims upon them, or who had the *least chance*, or was the *least potent* in urging their claims. This class of course was the colored people and Indians.

The Indians who in the early settlement of the continent, before an African captive had ever been introduced thereon, were reduced to the most abject slavery, toiling day and night in the mines, under the relentless hands of heartless Spanish taskmasters, but being a race of people raised to the sports of fishing, the chase, and of war, were wholly unaccustomed to labor, and therefore sunk under the insupportable weight, two millions and a half having fallen victims to the cruelty of oppression and toil suddenly placed upon their shoulders. And it was only this that prevented their farther enslavement as a class, after the provinces were absolved from the British Crown. It is true that their general enslavement took place on the islands and in the mining districts of South America, where indeed, the Europeans continued to enslave them, until a comparatively recent period; still, the design, the feeling, and inclination from policy, was the same to do so here, in this section of the continent.

Nor was it until their influence became too great, by the political position occupied by their brethren in the new republic, that the German and Irish peasantry ceased to be sold as slaves for a term of years fixed by law, for the repayment of their passage-money, the descendants of these classes of people for a long time being held as inferiors, in the estimation of the ruling class, and it was not until they assumed the rights and privileges guaranteed to them by the established policy of the country, among the leading spirits of whom were their relatives, that the policy towards them was discovered to be a bad one, and accordingly changed. Nor was it, as is frequently very erroneously asserted, by colored as well as white persons, that it was on account of hatred to the African, or in other words, on account of hatred to his color, that the African was selected as the subject of oppression in this country. This is sheer nonsense; being based on policy and nothing else, as shown in another place. The Indians, who being the most foreign to the sympathies of the Europeans on this continent, were selected in the first place, who, being unable to withstand the hardships, gave way before them.

But the African race had long been known to Europeans, in all ages of the world's history, as a long-lived, hardy race, subject to toil and labor of various kinds, subsisting mainly by traffic, trade, and industry, and consequently being as foreign to the sympathies of the invaders of the continent as the Indians, they were selected, captured, brought here as a laboring class, and as a matter of policy held as such. Nor was the absurd idea of natural inferiority of the African ever dreamed of, until recently adduced by the slave-holders and their abettors, in justification of the policy. This, with contemptuous indignation, we fling back into their face, as a scorpion to a vulture. And so did our patriots and leaders in the cause of regeneration know better, and never for a moment yielded to the base doctrine. But they had discovered the great fact, that a cruel policy was pursued towards our people, and that they possessed distinctive characteristics which made them the objects of proscription. These characteristics being strongly marked in the colored people, as in the Indians, by color, character of hair and so on, made them the more easily distinguished from other Americans, and the policies more effectually urged against us. For this reason they introduced the subject of emigration to Canada, and a proper institution for the education of the youth.

At this important juncture of their proceedings, the afore named white gentlemen were introduced to the notice of the Convention, and after gaining permission to speak, expressed their gratification and surprise at the qualification and talent manifested by different members of the Convention, all expressing their determination to give the cause of the colored people more serious reflection. Mr. Garrison, the youngest of them all, and none the less honest on account of his youthfulness, being but 26 years of age at the time, (1831) expressed his determination to change his course of policy at once, and espouse the cause of the elevation of the colored people here in their own country. We are not at present well advised upon this point, it now having escaped our memory, but we are under the impression that Mr. Jocelyn also, at once changed his policy.

During the winter of 1832, Mr. Garrison issued his

"Thoughts on African Colonization," and near about the same time or shortly after, issued the first number of the "Liberator," in both of which, his full convictions of the enormity of American slavery, and the wickedness of their policy towards the colored people, were fully expressed. At the sitting of the Convention in this year, a number, perhaps all of these gentlemen were present, and those who had denounced the Colonization scheme, and espoused the cause of the elevation of the colored people in this country, or the Anti-Slavery cause, as it was now termed, expressed themselves openly and without reserve.

Sensible of the high-handed injustice done to the colored people in the United States, and the mischief likely to emanate from the unchristian proceedings of the deceptious Colonization scheme, like all honest hearted penitents, with the ardor only known to new converts, they entreated the Convention, whatever they did, not to entertain for a moment, the idea of recommending emigration to their people, nor the establishment of separate institutions of learning. They earnestly contended, and doubtless honestly meaning what they said, that they (the whites) had been our oppressors and injurers, they had obstructed our progress to the high positions of civilization, and now, it was their bounden duty to make full amends for the injuries thus inflicted on an unoffending people. They exhorted the Convention to cease; as they had laid on the burden, they would also take it off; as they had obstructed our pathway, they would remove the hindrance. In a word, as they had oppressed and trampled down the colored people, they would now elevate them. These suggestions and promises, good enough to be sure, after they were made, were accepted by the Convention—though some gentlemen were still in favor of the first project as the best policy, Mr. A. D.

Shadd of West Chester, Pa., as we learn from himself, being one among that number—ran through the country like wild-fire, no one thinking, and if he thought, daring to speak above his breath of going any where out of certain prescribed limits, or of sending a child to school, if it should but have the name of "colored" attached to it, without the risk of being termed a "traitor" to the cause of his people, or an enemy to the Anti-Slavery cause.

At this important point in the history of our efforts, the colored men stopped suddenly, and with their hands thrust deep in their breeches-pockets, and their mouths gaping open, stood gazing with astonishment, wonder, and surprise, at the stupendous moral colossal statues of our Anti-Slavery friends and brethren, who in the heat and zeal of honest hearts, from a desire to make atonement for the many wrongs inflicted, promised a great deal more than they have ever been able half to fulfill, in thrice the period in which they expected it. And in this, we have no fault to find with our Anti-Slavery friends, and here wish it to be understood, that we are not laying any thing to their charge as blame, neither do we desire for a moment to reflect on them, because we heartily believe that all that they did at the time, they did with the purest and best of motives, and further believe that they now are, as they then were, the truest friends we have among the whites in this country. And hope, and desire, and request, that our people should always look upon *true* anti-slavery people, Abolitionists we mean, as their friends, until they have just cause for acting otherwise. It is true, that the Anti-Slavery, like all good causes, has produced some recreants, but the cause itself is no more to be blamed for that, than Christianity is for the malconduct of any professing hypocrite, nor the society of Friends, for the conduct of a broad-brimmed hat and shad-belly coated horsethief, because he spoke *thee* and *thou* before stealing the horse. But what is our condition even amidst our Anti-Slavery friends? And here, as our sole intention is to contribute to the elevation of our people, we must be permitted to express our opinion freely, without being thought uncharitable.

In the first place, we should look at the objects for which the Anti-Slavery cause was commenced, and the promises or inducements it held out at the commencement. It should be borne in mind, that Anti-Slavery took its rise among *colored men*, just at the time they were introducing their greatest projects for their own elevation, and that our Anti-Slavery brethren were converts of the colored men, in behalf of their elevation. Of course, it would be expected that being baptized into the new doctrines, their faith would induce them to embrace the principles therein contained, with the strictest possible adherence.

The cause of dissatisfaction with our former condition, was, that we were proscribed, debarred, and shut out from every respectable position, occupying the places of inferiors and menials.

It was expected that Anti-Slavery, according to its professions, would extend to colored persons, as far as in the power of its adherents, those advantages nowhere else to be obtained among white men. That colored boys would get situations in their shops and stores, and every other advantage tending to elevate them as far as possible, would be extended to them. At least, it was expected, that in Anti-Slavery establishments, colored men would have the preference. Because, there was no other ostensible object in view, in the commencement of the Anti-Slavery enterprise, than the *elevation* of the *colored man*, by facilitating his efforts in attaining to equality with the white man. It was urged, and it was true, that the colored people were susceptible of all that the whites were, and all that was required was to give them a fair opportunity, and they would prove their capacity. That it was unjust, wicked, and cruel, the result of an unnatural prejudice, that debarred them from places of respectability, and that public opinion could and should be corrected upon this subject. That it was only necessary to make a sacrifice of feeling, and an innovation on the customs of society, to establish a different order of things,—that as Anti-Slavery men, they were willing to make these sacrifices, and determined to take the colored man by the hand, making common cause with him in affliction, and bear a part of the odium heaped upon him. That his cause was the cause of God—that "In as much as ye did it not unto the least of these my little ones, ye did it not unto me," and that as Anti-Slavery men, they would "do right if the heavens fell." Thus, was the cause espoused, and thus did we expect much. But in all this, we were doomed to disappointment, sad, sad disappointment. Instead of realising what we had hoped for, we find ourselves occupying the very same position in relation to our Anti-Slavery friends, as we do in relation to the pro-slavery part of the community—a mere secondary, underling position, in all our relations to them, and any thing more than this, is not a matter of course affair—it comes not by established anti-slavery custom or right, but like that which emanates from the proslavery portion of the community, by mere sufferance.

It is true, that the "Liberator" office, in Boston, has got Elijah Smith, a colored youth, at the cases—the "Standard," in New York, a young colored man, and the "Freeman," in Philadelphia, William Still, another, in the publication office, as "packing clerk"; yet these are but three out of the hosts that fill these offices in their various departments, all occupying places that could have been, and as we once thought, would have been, easily enough, occupied by colored men. Indeed, we can have no other idea about anti-slavery in this country, than that the legitimate persons to fill any and every position about an anti-slavery establishment are colored persons. Nor will it do to argue in extenuation, that white men are as justly entitled to them as colored men; because white men do not from *necessity* become anti-slavery men in order to get situations; they being white men, may occupy any position they are capable of filling—in a word, their chances are endless, every avenue in the country being opened to them. They do not therefore become abolitionists, for the sake of employment—at least, it is not the song that anti-slavery sung, in the first love of the new faith, proclaimed by its disciples.

And if it be urged that colored men are incapable as yet to fill these positions, all that we have to say is, that the cause has fallen far short; almost equivalent to a failure, of a tithe, of what it promised to do in half the period of its existence, to this time, if it have not as yet, now a period of twenty years, raised up colored men enough, to fill the offices within its patronage. We think it is not unkind to say, if it had been half as faithful to itself, as it should have been—its professed principles we mean; it could have reared and tutored from childhood, colored men enough by this time, for its own especial purpose. These we know could have been easily obtained, because colored people in general, are favorable to the anti-slavery cause, and wherever there is an adverse manifestation, it arises from sheer ignorance; and we have now but comparatively few such among us. There is one thing certain, that no colored person, except such as would reject education altogether, would be adverse to putting their child with an anti-slavery person, for educational advantages. This then could have been done. But it has not been done, and let the cause of it be whatever it may, and let whoever may be to blame, we are willing to let all that pass, and extend to our anti-slavery brethren the right-hand of fellowship, bidding them God-speed in the propagation of good and wholesome sentiments—for whether they are practically carried out or not, the profession are in themselves all right and good. Like Christianity, the principles are holy and of divine origin. And we believe, if ever a man started right, with pure and holy motives, Mr. Garrison did; and that, had he the power of making the cause what it should be, it would all be right, and there never would have been any cause for the remarks we have made, though in kindness, and with the purest of motives. We are nevertheless, still occupying a miserable position in the community, wherever we live; and what we most desire is, to draw the attention of our people to this fact, and point out what, in our opinion, we conceive to be a proper remedy.

III | AMERICAN COLONIZATION

W HEN we speak of colonization, we wish distinctly to be understood, as speaking of the "American Colonization Society"—or that which is under its influence—commenced in Richmond, Virginia, in 1817, under the influence of Mr. Henry Clay of Ky., Judge Bushrod Washington of Va., and other Southern slaveholders, having for their express object, as their speeches and doings all justify us in asserting in good faith, the removal of the free colored people from the land of their birth, for the security of the slaves, as property to the slave propagandists.

This scheme had no sooner been propagated, than the old and leading colored men of Philadelphia, Pa., with Richard Allen, James Forten, and others at their head, true to their trust and the cause of their brethren, summoned the colored people together, and then and there, in language and with voices pointed and loud, protested against the scheme as an outrage, having no other object in view, than the benefit of the slave-holding interests of the country, and that as freemen, they would never prove recreant to the cause of their brethren in bondage, by leaving them without hope of redemption from their chains. This determination of the colored patriots of Philadelphia was published in full, authentically, and circulated throughout the length and breadth of the country by the papers of the day. The colored people every where received the news, and at once endorsed with heart and soul, the doings of the Anti-Colonization Meeting of colored freemen. From that time forth, the colored people generally have had no sympathy with the colonization scheme, nor confidence in its leaders, looking upon them all, as arrant hypocrites, seeking every opportunity to deceive them. In a word, the monster was crippled in its infancy, and has never as yet recovered from the stroke. It is true, that like its ancient sire, that was "more subtile than all the beasts of the field," it has inherited a large portion of his most prominent characteristic—an idiosyncrasy with the animal—that enables him to entwine himself into the greater part of the Church and other institutions of the country, which having once entered there, leaves his venom, which put such a spell on the conductors of those institutions, that is only on condition that a colored person consents to go to the neighborhood of his kindred brother monster the boa, that he may find admission in the one or the other. We look upon the American Colonization Society as one of the most arrant enemies of the colored man, ever seeking to discomfit him, and envying him of every privilege that he may enjoy. We believe it to be anti-Christian in its character, and misanthropic in its pretended sympathies. Because if this were not the case, men could not be found professing morality and Christianity—as to our astonishment we have found them—who unhesitatingly say, "I know it is right"—that is in itself—"to do" so and so, "and I am willing and ready to do it, but only on condition, that you go to Africa." Indeed, a highly talented clergyman, informed us in November last (three months ago) in the city of Philadelphia, that he was present when the Rev. Doctor J. P. Durbin, late President of Dickinson College, called on Rev. Mr. P. or B., to consult him

about going to Liberia, to take charge of the literary department of an University in contemplation, when the following conversation ensued: Mr. P.—"Doctor, I have as
much and more than I can do here, in educating the youth
of our own country, and preparing them for usefulness here
at home." Dr. D.—"Yes, but do as you may, you can never
be elevated here." Mr. P.—"Doctor, do you not believe that
the religion of our blessed Redeemer Jesus Christ, has
morality, humanity, philanthropy, and justice enough in it to
elevate us, and enable us to obtain our rights in this our own
country?" Dr. D.—"No, indeed, sir, I do not, and if you
depend upon that, your hopes are vain!" Mr. P.—Turning to
Doctor Durbin, looking him solemnly, though affectionately in the face, remarked—"Well, Doctor Durbin, we both
profess to be ministers of Christ; but dearly as I love the
cause of my Redeemer, if for a moment, I could entertain
the opinion you do about Christianity, I would not serve
him another hour!" We do not know, as we were not
advised, that the Rev. doctor added in fine,—"Well, you
may quit now, for all your serving him will not avail against
the power of the god (hydra) of Colonization." Will any one
doubt for a single moment, the justice of our strictures on
colonization, after reading the conversation between the
Rev. Dr. Durbin and the colored clergyman? Surely not. We
can therefore make no account of it, but that of setting it
down as being the worst enemy of the colored people.

Recently, there has been a strained effort in the city of
New York on the part of the Rev. J. B. Pinney and others,
of the leading white colonizationists, to get up a movement
among some poor pitiable colored men—we say pitiable, for
certainly the colored persons who are at this period capable
of loaning themselves to the enemies of their race, against
the best interest of all that we hold sacred to that race, are

pitiable in the lowest extreme, far beneath the dignity of an enemy, and therefore, we pass them by with the simple remark, that this is the hobby that colonization is riding all over the country, as the "tremendous" access of colored people to their cause within the last twelve months. We should make another remark here perhaps, in justification of governor Pinney's New York allies—that is, report says, that in the short space of some three or five months, one of his confidants, benefited himself to the "reckoning" of from eleven to fifteen hundred dollars, or "such a matter," while others were benefited in sums "pretty considerable" but of a less "reckoning." Well, we do not know after all, that they may not have quite as good a right, to pocket part of the spoils of this "grab game," as any body else. However, they are of little consequence, as the ever watchful eye of those excellent gentlemen and faithful guardians of their people's rights—the *Committee of Thirteen*, consisting of Messrs. John J. Zuille, *Chairman*, T. Joiner White, Philip A. Bell, *Secretaries*, Robert Hamilton, George T. Downing, Jeremiah Powers, John T. Raymond, Wm. Burnett, James McCuen Smith, Ezekiel Dias, Junius C. Morel, Thomas Downing, and Wm. J. Wilson, have properly chastised this pet-slave of Mr. Pinney, and made it "know its place," by keeping within the bounds of its master's enclosure.

In expressing our honest conviction of the designedly injurious character of the Colonization Society, we should do violence to our own sense of individual justice, if we did not express the belief, that there are some honest hearted men, who not having seen things in the proper light, favor that scheme, simply as a means of elevating the colored people. Such persons, so soon as they become convinced of their error, immediately change their policy, and advocate the elevation of the colored people, anywhere and everywhere, in common with other men. Of such were the early abolitionists as before stated; and the great and good Dr. F. J. Lemoyne, Gerrit Smith, and Rev. Charles Avery, and a host of others, who were Colonizationists, before espousing the cause of our elevation, here at home, and nothing but an honorable sense of justice, induces us to make these exceptions, as there are many good persons within our knowledge, whom we believe to be well wishers of the colored people, who may favor colonization.★ But the animal itself is the same "hydra-headed monster," let whomsoever may fancy to pet it. A serpent is a serpent, and none the less a viper, because nestled in the bosom of an honest hearted man. This the colored people must bear in mind, and keep clear of the hideous thing, lest its venom may be test upon them. But why deem any argument necessary to show the unrighteousness of colonization? Its very origin as before shown—the source from whence it sprung, being the off-spring of slavery—is in itself, sufficient to blast it in the estimation of every colored person in the United States, who has sufficient intelligence to comprehend it.

We dismiss this part of the subject, and proceed to consider the mode and means of our elevation in the United States.

★Benjamin Coates, Esq., a merchant of Philadelphia, we believe to be an honest hearted man, and real friend of the colored people, and a true, though as yet, rather undecided philanthropist. Mr. Coates, to our knowledge, has supported three or four papers published by colored men, for the elevation of colored people in the United States, and given, as he continues to do, considerable sums to their support. We have recently learned from himself, that, though he still advocates Colonization, simply as a means of elevating the colored race of the United States, that he has *left* the Colonization Society, and prefers seeing colored people located on this continent, to going to Liberia, or elsewhere off of it—though his zeal for the enlightenment of Africa, is unabated, as every good man's should be; and we are satisfied, that Mr. Coates is neither well understood, nor rightly appreciated by the friends of our cause. One thing we do know, that he left the Colonization Society, because he could not conscientiously subscribe to its measures.

IV | OUR ELEVATION IN THE UNITED STATES

THAT very little comparatively as yet has been done, to attain a respectable position as a class in this country, will not be denied, and that the successful accomplishment of this end is also possible, must also be admitted; but in what manner, and by what means, has long been, and is even now, by the best thinking minds among the colored people themselves, a matter of difference of opinion.

We believe in the universal equality of man, and believe in that declaration of God's word, in which it is there positively said, that "God has made of one blood all the nations that dwell on the face of the earth." Now of "the nations that dwell on the face of the earth," that is, all the people— there are one thousand millions of souls, and of this vast number of human beings, two-thirds are colored, from black, tending in complexion to the olive or that of the Chinese, with all the intermediate and admixtures of black and white, with the various "crosses" as they are physiologically, but erroneously termed, to white. We are thus explicit in stating these points, because we are determined to be understood by all. We have then, two colored to one white person throughout the earth, and yet, singular as it may appear, according to the present geographical and political history of the world, the white race predominates over the colored; or in other words, wherever there is one white person, that one rules and governs two colored persons. This is a living undeniable truth, to which we call the especial attention of the colored reader in particular. Now there is a cause for this, as there is no effect without a cause, a comprehensible remediable cause. We all believe in the justice of God, that he is impartial, "looking upon his children with an eye of care," dealing out to them all, the measure of his goodness; yet, how can we reconcile ourselves to the difference that exists between the colored and the white races, as they truthfully present themselves before our eyes? To solve this problem, is to know the remedy; and to know it, is but necesssary, in order successfully to apply it. And we shall but take the colored people of the United States, as a fair sample of the colored races everywhere of the present age, as the arguments that apply to the one, will apply to the other, whether Christians, Mahomedans, or pagans.

The colored races are highly susceptible of religion; it is a constituent principle of their nature, and an excellent trait in their character. But unfortunately for them, they carry it too far. Their hope is largely developed, and consequently, they usually stand still—hope in God, and really expect Him to do that for them, which it is necessary they should do themselves. This is their great mistake, and arises from a misconception of the character and ways of Deity. We must know God, that is understand His nature and purposes, in order to serve Him; and to serve Him well, is but to know him rightly. To depend for assistance upon God, is a *duty* and right; but to know when, how, and in what manner to obtain it, is the key to this great Bulwark of Strength, and Depository of Aid.

God himself is perfect; perfect in all his works and ways. He has means for every end; and every means used must be adequate to the end to be gained. God's means are laws—fixed laws of nature, a part of His own being, and as immutable, as unchangeable as Himself. Nothing can be accomplished but through the medium of, and conformable to these laws.

They are *three*—and like God himself, represented in the three persons in the God-head—the *Spiritual*, *Moral* and *Physical* Laws.

That which is Spiritual, can only be accomplished through the medium of the Spiritual law; that which is Moral, through the medium of the Moral law; and that which is Physical, through the medium of the Physical law. Otherwise than this, it is useless to expect any thing. Does a person want a spiritual blessing, he must apply through the medium of the spiritual law—*pray* for it in order to obtain it. If they desire to do a moral good, they must apply through the medium of the moral law—exercise their sense and feeling of *right* and *justice*, in order to effect it. Do they want to attain a physical end, they can only do so through the medium of the physical law—go to *work* with muscles, hands, limbs, might and strength, and this, and nothing else will attain it.

The argument that man must pray for what he receives, is a mistake, and one that is doing the colored people especially, incalculable injury. That man must pray in order to get to Heaven, every Christian will admit—but a great truth we have yet got to learn, that he can live on earth whether he is religious or not, so that he conforms to the great law of God, regulating the things of earth; the great physical laws. It is only necessary, in order to convince our people of their error and palpable mistake in this matter, to call their attention to the fact, that there are no people more religious in this Country, than the colored people, and none so poor and miserable as they. That prosperity and wealth, smiles upon the efforts of wicked white men, whom we know to utter the name of God with curses, instead of praises. That among the slaves, there are thousands of them religious, continually raising their voices, sending up their prayers to God, invoking His aid in their behalf, asking for a speedy deliverance; but they are still in chains, although they have thrice suffered out their three score years and ten. That "God sendeth rain upon the just and unjust," should be sufficieint to convince us that our success in life, does not depend upon our religions character, but that the physical laws governing all earthly and temporary affairs, benefit equally the just and the unjust. Any other doctrine than this, is downright delusion, unworthy of a free people, and only intended for slaves. That all men and women, should be moral, upright, good and religious—we mean *Christians*—we would not utter a word against, and could only wish that it were so; but, what we here desire to do is, to correct the long standing error among a large body of the colored people in this country, that the cause of our oppression and degradation, is the displeasure of God towards us, because of our unfaithfulness to Him. This is not true; because if God is just—and he is—there could be no justice in prospering white men with his fostering care, for more than two thousand years, in all their wickedness, while dealing out to the colored people, the measure of his displeasure, for not half the wickedness as that of the whites. Here then is our mistake, and let it forever henceforth be corrected. We are no longer slaves, believing any interpretation that our oppressors may give the word of God, for the purpose of deluding us to the more easy subjugation; but freemen, comprising some of the first minds of intelligence and rudimental qualifications, in the country. What then is the remedy, for our degradation and oppression? This appears now to be the only remaining question—the means of successful elevation in this our own native land? This depends entirely upon the application of the means of Elevation.

V | MEANS OF ELEVATION

MORAL theories have long been resorted to by us, as a means of effecting the redemption of our brethren in bonds, and the elevation of the free colored people in this country. Experience has taught us, that speculations are not enough; that the *practical* application of principles adduced, the thing carried out, is the only true and proper course to pursue.

We have speculated and moralised much about equality—claiming to be as good as our neighbors, and every body else—all of which, may do very well in ethics—but not in politics. We live in society among men, conducted by men, governed by rules and regulations. However arbitrary, there are certain policies that regulate all well organized institutions and corporate bodies. We do not intend here to speak of the legal political relations of society, for those are treated on elsewhere. The business and social, or voluntary and mutual policies, are those that now claim our attention. Society regulates itself—being governed by mind, which like water, finds its own level. "Like seeks like," is a principle in the laws of matter, as well as of mind. There is such a thing as inferiority of things, and positions; at least society has made them so; and while we continue to live among men, we must agree to all *just* measures—all those we mean, that do not necessarily infringe on the rights of others. By the regulations of society, there is no equality of attainments. By this, we do not wish to be understood as advocating the actual equal attainments of every individual; but we mean to say, that if these attainments be necessary for the elevation of the white man, they are necessary for the elevation of the colored man. That some colored men and women, in a like proportion to the whites, should be qualified in all the attainments possessed by them. It is one of the regulations of society the world over, and we shall have to conform to it, or be discarded as unworthy of the associations of our fellows.

Cast our eyes about us and reflect for a moment, and what do we behold! every thing that presents to view gives evidence of the skill of the white man. Should we purchase a pound of groceries, a yard of linen, a vessel of crockery-ware, a piece of furniture, the very provisions that we eat,—all, all are the products of the white man, purchased by us from the white man, consequently, our earnings and means, are all given to the white man.

Pass along the avenues of any city or town, in which you live—behold the trading shops—the manufactures—see the operations of the various machinery—see the stage-coaches coming in, bringing the mails of intelligence—look at the railroads interlining every section, bearing upon them their mighty trains, flying with the velocity of the swallow, ushering in the hundreds of industrious, enterprising travellers. Cast again your eyes widespread over the ocean—see the vessels in every direction with their white sheets spread to the winds of heaven, freighted with the commerce, merchandise and wealth of many nations. Look as you pass along through the cities, at the great and massive buildings—the beautiful and extensive structures of architecture—behold the ten thousand cupolas, with their spires all reared up towards heaven, intersecting the territory of the clouds—all standing as mighty living monuments, of the industry, enterprise, and intelligence of the white man. And yet, with all these living truths, rebuking us with scorn, we strut about, place our hands akimbo, straighten up ourselves to our greatest height, and talk loudly about being "as good as any body." How do we compare with them? Our fathers are their coachmen, our brothers their cookmen, and ourselves their waiting-men. Our mothers their nurse-women, our sisters their scrub-women, our daughters their maid-women, and our wives their washer-women. Until colored men, attain to a position above permitting their mothers, sisters, wives, and daughters, to do the drudgery and menial offices of other men's wives and daughters; it is useless, it is nonsense, it is pitiable mockery, to talk about equality and elevation in society. The world is looking upon us, with feelings of commisseration, sorrow, and contempt. We scarcely deserve sympathy, if we peremptorily refuse advice, bearing upon our elevation.

We will suppose a case for argument: In this city reside, two colored families, of three sons and three daughters each. At the head of each family, there is an old father and mother. The opportunities of these families, may or may not be the same for educational advantages—be that as it may, the children of the one go to school, and become qualified for the duties of life. One daughter becomes school-teacher, another a mantua-maker, and a third a fancy shop-keeper; while one son becomes a farmer, another a merchant, and a third a mechanic. All enter into business with fine prospects, marry respectably, and settle down in domestic comfort— while the six sons and daughters of the other family, grow up without educational and business qualifications, and the highest aim they have, is to apply to the sons and daughters of the first named family, to hire for domestics! Would there be an equality here between the children of these two families? Certainly not. This, then, is precisely the position of the colored people generally in the United States, compared with the whites. What is necessary to be done, in order to attain an equality, is to change the condition, and the person is at once changed. If, as before stated, a knowledge of all the various business enterprises, trades, professions, and sciences, is necessary for the elevation of the white, a knowledge of them also is necessary for the elevation of the colored man; and he cannot be elevated without them.

White men are producers—we are consumers. They build houses, and we rent them. They raise produce, and we consume it. They manufacture clothes and wares, and we garnish ourselves with them. They build coaches, vessels, cars, hotels, saloons, and other vehicles and places of accommodation, and we deliberately wait until they have got them in readiness, then walk in, and contend with as much assurance for a "right," as though the whole thing was bought by, paid for, and belonged to us. By their literary attainments, they are the contributors to, authors and teachers of, literature, science, religion, law, medicine, and all other useful attainments that the world now makes use of. We have no reference to ancient times—we speak of modern things.

These are the means by which God intended man to succeed: and this discloses the secret of the white man's success with all of his wickedness, over the head of the colored man, with all of his religion. We have been pointed and plain, on this part of the subject, because we desire our readers to see persons and things in their true position. Until we are determined to change the condition of things, and raise ourselves above the position in which we are now prostrated, we must hang our heads in sorrow, and hide our

faces in shame. It is enough to know that these things are so;
the causes we care little about. Those we have been examining, complaining about, and moralising over, all our life
time. This we are weary of. What we desire to learn now is,
how to effect a *remedy*; this we have endeavored to point
out. Our elevation must be the result of *self-efforts*, and work
of our *own hands*. No other human power can accomplish it.
If we but determine it shall be so, it will be so. Let each one
make the case his own, and endeavor to rival his neighbor,
in honorable competition.

These are the proper and only means of elevating ourselves and attaining equality in this country or any other,
and it is useless, utterly futile, to think about going any
where, except we are determined to use these as the necessary means of developing our manhood. The means are at
hand, within our reach. Are we willing to try them? Are we
willing to raise ourselves superior to the condition of slaves,
or continue the meanest underlings, subject to the beck and
call of every creature bearing a pale complexion? If we are,
we had as well remained in the South, as to have come to
the North in search of more freedom. What was the object
of our parents in leaving the south, if it were not for the
purpose of attaining equality in common with others of
their fellow citizens, by giving their children access to all the
advantages enjoyed by others? Surely this was their object.
They heard of liberty and equality here, and they hastened
on to enjoy it, and no people are more astonished and disappointed than they, who for the first time, on beholding
the position we occupy here in the free north—what is
called, and what they expect to find, the free States. They at
once tell us, that they have as much liberty in the south as
we have in the north—that there as free people, they are
protected in their rights—that we have nothing more—that

in other respects they have the same opportunity, indeed the preferred opportunity, of being their maids, servants, cooks, waiters, and menials in general, there, as we have here—that had they known for a moment, before leaving, that such was to be the only position they occupied here, they would have remained where they were, and never left. Indeed, such is the disappointment in many cases, that they immediately return back again, completely insulted at the idea, of having us here at the north, assume ourselves to be their superiors. Indeed, if our superior advantages of the free States, do not induce and stimulate us to the higher attainments in life, what in the name of degraded humanity will do it? Nothing, surely nothing. If, in fine, the advantages of free schools in Massachusetts, New York, Pennsylvania, Ohio, Michigan, and wherever else we may have them, do not give us advantages and pursuits superior to our slave brethren, then are the unjust assertions of Messrs. Henry Clay, John C. Calhoun, Theodore Frelinghuysen, late Governor Poindexter of Mississippi, George McDuffy, Governor Hammond of South Carolina, Extra Billy (present Governor) Smith, of Virginia, and the host of our oppressors, slave-holders and others, true, that we are insusceptible and incapable of elevation to the more respectable, honorable, and higher attainments among white men. But this we do not believe—neither do you, although our whole life and course of policy in this country are such, that it would seem to prove otherwise. The degradation of the slave parent has been entailed upon the child, induced by the subtle policy of the oppressor, in regular succession handed down from father to son—a system of regular submission and servitude, menialism and dependence, until it has become almost a physiological function of our system, an actual condition of our nature. Let this no longer be so, but let us determine to equal the whites among whom we live, not by declarations and unexpressed self-opinion, for we have always had enough of that, but by actual proof in acting, doing, and carrying out practically, the measures of equality. Here is our nativity, and here have we the natural right to abide and be elevated through the measures of our own efforts.

VI | THE UNITED STATES OUR COUNTRY

O UR common country is the United States. Here were we born, here raised and educated; here are the scenes of childhood; the pleasant associations of our school going days; the loved enjoyments of our domestic and fireside relations, and the sacred graves of our departed fathers and mothers, and from here will we not be driven by any policy that may be schemed against us.

We are Americans, having a birthright citizenship—natural claims upon the country—claims common to all others of our fellow citizens—natural rights, which may, by virtue of unjust laws, be obstructed, but never can be annulled. Upon these do we place ourselves, as immovably fixed as the decrees of the living God. But according to the economy that regulates the policy of nations, upon which rests the basis of justifiable claims to all freeman's rights, it may be necessary to take another view of, and enquire into the political claims of colored men.

CLAIMS OF COLORED MEN AS CITIZENS OF THE UNITED STATES

T HE political basis upon which rests the establishment of all free nations, as the first act in their organization, is the security by constitutional provisions, of the fundamental claims of citizenship.

The legitimate requirement, politically considered, necessary to the justifiable claims for protection and full enjoyment of all the rights and privileges of an unqualified freeman, in all democratic countries is, that each person so endowed, shall have made contributions and investments in the country. Where there is no investment there can be but little interest; hence an adopted citizen is required to reside a sufficient length of time, to form an attachment and establish some interest in the country of his adoption, before he can rightfully lay any claims to citizenship. The pioneer who leads in the discovery or settlement of a country, as the first act to establish a right therein, erects a building of whatever dimensions, and seizes upon a portion of the soil. The soldier, who braves the dangers of the battle-field, in defence of his country's rights, and the toiling laborer and husbandman, who cuts down and removes the forest, levels and constructs post-roads and other public highways—the mechanic, who constructs and builds up houses, villages, towns, and cities, for the conveniency of inhabitants—the farmer, who cultivates the soil for the production of breadstuffs and forage, as food and feed for man and beast—all of these are among the first people of a democratic state, whose claims are legitimate as freemen of the commonwealth. A freeman in a political sense, is a citizen of unrestricted rights in the state, being eligible to the highest position known to their civil code. They are the preferred persons in whom may be invested the highest privileges, and to whom may be entrusted fundamentally the most sacred rights of the country; because, having made the greatest investments, they necessarily have the greatest interests; and consequently, are the safest hands into which to place so high and sacred a trust. Their interest being the country's, and the interest of the country being the interest of the people; therefore, the protection of their own interests necessarily protects the interests of the whole country and people. It is this simple but great principle of primitive rights, that forms the fundamental basis of citizenship in all free countries, and it is upon this principle, that the rights of the colored man in this country to citizenship are fixed.

The object of this volume is, to enlighten the minds of a large class of readers upon a subject with which they are unacquainted, expressed in comprehensible language, therefore we have studiously avoided using political and legal phrases, that would serve more to perplex than inform them. To talk about the barons, king John, and the Magna Charta, would be foreign to a work like this, and only destroy the interest that otherwise might be elicited in the subject. Our desire is, to arrest the attention of the American people in general, and the colored people in particular, to great truths as heretofore but little thought of. What claims then have colored men, based upon the principles set forth, as fundamentally entitled to citizenship? Let the living records of history answer the enquiry.

When Christopher Columbus, in 1492, discovered America, natives were found to pay little or no attention to cultivation, being accustomed by hereditary pursuit, to war, fishing, and the sports of the chase. The Spaniards and Portuguese, as well as other Europeans who ventured here, came as mineral speculators, and not for the purpose of improving the country.

As the first objects of speculation are the developments of the mineral wealth of every newly discovered country, so was it with this. Those who came to the new world, were not of the common people, seeking in a distant land the means of livelihood, but moneyed capitalists, the grandees and nobles, who reduced the natives to servitude by confining them to the mines. To have brought large numbers of the peasantry at that early period, from the monarchies of Europe, to the wilds of America, far distant from the civil and military powers of the home governments, would have been to place the means of self-control into their own hands, and invite them to rebellion against the crowns. The capitalist miners were few, compared to the number of laborers required; and the difficulty at that time of the transportation of suitable provisions for their sustenance, conduced much to the objection of bringing them here. The natives were numerous, then easily approached by the wily seductions of the Europeans, easily yoked and supported, having the means of sustenance at hand, the wild fruits and game of the forest, the fish of the waters and birds of the country. All these as naturally enough, European adventurers would be cautious against introducing into common use among hundreds of thousands of laborers, under all the influences incident of a foreign climate in a foreign country, in its primitive natural state. The Indians were then preferred for many reasons, as the common laborers on the continent, where nothing but the mining interests were thought of or carried on. This noble race of Aborigines, continued as the common slaves of the new world, to bear the yoke of foreign oppression, until necessity induced a substitute for them. They sunk by scores under the heavy weight of oppression, and were fast passing from the shores of time. At this, the foreigners grew alarmed, and of necessity, devised ways and means to obtain an adequate substitute. A few European laborers were brought into the country, but the influence of climate and mode of living, operated entirely against them. They were as inadequate to stand the climate, as the nobles were themselves.

From the earliest period of the history of nations, the African race had been known as an industrious people, cultivators of the soil. The grain fields of Ethiopia and Egypt were the themes of the poet, and their garners, the subject of the historian. Like the present America, all the world went to Africa, to get a supply of commodities. Their massive piles of masonry, their skilful architecture, their subterranean vaults, their deep and mysterious wells, their extensive artificial channels, their mighty sculptured solid rocks, and provinces of stone quarries; gave indisputable evidence, of the hardihood of that race of people.

Nor was Africa then, without the evidence of industry, as history will testify. All travelers who had penetrated towards the interior of the continent, have been surprised at the seeming state of civilization and evidences of industry among the inhabitants of that vast country. These facts were familiar to Europeans, who were continually trading on coast of Africa, as it was then the most important part of adventure and research, known to the world. In later periods still, the history of African travelers, confirm all the former accounts concerning the industry of the people.

John and Richard Lander, two young English noblemen, in 1828, under the patronage of the English government, sailed to the western coast of Africa, on an expedition of research. In their voyage up the river Niger, their description of the scenes is extravagant. They represent the country on each side of the river, for several hundred miles up the valley, as being not only beautiful and picturesque, but the fields as in a high state of cultivation, clothed in the verdure of husbandry, waving before the gentle breezes, with the rich products of industry—maize, oats, rye, millet, and wheat, being among the fruits of cultivation. The fences were of various descriptions: hedge, wicker, some few pannel, and the old fashioned zig-zag, known as the "Virginia worm fence"—the hedge and worm fence being the most common. Their cattle were fine and in good order, looking in every particular, except perhaps in size, as well as European cattle on the best managed farms. The fruit groves were delightful to the eye of the beholder. Every variety common to the country, were there to be seen in a high state of cultivation. Their roads and public highways were in good condition, and well laid out, as by the direction of skillful supervising surveyors. The villages, towns, and cities, many of them, being a credit to the people. Their cities were well laid out, and presented evidence of educated minds and mechanical ingenuity. In many of the workshops in which they went, they found skillful workmen, in iron, copper, brass, steel, and gold; and their implements of husbandry and war, were as well manufactured by African sons of toil, as any in the English manufactories, save that they had not quite so fine a finish, garnish and embellishment. This is a description, given of the industry and adaptedness of the people of Africa, to labor and toil of every kind. As it was very evident, that where there were manufactories of various metals, the people must of necessity be inured to mining operations, so it was also very evident, that this people must be a very hardy and enduring people.

In 1442, fifty years previous to the sailing of Columbus in search of a new world, Anthony Gonzales, Portuguese, took from the gold coast of Guinea, ten Africans and a quantity of gold dust, which he carried back to Lisbon with him. These Africans were set immediately to work in the gardens of the emperor, which so pleased his queen, that the number were much augmented, all of whom were found to be skillful and industrious in agriculture.

In 1481, eleven years prior to the discovery by Columbus, the Portuguese built a fort on the Gold Coast, and there commenced mining in search of gold. During this time until the year 1502, a period of ten years, had there been no other evidence, there was sufficient time and opportunity, to give full practical demonstrations of the capacity of this people to endure toil, especially in the mining operations, and for this cause and this alone, were they selected in preference to any other race of men, to do the labor of the New World. They had proven themselves physically superior either to the European or American races—in fact, superior physically to any living race of men—enduring fatigue, hunger and thirst— enduring change of climate, habits, manners and customs, with infinitely far less injury to their physical and mental system, than any other people on the face of God's earth.

The following extract shows, that even up to the year 1676, the Indians were enslaved—but that little value were attached to them as laborers, as the price at which they were disposed and sold to purchasers, fully shows:

SLAVERY IN PROVIDENCE, R.I.—Immediately after the struggle between the natives and some of the New England settlers, known as "King Philip's war," it became necessary to dispose of certain Indian captives then in Providence. The method adopted was common in that day, but to us remarkable, as also the names of those who figured prominently therein. Only think of ROGER WILLIAMS sharing in the proceeds of a slave sale. The following is from the "Annals of Providence."

"A town meeting was held before Thomas Field's house, under a tree, by the water side, on the 14th of August, 1676. A committee was appointed to determine in what manner the Indians should be disposed of. They reported as follows:

"Inhabitants wanting, can have Indians at the price they sell at the Island of Rhode Island or elsewhere. All under five, to serve till thirty; above five and under ten, till twenty-eight; above ten to fifteen, till twenty-seven; above fifteen to twenty, till twenty-six; from twenty to thirty, shall serve eight years; all above thirty, seven years.

"We whose names are underwritten, being chosen by the town to see the disposal of the Indians now in town, we agree that Roger Williams, N. Waterman, T. Fenner, H. Ashton, J. Morey, D. Abbot, J. Olney, V. Whitman, J. Whipple, sen., E. Pray, J. Pray, J. Angell, Jas. Angell, T. Arnold, A. Man, T. Field, E. Bennett, T. Clemence, W. Lancaster, W. Hopkins, W. Hawkins, W. Harris, Z. Field, S. Winsor, and Capt. Fenner, shall each have a whole share in the product. I. Woodward and R. Pray, three-fourths of a share each. J. Smith, E. Smith, S. Whipple, N. Whipple, and T. Walling each half a share."

Signed, "Roger Williams, Thomas Harris, sen., Thomas [✕] Angell, Thomas Field, John Whipple, Jr."

To gratify curiosity as to the price of Indians on those terms, the following extracts are made from an account of sales about this time;

"To Anthony Low, five Indians, great and small, £8.

"To James Rogers, two, for twenty bushels of Indian corn.

"To Philip Smith, two, in silver, $4 10.
"To Daniel Allen, one, in silver, $2 10.
"To C. Carr, one, twelve bushels of Indian corn.
"To Elisha Smith, one, in wool, 100 lbs.
"To   "   " one, for three fat sheep."

From 1492, the discovery of Hispaniola, to 1502, the short space of but four years, such was the mortality among the natives, that the Spaniards then holding rule there, "began to employ a few" Africans in the mines of the Island. The experiment was effective—a successful one. The Indian and African were enslaved together, when the Indian sunk, and the African stood. It was not until June the 24th of the year 1498, that the Continent was discovered by John Cabot, a Venitian, who sailed in August of the previous year 1497, from Bristol, under the patronage of Henry VII., King of England, with two vessels, "freighted by the merchants of London and Bristol, with articles of traffic," his son Sebastian, and 300 men. In 1517, but the short period of thirteen years from the date of their first introduction, Carolus V., King of Spain, by the right of a patent, granted permission to a number of persons, annually, to supply to the Islands of Hispaniola, (St. Domingo,) Cuba, Jamaica, and Porto Rico, natives of Africa, to the number of four thousand annually. John Hawkins, an unprincipled Englishman—whose name should be branded with infamy—was the first person known to have engaged in so inhuman a traffic, and that living monster his mistress, Queen Elizabeth, engaged with him and shared in the profits.

The natives of Africa, on their introduction into a foreign country, soon discovered the loss of their accustomed food, and mode and manner of living. The Aborigines subsisted mainly by game and fish, with a few patches of maize or Indian corn near their wigwams, which were generally attended by the women, while the men were absent. The grains and fruits, such as they had been accustomed to, were not to be had among the Aborigines of the country, and this first induced the African to cultivate patches of ground in the neighborhood of the mines, for the raising of food for his own sustenance. This trait in their character was observed, and regarded by the Spaniards with considerable interest; and when on contracting with the English slave-dealer, Captain Hawkins, and others for new supplies of slaves, they were careful to request them to secure a quantity of the seeds and different products of the country, to bring with them to the New World. Many of these were cultivated to some extent, while those indigenous to America, were cultivated by them with considerable success. And up to this day, it is a custom on many of the slave plantations of the South, to allow the slave his "patch," and Saturday afternoon or Sabbath day, to cultivate it.

Shortly after the commencement of the shameful traffic in the blood and bones of men—the destiny and chastity of women by Captain Hawkins, and what was termed England's "Virgin Queen"; Elizabeth gave a license to Sir Walter Raleigh, to search for uninhabited lands, and seize upon all uninhabited by Christians. Sir Walter discovered the coast of North Carolina and Virginia, assigning the name of "Virginia" to the whole coast now composing the old state. A feeble colony was settled here, which did not avail, and it was not until the month of April, 1607, that the first permanent settlement was made in Virginia, under the patronage of letters patent from James I, King of England, to Thomas Gates and his associates.

This was the first settling of North America, and thirteen years anterior to the landing of the Pilgrims.

"No permanent settlement was effected in what is now

called the United States, till the reign of James the First."—
Ramsay's Hist. U. S., vol I., p. 38.

"The month of April, 1607, is the epoch of the first permanent settlement on the coast of Virginia; the name then
given to all that extent of country which forms thirteen
States."—*Ibid.*, p. 39. The whole coast of the country was
now explored, not for the purpose of trade and agriculture—because there were no products in the country—the
natives not producing sufficient provisions to supply present
wants, and, consequently, nothing to trade for; but like the
speculations of their Spanish and Portuguese predecessors,
on the islands and in South America, but for that of mining
gold. Trade and the cultivation of the soil was foreign to
their designs and intention on coming to the continent of
the new world, and they were consequently, disappointed
when failing of success. "At a time when the precious metals
were conceived to be the peculiar and only valuable productions of the new world, when every mountain was supposed to contain a treasure, and every rivulet was searched
for its golden sands, this appearance was fondly considered
as an infallible indication of the mine. Every hand was eager
to dig." . . .

"There was now," says Smith, "no talk, no hope, no
work; but dig gold, wash gold, refine gold. With this imaginary wealth, the first vessel returning to England was loaded,
while the *culture of the land*, and every useful occupation was
totally neglected." . . .

The colonists, thus left, were in miserable circumstances
for want of provisions. The remainder of what they had
brought with them, was so small in quantity, as to be soon
expended—and so damaged in the course of a long voyage,
as to be a source of disease. . . . In their expectation of getting gold, the people were disappointed, the glittering sub-

stance they had sent to England, proving to be a valueless mineral. "Smith, on his return to Jamestown, found the colony reduced to thirty-eight persons, who, in despair, were preparing to abandon the country. He employed caresses, threats, and even violence, in order to prevent them from executing this fatal resolution." *Ibid.*, pp. 45–46. In November, 1620, the Pilgrims or Puritans made the harbor of Cape Cod, and after solemn vows and organization previous to setting foot on shore, they landed safely on "Plymouth Rock," December the 20th, about one month after. They were one hundred and one in number, and from the toils and hardships consequent to a severe season, in a strange country, in less than six months after their arrival, "forty-four persons, nearly one-half of their original number," had died.

. . . "In 1618, in the reign of James I, the British government established a regular trade on the coast of Africa. In the year 1620, negro slaves began to be imported into Virginia: a Dutch ship bringing twenty of them for sale."— *Sampson's Hist. Dict.*, p. 348. The Dutch ship landed her cargo at New Bedford, (now Massachusetts,) as it will be remembered, that the whole coast, now comprising the "Old Thirteen," and original United States, was then called Virginia, so named by Sir Walter Raleigh, in honor of his royal Mistress and patron, Elizabeth, the Virgin Queen, under whom he received his royal patent commission of adventure and expedition.

Beginning their preparation in the slave-trade in 1618, just two years previous, giving time for successfully carrying out the project against the landing of the first emigrant settlers, it will be observed that the African captain, and the "Puritan" emigrants, landed upon the same section of the continent at the same time, 1620—the Pilgrims at Plymouth, and the captives at New Bedford, but a few miles comparatively south.

The country at this period, was one vast wilderness. "The continent of North America was then one continued forest." . . . There were no horses, cattle, sheep, hogs, or tame beasts of any kind. . . . There were no domestic poultry. . . . There were no gardens, orchards, public roads, meadows, or cultivated fields. . . . They "often burned the woods that they could advantageously plant their corn." . . . They had neither spice, salt, bread, butter, cheese, nor milk. . . . They had no set meals, but eat when they were hungry, and could find any thing to satisfy the cravings of nature. . . . Very little of their food was derived from the earth, except what it spontaneously produced. . . . The ground was both their seat and table. . . . Their best bed was a skin. . . . They had neither steel, iron, nor any metallic instruments. . . . —*Ramsay's Hist.*, pp. 39–40.

We adduce not these historical extracts to disparage our brother the Indian—far be it: whatever he may think of our race, according to the manner in which he has been instructed to look upon it, by our mutual oppressor the American nation; we admire his, for the many deeds of noble daring, for which the short history of his liberty-loving people are replete: we sympathise with them, because our brethren are the successors of their fathers in the degradation of American bondage—but we adduce them in evidence against the many aspersions charged against the African race, that their inferiority to the other races caused them to be reduced to servitude. For the purpose of proving that their superiority, and not inferiority, alone was the cause which first suggested to Europeans the substitution of Africans for that of aboriginal or Indian laborers in the mines; and that their superior skill and industry, first suggested to the colonists, the propriety of turning their attention to agricultural and other industrial pursuits, than that of mining.

It is very evident, from what has been adduced, the settlement of Captain John Smith, being in the course of a few months, reduced to thirty-eight, and that of Plymouth, from one hundred and one, to that of fifty-seven in six months— it is evident, that the whites nor the Indians were equal to the hard and almost insurmountable difficulties, that now stood wide-spread before them.

An endless forest, the impenetrable earth; the one to be removed, and the other to be excavated. Towns and cities to be built, and farms to be cultivated—all these presented difficulties too arduous for the European then here, and unknown to the Indian.

It is very evident, that at a period such as this, when the natives themselves had fallen victims to tasks imposed upon them by their usurpers, and the Europeans were sinking beneath the weight of climate and hardships; when food could not be had nor the common conveniences of life procured—when arduous duties of life were to be performed and none capable of doing them, but those who had previously by their labors, not only in their native country, but in the new, so proven themselves—as the most natural consequence, the Africans were resorted to, for the performance of every duty common to domestic life.

There were no laborers known to the colonists from Cape Cod to Cape Look Out, than those of the African race. They entered at once into the mines, extracting therefrom, the rich treasures that for a thousand ages lay hidden in the earth. And from their knowledge of cultivation, the farming interests in the North, and planting in the South, were commenced with a prospect never dreamed of before the introduction of this most extraordinary, hardy race of men: though pagans, yet skilled in all the useful duties of life. Farmers, herdsmen, and laborers in their own country, they required not to be taught to work, and how to do it—but it was only necessary to tell them to go to work, and they at once knew what to do, and how it should be done.

It is notorious, that in the planting States, the blacks themselves are the only skillful cultivators—the proprietor knowing little or nothing about the art, save that which he learns from the African husbandman, while his ignorant white overseer, who is merely there to see that the work is attended to, knows a great deal less. Tobacco, cotton, rice, hemp, indigo, the improvement in Indian corn, and many other important products, are all the result of African skill and labor in this country. And the introduction of the zigzag, or "Virginia Worm Fence," is purely of African origin. Nor was their skill as herdsmen inferior to their other attainments, being among the most accomplished trainers and horsemen in the world. Indeed, to this class of men may be indebted the entire country for the improvement South in the breed of horses. And any one who has travelled South, could not fail to have observed, that all of the leading trainers, jockies, and judges of horses, as well as riders, are men of African descent.

In speaking of the Bornouese, a people from among whom a great many natives have been enslaved by Arabian traders, and sold into foreign bondage, and of course many into this country, "It is said that Bornou can muster 15,000 Shonaas in the field mounted. They are the greatest breeders of cattle in the country, and annually supply Soudan with from two to three thousand horses." . . . "Our road lying along one of them, gave me an excellent view of beautiful villages all round, and herds of cattle grazing in the open country." . . . "Plantations of cotton or indigo now occupy the place where the houses formerly stood." . . . "The Souga market is well supplied with every necessary and luxury in request among the people of the interior." "The country still open and well cultivated, and the villages numerous. We met crowds of people coming from Karro with goods. Some carried them on their heads, others had asses or bullocks, according to their wealth." . . . "The country still highly cultivated." . . . "We also passed several walled towns, quite deserted, the inhabitants having been sold by their conquerors, the Felatohs." "Women sat spinning cotton by the road side, offering for sale to the passing caravans, gussub water, roast-meat, sweet potatoes, coshen nuts," &c. (*Dunham and Clapperton's Travels and Discoveries in North and Central Africa*, vol. 2, pp. 140, 230, 332, 333, 353.)

The forests gave way before them, and extensive verdant fields, richly clothed with produce, rose up as by magic before these hardy sons of toil. In the place of the unskillful and ill-constructed wigwam, houses, villages, towns and cities quickly were reared up in their stead. Being farmers, mechanics, laborers and traders in their own country, they required little or no instruction in these various pursuits. They were in fact, then, to the whole continent, what they are in truth now to the whole Southern section of the Union—the bone and sinews of the country. And even now, the existence of the white man, South, depends entirely on the labor of the black man—the idleness of the one, is sustained by the industry of the other. Public roads and highways are the result of their labor, as are also the first public works, as wharves, docks, forts, and all such improvements. Are not these legitimate investments in the common stock of the nation, which should command a proportionate interest?

We shall next proceed to review the contributions of

colored men to other departments of the nation, and as among the most notorious and historical, we refer to colored American warriors.

VIII | COLORED AMERICAN WARRIORS

AMONG the highest claims that an inhabitant has upon his country, is that of serving in its cause, and assisting to fight its battles. There is no responsibility attended with more personal hazard, and consequently, none for which the country owes a greater debt of gratitude. *Amor patria*, or love of country, is the first requisition and highest attribute of every citizen; and he who voluntarily ventures his own safety for that of his country, is a patriot of the purest character.

When the country's attention is arrested—her fears aroused—her peace disturbed, and her independence endangered—when in the dread and momentous hour, the tap of the drum, the roll of the reveille, the shrill sound of the bugler's trumpet, or the thunders of the cannon's roar, summons the warrior on to the pending conflict—upon whom then do the citizens place their dependence, and in whom the country her trust? Upon him who braves the consequences, and fights his country's battles for his country's sake. Upon whom does the country look, as the most eligible of her favored sons? Upon none more so than he, who shoulders his musket, girds on his sword, and faces the enemy on to the charge. The hero and the warrior, have long been estimated, the favorite sons of a favored people.

In the Convention for the formation of the national

compact, when the question arose on the priority of citizen's rights, an honorable member—Mr. Jefferson, if we mistake not—arose and stated, that for the purpose of henceforward settling a question of such moment to the American people, that nativity of birth, and the descendants of all who had borne arms in their country's struggle for liberty, should be always entitled to all the rights and privileges to which an American citizen could be eligible. This at once, enfranchised the native citizen, and the posterity of all those at the time, who may have been so fortunate as to have been born on the American continent. The question was at once settled, as regards American citizenship. And if we establish our right of equal claims to citizenship with other American people, we shall have done all that is desirable in this view of our position in the country. But if in addition to this, we shall be able to prove, that colored men, not only took part in the great scene of the first act for independence, but that they were the actors—a colored man was really the hero in the great drama, and actually the first victim in the revolutionary tragedy—then indeed, shall we have more than succeeded, and have reared a monument of fame to the history of our deeds, more lasting than the pile that stands on Bunker Hill.

For a concise historical arrangement of colored men, who braved the dangers of the battlefield, we are much indebted to William C. Nell, Esq., formerly of Boston, now of Rochester, N.Y., for a pamphlet, published by him during the last year, which should be read by every American the country through.

For ten years previous, a dissatisfaction had prevailed among the colonists, against the mother country, in consequence of the excessive draughts of supplies, and taxation, made upon them, for the support of the wars carried on in

Europe. The aspect began to change, the light grew dim, the sky darkened, the clouds gathered lower and lower, the lightning glimmered through the black elements around—the storm advanced, until on the fifth of March, 1773, it broke out in terrible blasts, drenching the virgin soil of America, with the blood of her own native sons—Crispus Attuck, a colored man, was the first who headed, the first who commanded, the first who charged, who struck the first blow, and the first whose blood was spilt, and baptized the colony, as a peace-offering on the altar of American liberty. "The people were greatly exasperated. The multitude, armed with clubs, ran towards King street, crying, 'Let us drive out the ribalds; they have no business here!' The rioters rushed furiously towards the Custom House; they approached the sentinel crying, 'Kill him, kill him!' They assaulted him with snowballs, pieces of ice, and whatever they could lay their hands upon. They encountered a band of the populace led by a mulatto named Attucks, who brandished their clubs and pelted them with snow-balls. The maledictions, the imprecations, the execrations of the multidudes were horrible. In the midst of a torrent of invectives from every quarter, the military were challenged to fire. The populace advanced to the points of the bayonets; the soldiers appeared like statues; the cries, the howlings, the menaces, the violent din of bells still sounding the alarm, increased the confusion and the horrors of these moments: at length the mulatto and twelve of his companions, pressing forward environed the soldiers, and striking their muskets with their clubs cried to the multitude: 'Be not afraid, they dare not fire; why do you hesitate, why do you not kill them, why not crush them at once?' The mulatto lifted his arm against Captain Preston, having turned one of the muskets, he seized the bayonet with his left hand, as if he intended to execute his threat. At this moment confused cries were heard: 'The wretches dare not fire!' Firing succeeds. Attucks is slain. Two other discharges follow. Three were killed, five severely wounded, and several others slightly." Attucks was killed by Montgomery, one of Captain Preston's soldiers. He had been foremost in resisting, and was first slain; as proof of front and close engagement, received two balls, one in each breast." "John Adams, counsel for the soldier, admitted that Attucks appeared to have undertaken to be the hero of the night, and to lead the army with banners. John Hancock, in 1774, invokes the injured shades of Maverick, Gray, Caldwell, *Attucks* and Carr." *Nell's Wars*, 1776 and 1812, pp. 5, 6.— RHODE ISLAND also contributes largely to the capital stock of citizenship. "In Rhode Island, the blacks formed an entire regiment, and they discharged their duty with zeal and fidelity. The gallant defence of Red Bank, in which the black regiment bore a part, is among the proofs of their valor." In this contest it will be recollected, that four hundred men met and repulsed, after a terrible sanguinary struggle, fifteen hundred Hessian troops, headed by count Donop." *Ibid.*, p. 10. CONNECTICUT next claims to be heard and given credit on the nation's books. In speaking of the patriots who bore the standard of their country's glory, Judge Goddard, who held the office of commissioner of pensions for nineteen colored soldiers, says, "I cannot refrain from mentioning one aged black man, Primus Babcock, who proudly presented to me an honorable discharge from service during the war, dated at the close of it, wholly in the hand-writing of GEORGE WASHINGTON. Nor can I forget the expression of his feelings, when informed that, after his discharge had been sent to the department, that it could not be returned. At his request it was written for, as he seemed to spurn the pension and reclaim the discharge." It is related of Babcock, that when the British in a successful charge took a number of the Americans prisoners, they were ordered to deliver up their arms by the British officer of the detachment, which demand was readily conceded to by all the prisoners except Babcock, who looking at the officer sternly—at the margin of a mud pond foot of Bunker Hill—turned his musket bayonet downwards, thrusting it into the mire up to the armpit, drawing out his muddy arm, turned to the British officer, and said, "Now dirty your silk glove, and take it—you red coat!" The officer raised his sword as if to cut him down for the impertinence, then replied, "You are too brave a soldier to be killed, you black devil!" A few years since, a musket evidently a relic of the Revolution, was found near the same spot in the singular position of that thrust down by Babcock, no doubt being the same, which was deposited among the relics in the archives at Washington. Babcock died but a few years ago, aged we believe 101 years.

"When Major Montgomery, one of the leaders in the expedition against the colonists, was lifted upon the walls of the fort by his soldiers, flourishing his sword and calling on them to follow him, Jordan Freeman received him on the point of a pike and pinned him dead to the earth." "NEW HAMPSHIRE gives her testimony to the deposit of colored interest. There was a regiment of blacks in the same situation, a regiment of negroes fighting for our liberty and independence, not a white man among them but the officers, in the same dangerous and responsible position. Had they been unfaithful, or given way before the enemy all would have been lost. Three times in succession were they attacked with most desperate fury by well disciplined and veteran troops, and three times did they successfully repel the assault, and thus preserve the army. They fought thus through the war. They were brave and hearty troops." *Nell*, pp. 11, 13.

NEW YORK comes bravely to the call, and sends her

investments by land and sea. In the convention of 1821, for revising the constitution of the State, the question of equal rights having been introduced, Doctor Clarke among other things said, "In the war of the Revolution, these people helped to fight our battles by land and by sea. Some of your states were glad to turn out corps of colored men, and to stand 'shoulder to shoulder' with them. In your late war, they contributed largely towards some of your most splendid victories. On lakes Erie and Champlain, where your fleets triumphed over a foe superior in numbers and engines of death, they were manned in a large proportion with men of color. And in this very house, in the fall of 1814, a bill passed receiving all the branches of your government, authorising the governor to accept the services of a corps of two thousand free people of color. These were times when a man who shouldered his musket did not know but he bared his bosom to receive a death wound from the enemy ere he laid it aside; and in these times these people were found as ready and as willing to volunteer in your service as any other. They were not compelled to go; they were not draughted. . . . They were volunteers. . . . Said Martindale of New York in congress 22 of first month 1828: "Slaves, or negroes who had been slaves, were enlisted as soldiers in the War of the Revolution; and I myself saw a battalion of them, as fine martial looking men as I ever saw, attached to the northern army in the last war, on its march from Plattsburg to Sackett's Harbor."

PENNSYLVANIA contributes an important share in the stock of Independence, as will be seen by the following historical reminiscence: "On the capture of Washington by the British forces, it was judged expedient to fortify without delay, the principal towns and cities exposed to similar attacks. The Vigilance Committee of Philadelphia waited upon three of the principal Colored citizens, namely, James Forten, Bishop Allen, and Absalom Jones, soliticing the aid of the people of Color in erecting suitable defences for the city. Accordingly two thousand five hundred Colored men assembled in the State House yard, and from thence marched to Gray's Ferry, where they labored for two days, almost without intermission. Their labors were so faithful and efficient, that a vote of thanks was tendered them by the Committee. A battalion of Colored troops were at the same time organized in the city, under an officer of the United States army; and they were on the point of marching to the frontier when peace was proclaimed."—*Ibid.*, pp. 14–17–18.★

And even in the slave States, where might reasonably be expected, nothing but bitter hate and burning revenge to

---

★Captain Jonathan Tudas, who led the 500 brave blacks out to build the Redoubt, is now living in Philadelphia, and since the commencement of this publication, we learned the following particulars: When the news arrived of the approach of the British under Major General Ross, upon Baltimore, the expectation ran high, that the city would be taken, and forced marches made, immediately upon Philadelphia. The whole City consequently was thrown into great alarm, when Captain Tudas, applied to the United States Engineer, and offered the services of colored men, who during the week, were summoned to meet at the African Methodist Episcopal Church, on the following Sabbath; when from the pulpit, the Right Rev. Richard Allen, Bishop of the Connexion, made known to the people the peril of the Country, and demands of the Commonwealth; when, the next day, Monday, five hundred volunteered, working incessantly during that day, and on Tuesday, six hundred more were added, swelling the number to eleven hundred men. William Stansberry, arrested and tried a few years ago, as a fugitive slave from Maryland, and Mr. Ignatius Beck, an old respectable colored man, who appeared as a witness, and by whose testimony alone, Mr. Stansberry was released from the grasp of the oppression of his Country, and thereby saved from endless bondage, were both under Captain Tudas, and belong to the faithful eleven hundred Philadelphia black warriors. He farther informs us, that the Engineer gave them credit for having thrown up superior works to any other men employed in the service, and having done more work in the same time, and *drank less*, by four-fifth, than twice their number of "Old Countrymen." The relics of the breastworks, still stand on or near the banks of the Schuylkill, as a living monument of the fidelity of the back race to their State and Country. Mr. Stansberry, is still living, and Captain Tudas, now quite an old man, about "turning the corner," as he expresses it, is a very intellegent old gentleman, and a living history of facts. There are few white men of his age and opportunities, that equal him at all in intelligence on any subject. He is a kind of living synoptic-historical Encyclopedia.

exist—where the displeasure of Heaven and anger of God was invoked—where it is thought the last glimmering spark of patriotic fire has been quenched, and every aid withheld—even there, in the hour of their country's danger, did they lay aside every consideration of the ten thousand wrongs inflicted —throw in their contributions, and make common cause.

Says Mr. Nell, "The celebrated Charles Pinkney, of South Carolina, in his speech on the Missouri question, in defence of the Slave representation of the South, made the following admission:—They (the colored people) were in numerous instances the pioneers, and in all the labors of our army. To their hands we are owing the greatest part of the fortifications raised for the protection of the country. Fort Moultrie gave, at an early period of inexperience and untried valor of our citizens, immortality to the American arms." And were there no other proof on record, the testimony given to the brave followers of the renowned hero of Chalmet Plains, would of itself be sufficient to establish the right of the colored man to eligibility in his native country. "In 1814," continues Mr. Nell, "when New Orleans was in danger, and the proud criminal distinctions of caste were again demolished by one of those emergencies in which nature puts to silence for the moment the base partialities of art, the free colored people were called into the field in common with the whites; and the importance of their services was thus acknowledged by General Jackson:—

"HEAD-QUARTERS SEVENTH MILITARY DISTRICT, MOBILE, SEPTEMBER 21, 1814.
"*To the Free Colored Inhabitants of Louisiana*:
"Through a mistaken policy, you have heretofore been deprived of a participation in the glorious struggle for national rights, in which *our* country is engaged. This no

longer shall exist. As sons of Freedom you are now called upon to defend your most estimable blessings. *As Americans*, your country looks with confidence to her adopted children, for a valorous support, as a faithful return for the advantages enjoyed under her mild and equitable government. As fathers, husbands, and brothers, you are summoned to rally round the standard of the Eagle, to defend all which is dear in existence.

"*Your country*, although calling for your exertions, does not wish you to engage in her cause, without remunerating you for the services rendered. Your intelligent minds are not to be led away by false representations—your love of honor would cause you to despise the man who should attempt to deceive you. In the sincerity of a soldier, and the language of truth I address you.

"To every noble hearted free man of color, volunteering to serve during the present contest with Great Britain, and no longer, there will be paid the same bounty in money and lands now received by white soldiers of the United States, namely, one hundred and twenty-four dollars in money and one hundred and sixty acres in land. The non-commissioned officers and privates will also be entitled to the same monthly pay and daily rations and clothes furnished to any American soldiers.

"On enrolling yourselves in companies, the Major General commanding will select officers for your government from your white fellow-citizens. Your non-commissioned officers will be appointed from among yourselves.

"Due regard will be paid to the feelings of free men and soldiers.

"You will not, by being associated with white men in the same corps, be exposed to improper comparison, or unjust sarcasm. As a distinct, independent battalion or regiment, pursuing the path of glory, you will, undivided, receive the applause and gratitude of your countrymen.

"To assure you of the sincerity of my intentions, and my anxiety to engage your invaluable services to our country, I have communicated my wish to the Governor of Louisiana, who is fully informed as to the manner of enrollments, and will give you every necessary information on the subject of this address.

"ANDREW JACKSON,
"Major General Commanding."

On the 18th of December, 1814, through his Aid-de-camp, Colonel Butler, the General issued another address to the colored soldiers, who had proven themselves, in every particular, worthy of their country's trust, and in every way worthy of the proudest position of enfranchised freemen. To deny to men and their descendants, who are capable of such deeds as are acknowledged in this proclamation, equal rights with other men, is a moral homicide—as assassination, which none but the most malicious and obdurate are capable of perpetrating. Surely, surely, it cannot be, that our fellow-citizens, who control the destiny of the country, one fully advised of the claims of their brethren in adversity—we cannot be persuaded that a people, claiming the self-respect and consideration of the American people, can be satisfied that the perils of war be encountered by them—their country's rights sustained—and their liberty, the liberty of their wives and children defended and protected; then, with a cool deliberation, unknown to any uncivilized people on the face of the earth, deny them a right—withhold their consent to their having equal enjoyment of human rights with other citizens, with those who have never contributed aid to our country—but we give the proclamation and let it speak for itself. Of it Mr. Nell says:—

"The second proclamation is one of the highest compliments ever paid by a military chief to his soldiers."

"SOLDIERS! When on the banks of the Mobile, I called you to take up arms, inviting you to partake the perils and glory of your *white fellow-citizens, I expected much* from you; for I was not ignorant that you possessed qualities most formidable to an invading enemy. I knew with what fortitude you could endure hunger and thirst, and all the fatigues of a campaign. *I knew well how you love your native country*, and that you, as well as ourselves, had to defend what *man* holds most dear—his parents, wife, children, and property. *You have done more than I expected.* In addition to the previous qualities I before knew you to possess, I found among you noble enthusiasm, which leads to the performance of geat things.

"Soldiers! The President of the United States shall hear how praise-worthy was your conduct in the hour of danger; and the representatives of the American people will give you the praise your exploits entitle you to. The General anticipates them in applauding your noble ardor.

"The enemy approaches; his vessels cover our lakes; our brave citizens are united, and all contentions have ceased among them. Their only dispute is, who shall win the prize of valor, or who the most glory, its noblest reward.

"By order,

"THOMAS BUTLER, Aid-de-camp."

A circumstance that reflects as well upon the devisor, as upon the commander, or the engineer of the army, is not generally known to the American people. The redoubt of cotton bales, has ever been attributed to the judgment, skill, quick perception, and superior tact of Major General Andrew Jackson; than whom, a braver heart, never beat in the breast of man. But this is a mistake. The suggestion of the cotton bales was made by a colored man, at the instant, when the city of New Orleans was put under martial law. The colored troops were gathering, and their recruiting officers (being colored,) were scouring the city in every direction, and particularly on the Levee, where the people throng for news—to hear, see, and be seen. At such times in particular, the blacks are found in great numbers. The cotton shipped down the Mississippi in large quantities to the city, is landed and piled in regular terrace walls, several thousand feet long, sometimes double rows—and fifteen or twenty feet high. When the sun shines in winter, the days become warm and pleasant after the morning passes off, and at such times, there may be found many of the idle blacks, lying upon the top, and in comfortable positions between or behind those walls of cotton bales. On the approach of the recruiting officer, a number of persons were found stretched out upon the bales, lying scattered upon the ground. On addressing them, they were found to be slaves, which the pride of the recently promoted free colored soldiers, nor the policy of the proclamation, then, justified them in enrolling. On questioning them respecting their fears of the approaching contest—they expressed themselves as perfectly satisfied and *safe*, while permitted to lie *behind* the bales. The idea was at once impressed—Chalmet Plain, the battle field, being entirely barren without trees, brush, or stone, and the ingenuity of the General-in-chief and engineer of the army, having been for several days taxed, without successful device; the officer determined that he would muster courage, and hazard the consequences of an approach to the General, and suggest the idea suggested to him, by the observation of a slave, who was indifferent to the safety of others, so that he was secure—and perhaps justly so—whether conscious or not of the importance of its bearing. General Jackson, whatever may be said to the contrary, though firm and determined, was pleasant, affable, and easily approached, and always set equal estimate upon the manhood of a colored man; believing every thing of him, that he expressed in his proclamation to the colored freemen of Louisiana. He did not pretend to justify the holding of slaves, especially on the assumed unjust plea of their incapacity for self-government—he always hooted at the idea; never would become a member of the Colonization Society, always saying "Let the colored people be—they were quiet now, in comparative satisfaction—let them be." But he held them as a policy, by which to make money—and would just as readily have held a white man, had it been the policy of the country, as a black one in slavery. The General was approached—the suggestion made—slaves set to work—the bales conveyed down—the breast-works raised—the Americans protected, as the musketry and artillery proved powerless against the elastic cushion-wall of cotton bales; the battle fought—the British vanquished—the Americans victorious, and Major General Andrew Jackson "all covered with glory," as the most distinguished and skillful captain of the age. It has always been thought by colored men familiar with this circumstance, that the reference of the General is directed to this, when he expresses himself in his last proclamation to them: "*You have done more than I expected.*" Doubtless this was the case. Whatever valor and capacity to endure hardships, the General knew colored men to possess, it *was* more than he expected of them, to bring skill to his aid, and assist in counseling plans for the defence of the army.

On the *Eighth* of January, 1851, the celebration of the Battle of New Orleans, in that city one year ago, "Ninety of the colored veterans who bore a conspicious part in the dangers of the day," (the day of battle,) held "a conspicuous place in the procession," in exaltation of their country's

glory. Nor was the NAVY without the representative of colored interest in the liberty of the country. In speaking of the
war of 1812, a colored veteran of Philadelphia, the late James
Forten, who had himself enlisted and was imprisoned on
board of a British man-of-war, the "Old Jersey Prison Ship,"
affirms: "The vessels of war of that period were all, to a
greater or less extent, manned with colored men." The
father-in-law of the writer, has often related to him that he
saw the three hundred and sixty colored marines, in military
pomp and navel array, when passing through Pittsburg in
1812 on their way to the frigate Constitution, then on lake
Erie under command of the gallant Commodore Perry. And
we cannot close this view of our subject, without reference
to one of the living veterans of the battle of New Orleans,
now residing where he has for many years, in the city of
Pittsburg, Pa., to whom we are indebted for more oral information concerning that memorable conflict, than to any
other living person. MR. JOHN JULIUS, was a member of the
valiant regiment of colored soldiers, who held so conspicuous a place in the estimation of their General, their
country's struggles for Liberty and Independence. He is a
tall, good-looking, brown skin creole of Louisiana, now
about sixty-three years of age, bearing the terrible gashes of
the bayonet still conspicuously in his neck. He was one of
the few Americans who encountered the British in single-
handed charges on top of the breast-works. *Julien Bennoit*,
(pronounced *ben wah*,) for such is his name, though com-
monly known as John Julius, is a man of uprightness and
strict integrity of character, having all the delicate sensibility
and pride of character known to the Frenchman; and
laments more at the injustice done him, in the neglect of the
authorities to grant him his claims of money and land,
according to the promises set forth in the Proclamation,

than at any reverse of fortune with which he has ever met. He is enthusiastic on the subject of the battle scenes of Chalmet Plains, and anxious that all who converse with him may know that he is one of the actors. Not so much for his own notoriety—as all soldiers have a right to—as for the purpose of making known and exposing the wrongs done to him and hundreds of his fellows, who fought shoulder to shoulder with him, in the conflict with Sir Edward Packenham. Mr. Julius is the only person in whose possession we have ever seen a complete draught of the plan of the battle fought on the 8th of January, 1815, drawn on the field, by the U.S. Engineer.

This consists of two charts, one quite large, and the other smaller; the larger giving the whole plan of battle, and the other being the key, which shows the position of the different battalions and regiments of troops, with the several officers of command, in which the Colored Regiment is beautifully and conspicuously displayed. He sets great estimate upon them. Col. Marshall John M. Davis, who was an officer under General Jackson at the battle of New Orleans, now still residing in Alleghany Co., near Pittsburg, bears testimony to the truthfulness of Mr. Julien Bennoit having been a soldier in the Army of the Mississippi in 1814. The deeds of these tried and faithful daring sons of Liberty, and defenders of their country, shall live triumphantly, long after the nation shall have repented her wrongs towards them and their descendants, and hung her head with shame, before the gaze of manhood's stern rebuke.

Mr. John B. Vashon, of Pittsburg, embarked in the service of the United States, and in an engagement of the American squadron in South America, was imprisoned, with Major Henry Bears, a respectable white citizen, still living in that city.

IX | CAPACITY OF COLORED MEN AND WOMEN AS CITIZEN MEMBERS OF COMMUNITY

THE utility of men in their private capacity as citizens, is of no less import than that of any other department of the community in which they live; indeed, the fitness of men for positions in the body politic, can only be justly measured by their qualification as citizens. And we may safely venture the declaration, that in the history of the world, there has never been a nation, that among the oppressed class of inhabitants—a class entirely ineligible to any political position of honor, profit or trust—wholly discarded from the recognition of citizens' rights—not even permitted to carry the mail, nor drive a mail coach—there never has, in the history of nations, been any people thus situated, who has made equal progress in attainments with the colored people of the United States. It would be as unnecessary as it is impossible, to particularize all the individuals; we shall therefore be satisfied, with a classification and a few individual cases. Our history in this country is well known, and quite sufficiently treated on in these pages already, without the necessity of repetition here; it is enough to know that by the most cruel acts of injustice and crime, our forefathers were forced by small numbers, and enslaved in the country—the great body now to the number of three millions and a half, still groaning in bondage—that the half million now free, are the descendants of the few who by various means, are fortunate enough to gain their liberty from Southern bondage—that no act of general emancipation has ever taken place, and no chance as yet for a general rebellion—we say in view of all these facts, we proceed to give a cursory history of the attainments—the civil, social, business and professional, and literary attainments of colored men and women, and challenge comparison with the world —according to circumstances—in times past and present.

Though shorn of their strength, disarmed of manhood, and stripped of every right, encouraged by the part performed by their brethren and fathers in the Revolutionary struggle—with no records of their deeds in history, and no means of knowing them save orally, as overheard from the mouths of their oppressors, and tradition as kept up among themselves—that memorable event, had not yet ceased its thrill through the new-born nation, until a glimmer of hope—a ray of light had beamed forth, and enlightened minds thought to be in total darkness. Minds of no ordinary character, but those which embraced business, professions, and literature—minds, which at once grasped the earth, encompassed the seas, soared into the air, and mounted the skies. And it is none the less creditable to the colored people, that among those who have stood the most conspicuous and shone the brightest in the earliest period of our history, there are those of pure and unmixed African blood. A credit—but that which is creditable to the African, cannot disgrace any into whose veins his blood may chance to flow. The elevation of the colored man can only be completed by the elevation of the pure descendants of Africa; because to deny his equality, is to deny in a like proportion, the equality of all those mixed with the African organization; and to establish his inferiority, will be to degrade every person related to him by consanguinity; therefore, to establish the equality of the African with the European race, establishes the equality of every person intermediate between the two races. This established beyond contradiction, the general equality of men.

In the year 1773, though held in servitude, and without the advantages or privileges of the schools of the day, accomplishing herself by her own perseverance; Phillis Wheatley appeared in the arena, the brilliancy of whose genius, as a poetess, delighted Europe and astonished America, and by a special act of the British Parliament, 1773, her productions were published for the Crown. She was an admirer of President Washington, and addressed to him lines, which elicited from the Father of his country, a complimentary and courteous reply. In the absence of the poem addressed to General Washington, which was not written until after her work was published, we insert a stanza from one addressed (intended for the students) "To the University at Cambridge." We may further remark, that the poems were originally written, not with the most distant idea of publication, but simply for the amusement and during the leisure moments of the author.

> "Improve your privileges while they stay,
> Ye pupils, and each hour redeem, that bears
> Or good or bad report of you to heav'n.
> Let sin, that baneful evil of the soul,
> By you be shunn'd, nor once remit your guard;
> Suppress the deadly serpent in its egg.
> Ye blooming plants of human race divine,
> An *Ethiop* tells you 'tis your greatest foe;
> Its transient sweetness turns to endless pain,
> And in immense perdition sinks the soul."

"CAMBRIDGE, FEBRUARY 28, 1776.

"MISS PHILLIS:

"Your favor of the 26th of October, did not reach my hands till the middle of December. Time enough, you will say, to have given an answer ere this. Granted. But a variety of important occurrences, continually interposing to divert the mind and withdraw the attention, I hope will apologise for the delay, and plead my excuse for the seeming, but not real neglect. I thank you most sincerely for your polite notice of me, in the elegant lines you enclosed; and however undeserving I may be of such encomium and panegyric, the style and manner exhibit a striking proof of your poetic talents; in honor of which, and as a tribute justly due to you, I would have published the poem, had I not been apprehensive, that, while I only meant to give the world this new instance of your genius, I might have incurred the imputation of vanity. This, and nothing else, determined me not to give it place in the public prints.

"If you should ever come to Cambridge, or near headquarters, I shall be happy to see a person so favored by the Muses, and to whom Nature has been so liberal and beneficent in her dispensations.

"I am, with great respect, your obedient servant,

                    "GEORGE WASHINGTON.

"Miss Phillis Wheatley."

The tenor, style, and manner of President Washington's letter to Miss Wheatley—the publication of her works, together with an accompanying likeness of the author, and her inscription and dedication of the volume to the "Right Honorable the Countess of Huntingdon," show, that she, though young, was a person of no ordinary mind, no common attainments; but at the time, one of the brightest ornaments among the American literati. She also was well versed in Latin, in which language she composed several pieces. Miss Wheatley died in 1780, at the age of 26 years, being seven years of age when brought to this country in 1761.

Doctor Peter, who married Miss Wheatley, 1775, was a man of business, tact, and talents—being first a grocer, and afterwards studied law, which he practised with great success, becoming quite wealthy by defending the cause of the oppressed before the different tribunals of the country. And who shone brighter in his day, than Benjamin Bannaker, of Baltimore county, Maryland, who by industry and force of character, became a distinguished mathematician and astronomer,—"for many years," says Davenport's Biographical Dictionary, "calculated and published the Maryland Ephemerides." He was a correspondent of the Honorable Thomas Jefferson, Secretary of State of the United States, taking the earliest opportunity of his acquaintanceship, to call his attention to the evils of American slavery, and doubtless his acquaintance with the apostle of American Democracy, had much to do with his reflections on that most pernicious evil in this country. Mr. Bannaker was also a naturalist, and wrote a treatise on locusts. He was invited by the Commission of United States Civil Engineers, to assist in the survey of the Ten Miles Square, for the District of Columbia. He assisted the Board, who, it is thought, could not have succeeded without him. His Almanac was preferred to that of Leadbeater, or any other calculator cotemporary with himself. He had no family, and resided in a house alone, but principally made his home with the Elliott family. He was upright, honorable, and virtuous; entertaining religious scruples similar to the Friends. He died in 1807, near Baltimore. Honorable John H. B. Latrobe, Esq., of Baltimore, is his biographer.

In 1812, Captain Paul Cuffy was an extensive trader and mariner, sailing out of Boston, to the West Indies and Europe, by which enterprise, he amassed an immense fortune. He was known to the commercial world of his day, and, if not so wealthy, stood quite as fair, and as much respected, as Captain George Laws or Commodore Vanderbilt, the Cunards of America. Captain Cuffy went to Africa, where he died in a few years.

James Durham, originally of Philadelphia, in 1778, at the early age of twenty-one, was the most learned physician in New Orleans. He spoke English, French and Spanish, learnedly, and the great Dr. Rush said of him, "I conversed with him on medicine, and found him very learned. I thought I could give him information concerning the treatment of diseases; but I learned from him more than he could expect from me." And it must be admitted, he must have been learned in his profession, to have elicited such an encomium from Dr. Rush, who stood then at the head of his profession in the country.

We have designed nothing here, but merely to give an individual case of the various developments of talents and acquirements in the several departments of respectability, discarding generalization, and name none but the Africo-American of unmixed extraction, who rose into note subsequent to the American Revolution. In the persons of note and distinction hereafter to be given, we shall not confine ourselves to any such narrow selections, but shall name persons, male and female, regardless of their extraction, so that they are colored persons, which is quite enough for our purpose. And our only excuse for the policy in the above course is, that we desire to disarm the villifiers of our race, who disparage us, giving themselves credit for whatever is commendable that may emanate from us, if there be the least opportunity of claiming it by "blood." We shall now proceed to review the attainments of colored men and women of the present day.

X PRACTICAL UTILITY OF COLORED PEOPLE OF THE PRESENT DAY AS MEMBERS OF SOCIETY—BUSINESS MEN AND MECHANICS

I N calling attention to the practical utility of colored people of the present day, we shall not be general in our observations, but simply, direct attention to a few particular instances, in which colored persons have been reponsibly engaged in extensive business, or occupying useful positions, thus contributing to the general welfare of community at large, filling their places in society as men and women.

It will studiously be borne in mind, that our sole object in giving these cases publicity, is to refute the objections urged against us, that we are not useful members of society. That we are consumers and non-producers—that we contribute nothing to the general progress of man. No people who have enjoyed no greater opportunity for improvement, could possibly have made greater progress in the same length of time than have done the colored people of the present day.

A people laboring under many disadvantages, may not be expected to present at once, especially before they have become entirely untrammeled, evidence of entire equality with more highly favored people.

When Mr. Jefferson, the great American Statesman and philosopher, was questioned by an English gentleman, on the subject of American greatness, and referred to their literature as an evidence of inferiority to the more highly

favored and long-existing European nations; Mr. Jefferson's
reply was—"When the United States have existed as long as
a nation, as Greece before she produced her Homer and
Socrates; Rome, before she produced her Virgil, Horace,
and Cicero; and England, before she produced her Pope,
Dryden, and Bacon"; then he might consider the comparison a just one. And all we shall ask, is not to wait so long as
this, not to wait until we become a nation at all, so far as the
United States are concerned, but only to unfetter our
brethren, and give us, the freemen, an equal chance for emu-
lation, and we will admit any comparison you may please to
make in a quarter of a century after.

For a number of years, the late James Forten, of Philadelphia, was the proprietor of one of the principal sail manufactories, constantly employing a large number of men,
black and white, supplying a large number of masters and
owners of vessels, with full rigging for their crafts.

On the failure of an extensive house, T. & Co., in that
city, during the pressure which followed a removal of the
deposits of the United States Treasury in 1837, Mr. Forten
lost by that firm, nine thousand dollars. Being himself in
good circumstances at the time, hearing of the failure of old
constant patrons, he called at the house; one of the proprietors, Mr. T., on his entering the warehouse door, came forward, taking him by the hand observed, "Ah! Mr. Forten, it
is useless to call on us—we are gone—we can do nothing!"
at which Mr. Forten remarked, "Sir, I hope you think better
of me than to suppose me capable of calling on a friend to
torture him in adversity! I came, sir, to express my regret at
your misfortune, and if possible, to cheer you by words of
encouragement. If your liabilities were all in my hands, you
should never be under the necessity of closing business." Mr.
Forten exchanged paper and signatures with some of the

first business men in Philadelphia, and raised and educated a large and respectable family of sons and daughters, leaving an excellent widow.

Joseph Cassey, recently deceased, was the "architect of his own fortune," and by industry and application to business, became a money broker in the city of Philadelphia; who becoming indisposed from a chronic affection, was obliged to retire from business for many years previous to his death. Had Mr. Cassey been favored with health, he doubtless would have become a very wealthy man. His name and paper was good in any house in the city, and there was no banker of moderate capital, of more benefit to the business community than was Joseph Cassey. He also left a young and promising family of five sons, one daughter, a most excellent widow, and a fortune of seventy-five thousand dollars, clear of all encumbrance.

Stephen Smith, of the firm of Smith and Whipper, is a remarkable man in many respects, and decidedly the most wealthy colored man in the United States. Mr. Smith commenced business after he was thirty years of age, without the advantages of a good business education, but by application, qualified himself for the arduous duties of his vocation. For many years, he has been known as the principal lumber merchant in Columbia, Lancaster Co., Pa., and for several years past associated with W. Whipper, a gentleman of great force of character, talents, and business qualifications, Mr. Smith residing in Philadelphia. Smith and Whipper, are very extensive business men, and very valuable members of the community, both of Lancaster and Philadelphia counties. By the judicious investment of their capital, they keep in constant employment a large number of persons; purchasing many rafts at a time, and many thousand bushels of coal. It is not only the laborer in "drawing boards," and the coal hauler and heaver, that are here benefitted by their capital, but the original owners of the lumber and coal purchased by them, and the large number of boatmen and raftsmen employed in bringing these commodities to market.

In the winter of 1849, these gentlemen had in store, several thousand bushels of coal, two million two hundred and fifty thousand feet of lumber; twenty-two of the finest merchantmen cars running on the railway from Philadelphia to Baltimore; nine thousand dollars' worth of stock in the Columbia Bridge; eighteen thousand dollars in stock in the Columbia Bank; and besides this, Mr. Smith was then the reputed owner of fifty-two good brick houses of various dimensions in the city of Philadelphia, besides several in the city of Lancaster, and the town of Columbia. Mr. Smith's paper, or the paper of the firm, is good for any amount wherever they are known; and we have known gentlemen to present the paper of some of the best men in the city, which was cashed by him at sight. The principal active business attended to by Mr. S. in person, is that of buying good negotiable and other paper, and speculating in real estate. The business of the firm is attended to by Mr. Whipper, who is a relative. Take Smith and Whipper from Lancaster and Philadelphia counties, and the business community will experience a hiatus in its connexion, that may not be easily filled.

Samuel T. Wilcox, of Cincinnati, Ohio, also stands conspicuously among the most respectable business men of the day. Being yet a young man, just scanning forty, he is one among the extraordinary men of the times. Born, like the most of colored men in this country, in obscurity, of poor parents, raised without the assistance of a father, and to a commonplace business, without the advantages of schools, by his own perseverance, he qualified himself to the extent that gave him an inclination to traffic, which he did for several years on the Mississippi and Ohio rivers, investing his gains in real estate, until he acquired a considerable property. For the purpose of extending his usefulness, and at the same time pursuing a vocation more in accordance with his own desires, a few years since, he embarked in the wholesale and retail Family Grocery business, and now has the best general assortment and most extensive business house of the kind, in the city of Cincinnati. The establishment is really beautiful, having the appearance more of an apothecary store, than a Grocery House. Mr. Wilcox has a Pickling and Preserving establishment besides, separate from his business house, owning a great deal of first class real estate. There is no man in the community in which he lives, that turns money to a greater advantage than Mr. Wilcox, and none by whom the community is more benefited for the amount of capital invested. He makes constant and heavy bills in eastern houses, and there are doubtless now many merchants in New York, Boston, and Baltimore cities, who have been dealing with S. T. Wilcox, and never until the reading of this notice of him, knew that he was a colored man. He has never yet been east after his goods, but pursuing a policy which he has adopted, orders them; but if deceived in an article, never deals with the same house again. He always gets a good article. The paper of Mr. Wilcox, is good for any amount.

Henry Boyd, is also a man of great energy of character, the proprietor of an extensive Bedstead manufactory, with a large capital invested, giving constant employment to eighteen or twenty-five men, black and white. Some of the finest and handsomest articles of the bedstead in the city, are at the establishment of Mr. Boyd. He fills orders from all parts of the West and South, his orders from the South being very heavy. He is the patentee, or holds the right of the Patent Bedsteads, and like Mr. Wilcox, there are hundreds who deal with Mr.

Boyd at a distance, who do not know that he is a colored man. Mr. Boyd is a useful member of society, and Cincinnati would not, if she could, be without him. He fills a place that every man is not capable of supplying, of whatever quarter of the globe his forefathers may have been denizens.

Messrs. Knight and Bell of the same place, Cincinnati, Ohio, are very successful and excellent mechanics. In the spring of 1851, (one year ago) they put in their "sealed proposal" for the plastering of the public buildings of the county of Hamilton—alms-house, &c.—and got the contract, which required ten thousand dollars' security. The work was finished in fine artistic style, in which a large number of mechanics and laborers were employed, while at the same time, they were carrying on many other contracts of less extent, in the city—the public buildings being some four miles out. They are men of stern integrity, and highly respected in the community.

David Jenkins of Columbus, Ohio, a good mechanic, painter, glazier, and paper-hanger by trade, also received by contract, the painting, glazing, and papering of some of the public buildings of the State, in autumn 1847. He is much respected in the capital city of his state, being extensively patronised, having on contract, the great "Neill House," and many of the largest gentlemen's residences in the city and neighborhood, to keep in finish. Mr. Jenkins is a very useful man and member of society.

John C. Bowers, for many years, has been the proprietor of a fashionable merchant tailor house, who has associated with him in business, his brother Thomas Bowers, said to be one of the best, if not the very best, mercers in the city. His style of cutting and fitting, is preferred by the first business men, and other gentlemen of Philadelphia, in whom their patrons principally consist.

Mr. Cordovell, for more than twenty-five years, was the leading mercer and tailor, reporter and originator of fashions in the city of New Orleans, Louisiana. The reported fashions of Cordovell, are said to have frequently become the leading fashions of Paris; and the writer was informed, by Mr. B., a leading merchant tailor in a populous city, that many of the eastern American reports were nothing more than a copy, in some cases modified, of those of Cordovell. Mr. Cordovell, has for the last four or five years, been residing in France, living on a handsome fortune, the fruits of his genius; and though "retired from business," it is said, that he still invents fashions for the Parisian reporters, which yields him annually a large income.

William H. Riley, of Philadelphia, has been for years, one of the leading fashionable gentlemen's boot-makers. Riley's style and cut of boots, taking the preeminence in the estimation of a great many of the most fashionable, and business men in the city. Mr. Riley is much of a gentleman, and has acquired considerable means.

James Prosser, Sen., of Philadelphia, has long been the popular proprietor of a fashionable restaurant in the city. The name of James Prosser, among the merchants of Philadelphia, is inseparable with their daily hours of recreation, and pleasure. Mr. Prosser, is withal, a most gentlemanly man, and has the happy faculty of treating his customers in such a manner, that those who call once, will be sure to call at his place again. His name and paper is good among the business men of the city.

Henry Minton also is the proprietor of a fashionable restaurant and resort of business men and gentlemen of the city. The tables of Mr. Henry Minton are continually laden with the most choice offerings to epicures, and the saloon during certain hours of the day, presents the appearance of a bee hive, such is the stir, din, and buz, among the throng of Chesnut street gentlemen, who flock in there to pay tribute at the shrine of bountifulness. Mr. Minton has acquired a notoriety, even in that proud city, which makes his house one of the most popular resorts.

Mr. Hill, of Chillicothe, Ohio, was for years, the leading tanner and currier in that section of country, buying up the hides of the surrounding country, and giving employment to large numbers of men. Mr. Hill kept in constant employment, a white clerk, who once a year took down, as was then the custom, one or more flatboats loaded with leather and other domestic produce, by which he realised large profits, accumulating a great deal of wealth. By endorsement, failure, and other mistransactions, Mr. Hill became reduced in circumstances, and died in Pittsburgh, Pennsylvania, in 1845. He gave his children a liberal business education.

Benjamin Richards, sen., of Pittsburgh, Pennsylvania, forty years ago, was one of the leading business men of the place. Being a butcher by trade, he carried on the business extensively, employing a white clerk, and held a heavy contract with the United States, supplying the various military posts with provisions. Mr. Richards possessed a large property in real estate, and was at one time reputed very wealthy, he and the late general O'H. being considered the most wealthy individuals of the place,—Mr. Richards taking the precedence; the estate of general O'H. now being estimated at seven millions of dollars. Mr. Richards has been known, to buy up a drove of cattle at one time. By mismanagement, he lost his estate, upon which many gentlemen are now living at ease in the city.

William H. Topp, of Albany, N.Y., has for several years been one of the leading merchant tailors of the city. Starting in the world without aid, he educated and qualified himself for business; and now has orders from all parts of the state, the city of New York not excepted, for "Topp's style of clothing." Mr. Topp stands high in his community as a business man, and a useful and upright member of society. His paper or endorsement is good at any time.

Henry Scott & Co., of New York city, have for many years been engaged extensively in the pickling business, keeping constantly in warehouse, a very heavy stock of articles in their line. He, like the most of others, had no assistance at the commencement, but by manly determination and perseverance, raised himself to what he is. His business is principally confined to supplying vessels with articles and provisions in his line of business, which in this great metropolis is very great. There have doubtless been many a purser, who cashed and filed in his office the bill of Henry Scott, without ever dreaming of his being a colored man. Mr. Scott is extensively known in the great City, and respected as an upright, prompt, energetic business man, and highly esteemed by all who know him.

Mr. Hutson, for years, kept in New York, an intelligence office. At his demise, he was succeeded by Philip A. Bell, who continues to keep one of the leading offices in the city. Mr. Bell is an excellent business man, talented, prompt, shrewd, and full of tact. And what seems to be a trait of character, only to be found associated with talent, Mr. Bell is highly sensitive, and very eccentric. A warm, good hearted man, he has not only enlisted the friendship of all his patrons, but also endeared himself to the multitude of persons who continually throng his office seeking situations. One of his usual expressions to the young women and men in addressing himself to them is, "My child"—this is kind, and philanthropic, and has a tendency to make himself liked. His business is very extensive, being sought from all parts of the city, by the first people of the community. It is said to be not unusual, for the peasantry of Liverpool, to speak of Mr. Bell, as a benefactor of the emigrant domestics. Mr. Bell is extensively known in the business community—none more so—and highly esteemed as a valuable citizen.

Thomas Downing, for thirty years, in the city of New York, has been proprietor of one of the leading restaurants. His establishment situated in the midst of the Wall street bankers, the business has always been of a leading and profitable character. Mr. Downing has commanded great influence, and much means, and it is said of him that he has made "three fortunes." Benevolent, kind, and liberal minded, his head was always willing, his heart ready, and his hands open to "give." Mr. Downing is still very popular, doing a most excellent business, and highly respected throughout New York. Indeed, you scarcely hear any other establishment of the kind spoken of than Downing's.

Henry M. Collins, of the City of Pittsburg, stands among the men of note; and we could not complete this list of usefulness, without the name of Mr. Collins. Raised a poor boy, thrown upon the uncertainties of chance, without example of precept, save such as the public at large presents; Mr. Collins quit his former vocation of a riverman, and without means, except one hundred and fifty dollars, and no assistance from any quarter, commenced speculating in real estate. And though only rising forty, has done more to improve the Sixth Ward of Pittsburg, than any other individual, save one, Captain W., who built on Company capital. Mr. Collins was the first person who commenced erecting an improved style of buildings; indeed, there was little else than old trees in that quarter of the city when Mr. Collins began. He continued to build, and dispose of handsome dwellings, until a different class of citizens entirely, was attracted to that quarter of the town, among them, one of the oldest and most respectable and wealthy citizens, an ex-Alderman. After this, the wealthy citizens turned their attention to the District; and now, it is one of the most fashionable quarters of the City, and bids fair to become, the preferred part for family residences. Mr. Collins' advice and counsel was solicited by some of the first lawyers, and land speculators, in matters of real estate. He has left or contemplates leaving Pittsburg, in April, for California, where he intends entering extensively into land speculation, and doubtless, with the superior advantages of this place, if his success is but half what it was in the former, but a few years will find him counted among the wealthy. Mr. Collins is a highly valuable man in any community in which he may live, and he leaves Pittsburg much to the regret of the leading citizens. Without capital, he had established such a reputation, that his name and paper were good in some of the first Banking houses.

Owen A. Barrett of Pittsburg, Pa., is the original proprietor of "B. A. Fahnestock's Celebrated Vermifuge." Mr. Fahnestock raised Mr. Barrett from childhood, instructing him in all the science of practical pharmacy, continuing him in his employment after manhood, when Mr. Barrett discovered the "sovereign remedy" for *lumbricalii*, and as an act of gratitude to his benefactor, he communicated it to him, but not until he had fully tested its efficacy. The proprietor of the house, finding the remedy good, secured his patent, or copy right, or whatever is secured, and never in the history of remedies in the United States, has any equaled, at least in sale, this of "B. A. Fahnestock's Vermifuge." Mr. Fahnestock, like a gentleman and Christian, has kept Mr. Barrett in his extensive House, compounding this and other medicines, for sixteen or eighteen years.

In 1840 it was estimated, that of this article alone, the

concern had realized eighty-five thousand dollars. Doubtless, this is true, and certainly proves Mr. Barrett to be of benefit, not only in his community, but like many others we have mentioned, to the country and the world.

Lewis Hayden, of Boston, is well deserving a place among the examples of character here given. But eight years ago, having emerged from bondage, he raised by his efforts, as an act of gratitude and duty, six hundred and fifty dollars, the amount demanded by mutual agreement, by the authorities in Kentucky, as a ransom for Calvin Fairbanks, then in the State Prison, at Frankfort, accused for assisting him in effecting his escape. In 1848, he went to Boston, and having made acquaintance, and gained confidence with several business men, Mr. Hayden opened a fashionable Clothing House in Cambridge street, where he has within the last year, enlarged his establishment, being patronized by some of the most respectable citizens of that wealthy Metropolis. Mr. Hayden has made considerable progress, considering his disadvantages, in his educational improvements. He has great energy of character, and extensive information. Lewis Hayden by perseverance, may yet become a very wealthy man. He is generally esteemed by the Boston people—all seeming to know him.

George T. Downing, a gentleman of education and fine business attainments, is proprietor of one of the principal Public houses and places of resort, at Newport, Rhode Island, during the watering Season. This fashionable establishment is spoken of as among the best conducted places in the country—the Proprietor among the most gentlemanly.

Edward V. Clark, is among the most deserving and active business men in New York, and but a few years are required, to place Mr. Clark in point of business importance, among the first men in the city. His stock consists of Jewelry and Silver Wares, and consequently, are always valuable, requiring a heavy capital to keep up business. His name and paper, has a respectable credit, even among the urbane denizens of Wall street.

John Julius and Lady, were for several years, the Proprietors of Concert Hall, a *Caffé*, then the most fashionable resort for ladies and gentlemen in Pittsburg. Mr. and Mrs. Julius, held Assemblies and Balls, attended by the first people of the city—being himself a fine violinist and dancing master, he superintended the music and dancing. When General William Henry Harrison in 1840, then the President elect of the United States, visited that city, his levee to and reception of the Ladies were held at Concert Hall, under the superintendence of Monsieur John and Madame Edna Julius, the colored host and hostess. No House was ever better conducted than under their fostering care, and excellent management, and the citizens all much regretted their retirement from the establishment.

In Penyan, Western New York, Messrs. William Platt and Joseph C. Cassey, are said to be the leading Lumber Merchants of the place. Situated in the midst of a great improving country, their business extends, and increases in importance every year. The latter gentleman was raised to the business by Smith and Whipper, the great Lumber Merchants of Columbia, Pa., where he was principal Book-Keeper for several years. Mr. Cassey has the credit of being one of the best Accountants, and Business Men in the United States of his age. Doubtless, a few years' perseverance, and strict application to business, will find them ranked among the most influential men of their neighborhood.

Anthony Weston, of Charleston, South Carolina, has acquired an independent fortune, by his mechanical ingenuity, and skillful workmanship. About the year 1831, William Thomas Catto, mentioned in another place, commenced an improvement on a Thrashing Machine, when on taking sick, Mr. Weston improved on it, to the extent of thrashing a thousand bushels a day. This Thrashing Mill, was commenced by a Yankee, by the name of Emmons, who failing to succeed, Mr. Catto, then a Millwright—since a Minister—improved it to the extent of thrashing five hundred bushels a day; when Mr. Weston, took it in hand, and brought it to the perfection stated, for the use of Col. Benjamin Franklin Hunt, a distinguished lawyer of Charleston, upon whose plantation, the machine was built, and to whom it belonged. Anthony Weston, is the greatest Millwright in the South, being extensively employed far and near, and by Southern people, thought the best in the United States.

Dereef and Howard, are very extensive Wood-Factors, keeping a large number of men employed, a regular Clerk and Book-Keeper, supplying the citizens, steamers, vessels, and factories of Charleston with fuel. In this business a very heavy capital is invested: besides which, they are the owners and proprietors of several vessels trading on the coast. They are men of great business habits, and command a great deal of respect and influence in the city of Charleston.

There is nothing more common in the city of New Orleans, than Colored Clerks, Salesmen and Business men. In many stores on Chartier, Camp and other business streets, there may always be seen colored men and women, as salesmen, and saleswomen, behind the counter. Several of the largest Cotton-Press houses, have colored Clerks in them; and on the arrival of steamers at the Levees, among the first to board them, and take down the Manifestos to make their transfers, are colored Clerks. In 1839–40, one of the most respectable Brokers and Bankers of the City, was a black gentleman.

Mr. William Goodrich of York, Pennsylvania, has considerable interest in the branch of the Baltimore Railroad, from Lancaster. In 1849, he had a warehouse in York, and owned ten first-rate merchandise cars on the Road, doing a fine business. His son, Glenalvon G. Goodrich, a young man of good education, is a good artist, and proprietor of a Daguerreo-type Gallery.

Certainly, there need be no further proofs required, at least in this department, to show the claims and practical utility of colored people as citizen members of society. We have shown, that in proportion to their numbers, they vie and compare favorably in point of means and possessions, with the class of citizens who from chance of superior advantages, have studiously contrived to oppress and deprive them of equal rights and privileges, in common with themselves.

XI | LITERARY AND PROFESSIONAL COLORED MEN AND WOMEN

D R. JAMES MCCUNE SMITH, a graduate of the Scientific and Medical Schools of the University of Glasgow, has for the last fifteen years, been a successful practitioner of medicine and surgery in the city of New York. Dr. Smith is a man of no ordinary talents, and stands high as a scholar and gentleman in the city, amidst the *literati* of a hundred seats of learning.

In 1843, when the character of the colored race was assailed to disparagement, by the representative of a combination of maligners, such was the influence of the Doctor, that the citizens at once agreed to give their presence to a fair public discussion of the subject—the Comparative Anatomy and Physiology of the races. This discussion was kept up for several evenings, attended by large and fashionable assemblages of ladies and gentlemen, until it closed. Doctor Smith, in the estimation of the audience, easily triumphed over his antagonist, who had made this a studied subject. The Doctor is the author of several valuable productions, and in 1846, a very valuable scientific paper, issued from the press in pamphlet form, on the "Influence of Climate on Longevity, with special reference to Life Insurance." This paper, we may surmise, was produced in refutation of the attempt at a physiological disquisition on the part of Hon. John C. Calhoun, United States Senator, on the colored race, which met with considerable favor from some quarters, until the appearance of Dr. Smith's pamphlet—since when, we have heard nothing about Calhoun's learned argument. It may be well to remark, that Senator Calhoun read medicine before he read law, and it would have been well for him if he had left medical subjects remain where *he left* them, for law. We extract a simple note of explanation without the main argument, to show with what ease the Doctor refutes an absurd argument: "The reason why the proportion of mortality is not a measure of longevity, is the following:—The proportion of mortality is a statement of how many persons die in a population; this, of course, does not state the age at which those persons die. If 1 in 45 die in Sweden, and 1 in 22 in Grenada, the ages of the dead might be alike in both countries; here the greater mortality might actually accompany the greater longevity."—Note to page 6.

About three months since, at a public meeting of scientific gentlemen, for the formation of a "Statistic Institute," Doctor Smith was nominated as one of five gentlemen, to draught a constitution. This, of course, anticipated his membership to the Institution. He, for a number of years, has held the office of Physician to the Colored Orphan Asylum, an excellent institution, at which he is the only colored officer. The Doctor is very learned.

Rev. Samuel Ringgold Ward was, for several years, pastor of a white congregation, in Courtlandville, N. Y., of the Congregational persuasion, and editor of an excellent newspaper, devoted to the religious elevation of that denomination. Mr. Ward is a man of great talents—his fame is widespread as an orator and man of learning, and needs no encomium from us. His name stood on nomination for two or three years, as Liberty-party candidate for Vice President of the United States.

Mr. Ward has embraced the legal profession, and intends to practise law. Governor Seward said of him, that he "never heard true eloquence until he heard Samuel R. Ward speak." Mr. Ward has recently left the United States, for Canada West, and is destined to be a great statesman.

Rev. Henry Highland Garnett, was also the pastor of a white congregation, in Troy, N. Y. Mr. Garnett is a graduate of Oneida Institute, a speaker of great pathetic eloquence, and has written several valuable pamphlets. In 1844, Mr. Garnett appeared before the Judiciary Committee of the Legislature at the capital, in behalf of the rights of the colored citizens of the State, and in a speech of matchless eloquence, he held them for four hours spell-bound.

He has also been co-editor of a newspaper, which was conducted with ability. As a token of respect, the "Young Men's Literary Society of Troy," elected him a life-member—and he was frequently solicited to deliver lectures before different lyceums. Mr. Garnett left the United States in the summer of 1849, and now resides in England, where he is highly esteemed.

Rev. James William Charles Pennington, D.D., a clergyman of New York city, was born in Maryland,—left when young—came to Brooklyn—educated himself—studied divinity—went to Hartford, Conn.;—took charge of a Presbyterian congregation of colored people—went to England—returned—went to the West Indies—returned—was called to the Shiloh Presbyterian Colored Congregation—was sent a Delegate to the Peace Congress at Paris, in 1849, preached there, and attended the National Levee at the mansion of the Foreign Secretary of State, Minister De Tocqueville; and had the degree of *Doctor of Divinity* conferred on him by the ancient time-honored University of Heidleburg, in Germany.

Dr. Pennington is very learned in theology, has fine literacy attainments, and has written several useful pamphlets, and contributed to science, by the delivery of lectures before several scientific institutions in Europe.

He has, by invitation, delivered lectures before the "Glasgow Young Men's Christian Association"; and "St. George's Biblical, Literary, and Scientific Institute," London. In one of the discourses, the following extract will give an idea of the style and character of the speaker:—"One of the chief attributes of the mind is a desire for freedom; but it has been the great aim of slavery to extinguish that desire."

"To extinguish this attribute would be to extinguish mind itself. Every faculty which the master puts forth to subdue the slave, is met by a corresponding one in the latter." . . . "Christianity is the highest and most perfect form of civilization. It contains the only great standard of the only true and perfect standard of civilization. When tried by this standard, we are compelled to confess, that we have not on earth, one strictly civilized nation; for so long as the sword is part of a nation's household furniture, it cannot be called strictly civilized; and yet there is not a nation, great or small, black or white, that has laid aside the sword."—pp. 7–14. The Doctor has been editor of a newspaper, which was ably conducted. He belongs to the Third Presbytery of New York, and stands very high as a minister of the Gospel, and gentleman.

Rev. John Francis Cook, a learned clergyman of Washington City, has taught an academy in the District of Columbia for years, under the subscribed sanction and patronage of many of the members of Congress, the Mayor of Washington, and some of the first men of the nation, for the education of colored youth of both sexes. Mr. Cook has done a great deal of good at the Capitol; is highly esteemed,

and has set as Moderator of a body of Presbyterian Clergymen, assembled at Richmond, Va., all white, except himself.

Charles L. Reason, Esq., a learned gentleman, for many
years teacher in one of the Public Schools in New York, in
1849, was elected by the trustees of that institution, Professor of Mathematics and Belles Lettres in Centre College,
at McGrawville, in the State of New York. After a short connection with the College, Professor Reason, for some cause,
retired from the Institution, much to the regret of the students, who, though a young man, loved him as an elder
brother—and contrary to the desire of his fellow-professors.

Mr. Reason is decidedly a man of letters, a high-souled
gentleman, a most useful citizen in any community—much
respected and beloved by all who know him, and most
scrupulously modest—a brilliant trait in the character of a
teacher. We learn that Professor Reason, is about to be called
to take charge of the High School for the education of colored youth of both sexes, now in course of completion in
Philadelphia. The people of New York will regret to part
with Professor Reason.

Charles Lenox Remond, Esq., of Salem, Massachusetts,
is among the most talented men of the country. Mr.
Remond is a native of the town he resides in, and at an early
age, evinced more than ordinary talents. At the age of
twenty-one, at which time (1832) the cause of the colored
people had just begun to attract public attention, he began
to take an interest in public affairs, and was present for the
first time, at the great convention of colored men, of that
year, at which the distinguished colonization gentlemen
named in another part of this work, among them, Rev.
R. R. Gurley, and Elliot Cresson, Esqs., were present. At this
convention, we think, Mr. Remond made his virgin speech.
From that time forth he became known as an orator, and

now stands second to no living man as a declaimer. This is his great forte, and to hear him speak, sends a thrill through the whole system, and a tremor through the brain.

In 1835, he went to England, making a tour of the United Kingdom, where he remained for two years, lecturing with great success; and if we mistake not was presented the hospitality of one of the towns of Scotland, at which he received a token of respect, in a code of resolutions adopted expressive of the sentiments of the people, signed by the town officers, inscribed to "Charles Lenox Remond, Esq.," a form of address never given in the United Kingdom, only where the person is held in the highest esteem for their attainments; the "Mr." always being used instead.

To C. L. Remond, are the people of Massachusetts indebted for the abolition of the odious distinction of caste, on account of condition. For up to this period, neither common white, nor genteel colored persons, could ride in first class cars; since which time, all who are able and willing to pay, go in them. In fact, there is but one class of cars, (except the emigrant cars which are necessary for the safety and comfort of other passengers) in Massachusetts.

Mr. Remond, appeared at one time before the legislature of Massachusetts, in behalf of the rights of the people above named, where with peals of startling eloquence, he moved that great body of intelligent New Englanders, to a respectful consideration of his subject; which eventually resulted as stated. The distinguished Judge Kelley, of Philadelphia, an accomplished scholar and orator, in 1849, in reply to an expression that Mr. Remond spoke like himself, observed, that it was the greatest compliment he ever had paid to his talents. "Proud indeed should I feel," said the learned Jurist, "were I such an orator as Mr. Remond." Charles Lenox Remond is the soul of an honorable gentleman.

Robert Morris, Jr., Esq., attorney and counsellor at law, is a member of the Essex county bar in Boston. Mr. Morris has also had the commission of magistracy conferred upon him, by his excellency George N. Briggs, recent governor of the commonwealth of Massachusetts, a high honor and compliment to an Attorney; the commission usually being conferred on none but the oldest or most meritorious among the members of the bar. He also keeps the books of one of the wealthy rail road companies, a business almost entirely confined to lawyers in that city. Mr. Morris is a talented gentleman, and stands very high at the Boston bar. He sometimes holds the magistrate's court in Chelsea, where his family resides, and is very highly esteemed by the whole community of both cities, and has a fine practice.

Macon B. Allen, Esq., attorney and counsellor at law, is also a member of the Essex bar. He is spoken of as a gentleman of fine education.

Robert Douglass, Jr., for many years, has kept a study and gallery of painting and daguerreotype in the city of Philadelphia. Mr. Douglass is an excellent artist—being a fine portrait and landscape painter, which art he practised before the discovery of daguerreotype. He is also a good lithographer, a gentleman of fine educational attainments, very clever talents, and highly esteemed in that city. Mr. Douglass has been twice to the West Indies and Europe.

J. Presley Ball is the principal daguerreotypist of Cincinnati, Ohio. Mr. Ball commenced the practice of his art about seven years ago, being then quite young, and inexperienced, as all young beginners are, laboring under many difficulties. He nevertheless, persevered, until he made a business, and established confidence in his skill; and now he does more business than any other artist in the profession in that city. His gallery, which is very large, finely skylighted, and handsomely furnished, is literally crowded from morning until evening with ladies, gentlemen, and children. He made some valuable improvements in the art, all for his own convenience. There is none more of a gentleman than J. Presley Ball. He has a brother, Mr. Thomas Ball, and a white gentleman to assist him. Few go to Cincinnati, without paying the daguerrean gallery of Mr. Ball, a visit.

The great organ of the "Liberty Party" in the United States, is now conducted by one who requires not a notice from such an obscure source—we mean Frederick Douglass, of Rochester, N. Y. His history is well known—it was written by more faithful hands than ours—it was written by himself. It stands enrolled on the reminiscences of Germany, and France, and in full length oil, in the academy of arts, and in bust of bronze or marble, in the museum of London. Mr. Douglass is also the sole owner of the printing establishment from which the paper is issued, and was promoted to this responsible position, by the power of his talents. He is a masterly letter writer, ably edits his paper, and as a speaker, and orator, let the scenes of a New York tabernacle, within two years, answer instead. Mr. Douglass is highly respected as a citizen and gentleman in Rochester.

In Syracuse, N. Y., resides George Boyer Vashon, Esq., A.M., a graduate of Oberlin Collegiate Institute, Attorney at Law, Member of the Syracuse Bar. Mr. Vashon, is a ripe scholar, an accomplished Essayist, and a chaste classic Poet; his style running very much in the strain of Byron's best efforts. He probably takes Byron as his model, and Childe Harold, as a sample, as in his youthful days, he was a fond admirer of GEORGE GORDON NOEL BYRON, always calling his whole name, when he named him. His Preceptor in Law, was the Honorable Walter, Judge Forward, late Controller, subsequently, Secretary of the Treasury of the United States, and recently *Charge de*

Affaires to Denmark, now President of the Bench of the District Court of the Western District of Pennsylvania.

Mr. Vashon was admitted to the Bar of the city of New York, in the fall of 1847, to practise in all the Courts of the State. He immediately subsequently, sailed to the West Indies, from whence he returned in the fall of 1850. He has contributed considerably to a number of the respectable journals of the country.

Mrs. Ann Maria Johnson, of the School of Mrs. Tillman and Mrs. Johnson, Teachers in French Worsted Needle Work, at the Exhibition of the Mechanics' Institute in Chicago, Ill., 1846, took the First Prize, and got her Diploma, for the best embroidery in cloth. This was very flattering to those ladies, especially the Diplomast, considering the great odds they had to contend with. The ladies were very successful teachers—their classes were always large.

In Williamsburg there is T. Joiner White, M.D.; in Brooklyn Peter Ray, M.D.; and in the city of New York, also, John Degrass, M.D., all young Physicians, who have time and experience yet before them, and promise fair to be good and useful members of society.

Miss Eliza Greenfield the BLACK SWAN, is among the most extraordinary persons of the present century. Being raised in obscurity, inured to callings far beneath her propensity, and unsuited to her taste, she had a desire to cultivate her talents, but no one to encourage her. Whenever she made the effort, she was discouraged—perhaps ridiculed; and thus discouraged, she would shrink again from her anxious task. She knew she could sing, and knew she could sing unlike any body else; knew she sung better than any whom she had heard of the popular singers, but could not tell why others could not think with, and appreciate her. In this way it seems, she was thrown about for three years, never meeting with a person who could fully appreciate her talents; and we have it from her own lips, that not until after the arrival of Jenny Lind and Parodi in the country, was she aware of the high character of her own talents. She knew she possessed them, because they were inherent, inseparable with her being. She attended the Concerts of Mad'll. Jenny Lind, and Operas of Parodi, and at once saw the "secret of their success"—they possessed talents, that no other popular singers mastered.

She went home; her heart fluttered; she stole an opportunity when no one listened, to mock or gossip; let out her voice, when *ecce!* she found her strains *four* notes *above* Sweden's favored Nightingale; she descended when lo! she found her tones *three* notes *below!* she thanked God with a "still small voice"; and now, she ranks second in point of voice, to no vocalist in the world. Miss Greenfield, if she only be judicious and careful, may become yet, in point of popularity, what Miss Lind was. The Black Swan, is singing to fine fashionable houses, and bids fair to stand unrivalled in the world of Song.

Patrick Henry Reason, a gentleman of ability and fine artist, stands high as an Engraver in the city of New York. Mr. Reason has been in business for years, in that city, and has sent out to the world, many beautiful specimens of his skillful hand. He was the first artist, we believe in the United States, who produced a plate of that beautiful touching little picture, the Kneeling Slave; the first picture of which represented a handsome, innocent little girl upon her knees, with hands outstretched, leaving the manacles dangling before her, anxiously looking and wishfully asking, "*Am I not a sister?*" It was beautiful—sorrowfully beautiful. He has we understand, frequently done Government engraving. Mr. P. H. is a brother of Professor Charles L. Reason.

David Jones Peck, M.D., a graduate of Rush Medical College, a talented young gentleman, practised Medicine for two years in Philadelphia. He left there in 1850.

William H. Allen, Esq., A.B., successor to Professor C. L. Reason, is Professor of Languages in Centre College, at McGrawville, N. Y. Professor Allen, is a gentleman of fine education, a graduate of Oneida Institute, and educated himself entirely by his own industry, having the aid of but fifty dollars during the whole period. The Professor is a talented Lecturer on Ancient History, and much of a gentleman.

Martin H. Freeman, A.B., a young gentleman, graduate of Rutland College, in Vermont, is "Junior Professor," in Allegheny Institute, Allegheny county, Pa. The Professor is a gentleman of talents, and doing much good in his position.

Rev. Molliston Madison Clark, a gentleman of great talents, a noble speaker, educated at Jefferson College, Pa., sailed to Europe in 1846, and was a member of the Evangelical Alliance. Mr. Clark kept a regular Journal of his travels through the United Kingdom of England, Scotland and Ireland. As well as a Greek and Latin, he is also a French and Spanish Linguist. He has all the eccentricity of Rowland Hill, manifested only in a very different manner.

William C. Nell, of Rochester, N.Y., formerly of Boston, has long been known as a gentleman of chaste and lofty sentiments, and a pure philanthropist. Mr. Nell, in company with Mr. Frederick Douglass, was present by invitation, and took his seat at table, at the celebration of Franklin's Birth Day, by the Typographical and Editorial corps of Rochester. In 1850, being again residing in Boston, he was nominated and ran for the Legislature of Massachusetts, by the Free Soil party of Essex county. Mr. Nell stood even with his party vote in the District.

He recently issued from the Boston press a Pamphlet, on the colored men who served in the wars of the United States of 1776, and 1812. This pamphlet is very useful as a book of reference on this subject, and Mr. Nell, of course does not aim at a full historical view. The circumstances under which it was got out, justify this belief. He was collecting materials in the winter of 1850-51, when he was taken down to his bed with a severe attack of disease of one of his lungs, with which he lingered, unable to leave his room for weeks. In the Spring, recovering somewhat his health, so as to go out—during this time, he had the little pamphlet published, as a means of pecuniary aid, promising another part to be forthcoming some subsequent period, which the writer hopes may soon be issued. Mr. Nell, is an excellent man, and deserves the patronage of the public.

Joseph G. Anderson, successor to Captain Frank Johnson, of Philadelphia, is now one of the most distinguished musicians in the country. Mr. Anderson is an artist professionally and practically, mastering various instruments, a composer of music, and a gentleman of fine accomplishments in other respects. His musical fame will grow with his age, which one day must place him in the front ranks of his profession, among the master in the world.

William Jackson, is among the leading musicians of New York city, and ranks among the most skillful violinists of America. This gentleman is a master of his favorite instrument, executing with ease the most difficult and critical composition. He is generally preferred in social and private parties, among the first families of the city, where the amateur and gentleman is more regarded than the mere services of the musician. Mr. Jackson is a teacher of music, and only requires a more favorable opportunity to vie with Ole Bull or Paganini.

Rev. Daniel A. Payne, commenced his literary career in Charleston, South Carolina, where he taught school for some time. In 1833 or 1834, he came North, placing himself in the Lutheran Theological Seminary, at Gettysburg, under the tutorage of the learned and distinguished Dr. Schmucker, where he finished his education as a Lutheran clergyman. To extend his usefulness, he joined the African Methodist Connexion, and for several years resided in Baltimore, where he taught an Academy for colored youth and maidens, gaining the respect and esteem of all who had the fortune to become acquainted with him. He is now engaged travelling and collecting information, for the publication of a history of one of the colored Methodist denominations in the United States. Mr. Payne is a pure and chaste poet, having published a small volume of his productions in 1850, under the title of "Pleasures and other Miscellaneous Poems, by Daniel A. Payne," issued from the press of Sherwood and Company, Baltimore, Maryland.

Rev. William T. Catto, a clergyman of fine talents, finished his education in the Theological Seminary in Charleston, South Carolina. He was ordained by the Presbytery of Charleston, and in 1848, under the best recommendations for piety, acquirements, and all the qualifications necessary to his high mission as a clergyman, was sent out as a missionary to preach the Gospel to all who needed it; but to make himself more useful, he joined the African Methodist Episcopal Church Connexion, and is now a useful and successful preacher in Philadelphia.

The musical profession of Philadelphia has long had a valuable votary in the person of William Appo, an accomplished pianist. Mr. Appo has been a teacher of the piano forte, for more than twenty years, alternately in the cities of New York and Philadelphia, and sometimes in Baltimore.

His profession extends amongst the citizens generally, from the more moderate in circumstances, to the ladies and daughters of the most wealthy gentlemen in community. This gentleman is a fine scholar, and as well as music, teaches the French langauge successfully. His young daughter, Helen, a miss of fourteen years of age, inherits the musical talents of her father, and is now organist in the central Presbyterian Church. The name of William Appo, is generally known as a popular teacher of music, but few who are not personally acquainted with him, know that he is a colored gentleman.

Augustus Washington, an artist of fine taste and perception, is numbered among the most successful Daguerreotypists in Hartford, Connecticut. His establishment is said to be visited daily by large numbers of the citizens of all classes; and this gallery is perhaps, the only one in the country, that keeps a female attendant, and dressing-room for ladies. He recommends, in his cards, black dresses to be worn for sitting; and those who go unsuitably dressed, are supplied with drapery, and properly enrobed.

John Newton Templeton, A.M., for fifteen years an upright, active, and very useful citizen of Pittsburg, Pennsylvania, was a graduate of Athens College, in the State of Ohio. Mr. Templeton, after an active life of more than twenty years, principally spent in school teaching, died in Pittsburg, in July, 1851, leaving an amiable widow and infant son.

Thomas Paul, A.B., of Boston, a gentleman of fine talents and amiable dispostion, whose life has been mainly devoted to teaching, is a graduate of Bowdoin College, in Maine. Mr. Paul is now the recipient of a salary of fifteen hundred dollars a year as teacher of a school in Boston.

Rev. Benjamin Franklin Templeton, pastor of St. Mary

street Church, Philadelphia, was educated at Hanover College, near Madison, Indiana. In 1838, Mr. Templeton was ordained a minister of the Ripley Presbytery, in Ohio; subsequently, in 1841, established a church, the Sixth Presbyterian, in Pittsburg, Pennsylvania, from which place he was called, in 1844, to take charge of his present pastorate. Mr. Templeton is a beautiful speaker, and an amiable gentleman.*

John B. Russworm, a gentleman of splendid talents, graduated at Bowdoin College, many years ago. Mr. Russworm was a class-mate of Honorable John P. Hale, United States

---

*During the last twenty years, there have been, at different periods, published among the colored people of the United States, twenty odd newspapers, some of which were conducted with ability. Among them, the "Colored American," in New York city; Samuel E. Cornish, Philip A. Bell, and Charles B. Ray, at different times, Editors. "The Demosthenian Shield," issued from a Literary Society of young colored men, in the city of Philadelphia. "The Struggler," by Philip A. Bell, New York, out of which the Colored American took its origin. The "National Reformer," an able monthly periodical, in pamphlet form, in Philadelphia; William Whipper, Editor. "The Northern Star," a Temperance monthly newspaper, published in Albany, N.Y.; Stephen Myers, Editor, still in existence—changed to ————————————————. "The Mystery," of Pittsburg, Pa.; Martin Robison Delany, Editor—succeeded by a committee of colored gentlemen as Editors. The "Palladium of Liberty," issued in Columbus, O., by a committee of colored gentlemen; David Jenkins, Editor. "The Disfranchised American," by a committee of colored gentlemen, Cincinnati, O.; A. M. Sumner, Editor—succeeded by the "Colored Citizen"; Rev. Thomas Woodson, and William Henry Yancey, Editors. The "National Watchman," Troy, N. Y.; William H. Allen and Henry Highland Garnett, Editors. Another issued in New York city, the name of which, we cannot now remember; James William Charles Pennington, D. D., and James McCuen Smith, M.D., Editors: the issue being alternately at Hartford, the then residence of Dr. Pennington—and New York city, the residence of Dr. Smith. The "Excelsior," an ephemeral issue, which appeared but once, in Detroit, Mich.; William H. Day, Editor.

The "Christian Herald," the organ of the A. M. Episcopal Church, published under the auspices of the General Conference of that body; Augustus Richardson Green, Editor, and General Book Steward. This gentleman has, also, written and published several small volumes of a religious character; a pamphlet on the Episcopacy and Infant Baptism, and the Lives of Reverends Fayette Davis and David Canyou. The "Elevator," of Philadelphia; James McCrummill, Editor. The "Ram's Horn," New York city; Thomas Vanrensellear, Editor. There is now a little paper, the name of which we cannot recollect, issued at Newark, N.J., merely a local paper, very meager in appearance. "The Farmer and Northern Star," in Courtland, N. Y., afterwards changed to the "Impartial Citizen," and published in Boston; Samuel Ringgold Ward, Editor. "The North Star," published in Rochester, N.Y.; Frederick Douglass, and Martin Robinson Delany, Edi-

Senator, and after leaving College as his first public act, commenced the publication of a newspaper, for the elevation of colored Americans, called "Freedom's Journal." Subsequently to the publication of his paper, Mr. Russworm became interested in the Colonization scheme, then in its infancy, and

---

tors—subsequently changed to the "Frederick Douglass' Paper"; Frederick Douglass, Editor.

A number of gentlemen have been authors of narratives, written by themselves, some of which are masterly efforts, manifesting great force of talents. Of such, are those by Frederick Douglass, William Wells Brown, and Henry Bibb.

Of the various churches and clergy we have nothing to say, as these do not come within our province; except where individuals, from position, come within the sphere of our arrangement.

There have been several inventors among the colored people. The youth Henry Blair, of Maryland, some years ago, invented the Corn-Planter, and Mr. Roberts of Philadelphia, 1842, a machine for lifting cars off the railways.

It may be expected that we should say something about a book issued in Boston, purporting to be a history of ancient great men of African descent, by one Mr. Lewis, entitled "Light and Truth." This book is nothing more than a compilation of selected portions of Rollin's, Goldsmith's, Furguson's, Hume's, and other ancient histories; added to which, is a tissue of historical absurdities and literary blunders, shamefully palpable, for which the author or authors should mantle their faces.

If viewed in the light of a "Yankee trick," simply by which to make money, it may, peradventure, be a very clever trick; but the publisher should have recollected, that the ostensible object of his work was, the edification and enlightenment of the public in general and the colored people in particular, upon a great and important subject of truth; and that those who must be the most injured by it, will be the very class of people, whom he professes a desire to benefit. We much regret the fact, that there are but too many of our brethren, who undertake to dabble in literary matters, in the shape of newspaper and book-making, who are wholly unqualified for the important work. This, however, seems to be called forth by the palpable neglect, and indifference of those who have had the educational advantages, but neglected to make such use of them.

There is one redeeming quality about "Light and Truth." It is a capital offset to the pitiable literary blunders of Professor George R. Gliddon, late Consul to Egypt, from the United States, Lecturer on Ancient Egyptian Literature, &c., &c., who makes all ancient black men, *white*; and asserts the Egyptians and Ethiopians to have been of the *Caucasian* or white race!—So, also, this colored gentleman, makes all ancient great white men, *black*—as Diogenes, Socrates, Themistocles, Pompey, Caesar, Cato, Cicero, Horace, Virgil, et cetera. Gliddon's idle nonsense has found a capital match in the production of Mr. Lewis' "Light and Truth," and both should be sold together. We may conclude by expressing our thanks to our brother Lewis, as we do not think that Professor Gliddon's learned ignorance, would have ever met an equal but for "Light and Truth." Reverends D. A. Payne, M. M. Clark, and other learned colored gentlemen, agree with us in the disapproval of this book.—Editor.

went to Liberia; after which he went to Bassa Cove, of which place he was made governor, where he died in 1851.

Benjamin Coker, a colored Methodist clergyman, forty years ago, wrote and issued, in the city of Baltimore, Maryland, a pamphlet, setting forth in glowing terms, the evils of American slavery, and the wrongs inflicted on the colored race. Rev. Daniel A. Payne, a talented clergyman, mentioned in this work, has now in his possession a copy of the pamphlet, and informs us, that the whole ground assumed by the modern abolitionists, was taken and reviewed in this pamphlet, by Daniel Coker. We may reasonably infer, that the ideas of Anti-Slavery, as taught by the friends of the black race at the present day, were borrowed from Mr. Coker; though, perhaps, policy forbade due credit to the proper source. Coker, like Russworm, became interested in the cause of African Colonization, and went to Africa; where he subsequently became an extensive coast trader, having several vessels, one of which he commanded in person, taking up his residence on the island of Sherbro, where he is said to have lived in great splendor. He died in 1845 or 1846, at an advanced age, leaving a family of sons and daughters.

Henry Bibb, an eloquent speaker, for several years, was the principal traveling lecturer for the Liberty Party of Michigan. Mr. Bibb, with equal advantages, would equal many of those who fill high places in the country, and now assume superiority over him and his kindred. He fled an exile from the United States, in 1850, to Canada, to escape the terrible consequences of the Republican Fugitive Slave Law, which threatened him with a total destruction of liberty. Mr. Bibb established the "Voice of the Fugitive," a newspaper, in Sandwich, Canada West, which is managed and conducted with credit.

Titus Basfield, graduated at Franklin College, New

Athens, Ohio, receiving his religious instruction from the late Dr. Jonathan Walker, of that place, a physician and Covenanter clergyman. He afterwards graduated in theology at the Theological Seminary of Cannonsburg, Pennsylvania, was ordained, and traveled preaching and lecturing to the people of his peculiar faith and the public, for several years. He went to New London, Canada West, where he has charge of a Scotch congregation of religious votaries to that ancient doctrine of salvation.

Mary Ann Shadd, a very intelligent young lady, peculiarly eccentric, published an excellent pamphlet, issued from the press in Wilmington, Delaware, in 1849, on the elevation of the colored people. The writer of this work, was favored with an examination of it before publication, which he then highly approved of, as an excellent introduction to a great subject, fraught with so much interest. Miss Shadd has traveled much, and now has charge of a school in Sandwich, Canada West.

James McCrummill, of Philadelphia, is a skillful surgeon-dentist, and manufacturer of porcelain teeth, having practised the profession for many years in that city. He is said to be equal to the best in the city, and probably only requires an undivided attention to establish the reality.

Joseph Wilson, Thomas Kennard, and William Nickless, are also practising dentists in the city of Philadelphia. Mr. Kennard is said to be one of the best *workmen* in the manufacture of artificial teeth, and *gums*—a new discovery, and very valuable article, in this most beautiful and highly useful art. He devotes several hours a day, to the manufacture of these articles for one of the principal surgeon-dentists of Arch street.

James M. Whitfield, of Buffalo, New York, though in an humble position, (for which we think he is somewhat reprehensible), is one of the purest poets in America. He has written much for different newspapers; and, by industry and application—being already a good English scholar—did he but place himself in a favorable situation in life, would not be second to John Greenleaf Whittier, nor the late Edgar A. Poe.

Mary Elizabeth Miles, in accordance with the established rules, graduated as a teacher, in the Normal School, at Albany, New York, several years ago. Miss Miles (now Mrs. Bibb) was a very talented young lady and successful teacher. She spent several years of usefulness in Massachusetts, and Philadelphia, Pennsylvania, after which she went to Cincinnati, as assistant-teacher in Gilmore's "High School for Colored Children," which ended her public position in life. She now resides in Sandwich, Canada West.

Lucy Stanton, of Columbus, Ohio, is a graduate of Oberlin Collegiate Institute, in that State. She is now engaged in teaching school in that city, in which she is reputed to be successful. She is quite a young lady, and has her promise of life all before her, and bids fair to become a woman of much usefulness in society.

Doctor Bias, of Philadelphia, spoken of in another place, graduated at the close of the session of 1851–52, in the Eclectic Medical College, in that city. The doctor is highly esteemed by the physicians of his system, who continually interchange calls with him. He is also a practical phrenologist,—which profession he does not now attend to, giving his undivided attention to the practice of medicine,—and has written a pamphlet on that subject, entitled, "Synopsis of Phrenology, and the Phrenological Developments, as given by J. J. Gould Bias." No man perhaps, in the community of Philadelphia, possesses more self-will, and determination of character, than Dr. James Joshua Gould Bias. Mr. Whipper says of him, that he is "a Napoleon in character."

The sterling trait in his character is, that he grasps after *originality*, and grapples with every difficulty. Such a man, must and will succeed in his undertakings.

XII | STUDENTS OF VARIOUS PROFESSIONS

T HERE are a number of young gentlemen who have finished their literary course, who are now studying for the different learned professions, in various parts of the country.

Jonathan Gibbs, A.B., a very talented young gentleman, and fine speaker, is now finishing his professional studies in the Theological School at Dartmouth University. Mr. Gibbs also studied in the Scientific Department of the same Institution.

William H. Day, Esq., A.B., a graduate of Oberlin Collegiate Institute, is now in Cleveland Ohio, preparing for the Bar. Mr. Day is, perhaps, the most eloquent young gentleman of his age in the United States.

John Mercer Langston, A.B., of Chillicothe, Ohio, also a graduate of Oberlin College, a talented young gentleman, and promising orator, is completing a Theological course at the School of Divinity at Oberlin. It is said, that Mr. Langston intends also to prepare for the Bar. He commenced the study of Law previous to that of Theology, under Judge Andrews of Cleveland.

Charles Dunbar, of New York city, a promising, very intelligent young gentleman, is now in the office of Dr. Childs, and having attended one course of Lectures at Bowdoin Medical School in Maine, will finish next fall and winter, for the practice of his profession.

Isaac Humphrey Snowden, a promising young gentleman of talents, is now reading Medicine under Dr. Clarke of Boston, and attended the session of the Medical School of Harvard University, of 1850–51.

Daniel Laing, Jr., Esq., a fine intellectual young gentleman of Boston, a student also of Dr. Clarke of that city, one of the Surgeons of the Massachusetts General Hospital, who attended the course of Lectures the session of 1850–51, at the Medical School of Harvard University, is now in Paris, to spend two years in the hospitals, and attend the Medical Lectures of that great seat of learning. Mr. Laing, like most medical students, has ever been an admirer, and anxious to sit under the teachings of that great master in Surgery, Velpeau.

Dr. James J. Gould Bias, a Botanic Physician, and talented gentleman of Philadelphia, is a member of the class of 1851–52, of the Eclectic Medical School of that city. Dr. Bias deserves the more credit for his progress in life, as he is entirely self-made.

Robert B. Leach, of Cleveland, Ohio, a very intelligent young gentleman, is a member of the medical class for 1851–52, of the Homeopathic College, in that City. Mr. Leach, when graduated, will be the *First Colored Homeopathic* Physician in the United States.

Dr. John Degrass, of New York city, named in another place, spent two years in Paris Hospitals, under the teaching of the great lecturer and master of surgery, Velpeau, to whom he was assistant and dresser, in the hospital—the first position—for advantages, held by a student. The Doctor has subsequently been engaged as surgeon on a Havre packet, where he discharged the duties of his office with credit.

Also Dr. Peter Ray, of Brooklyn, named on the same page, graduated at Castleton Medical School, Vermont, spent some time at the Massachusetts General Hospital, Boston, where he held the position of assistant and dresser to Surgeon Parkman, in his ward of the hospital.

Dr. John P. Reynolds, has for a number of years been one of the most popular and successful physicians in Vincennes, Indiana. We believe Dr. Reynolds, was not of the "regular" system, but some twenty-three or -four years ago, studied under an "Indian physician," after which, he practised very successfully in Zanesville, Ohio, subsequently removing to Vincennes, where he has for the last sixteen years, supported an enviable reputation as a physician. We understand Doctor Reynolds has entered into all the scientific improvements of the "eclectic school" of medicine, which has come into being in the United States, long since his professional career commenced. His popularity is such, that he has frequently been entrusted, with public confidence, and on one occasion, in 1838, was appointed by the court, sole executor of a very valuable orphans' estate. The Doctor has grown quite wealthy it is said, commanding a considerable influence in the community.

Dr. McDonough, a skillful young physician, graduated at the Institute, Easton, Pennsylvania, and finished his medical education at the University of New York. The Doctor is one of the most thorough of the young physicians; has been attached to the greater part of the public institutions of the city of New York, and is a good practical chemist.

Of course, there are many others, but as we have taken no measures whatever, to collect facts or information from abroad, only getting such as was at hand, and giving the few sketches here, according to our own recollection of them, we close this short chapter at this point.

A SCAN AT PAST THINGS

I T may not be considered in good taste to refer to those still living, who formerly occupied prominent business positions, and by dint of misfortune or fortune, have withdrawn. Nevertheless, we shall do so, since our simple object in this hasty sketch of things, is to show that the colored people of the country have not as has been charged upon them, always been dregs on the community and excrescences on the body politic, wherever they may have lived. We only desire to show that they have been, all things considered, just like other people.

Several years ago, there lived in the city of St. Louis, Missouri, Mr. Berry Mechum. This gentleman was very wealthy, and had at one time, two fine steamers plying on the Mississippi, all under the command and management of white men, to whom he trusted altogether. As late as 1836, he sent two sons to the Oberlin Collegiate Institute, desiring that they might become educated, in order to be able to manage his business; who, although he could read and write, was not sufficiently qualified and skilled in the arts of business to vie with the crafty whites of the Valley. But before his sons were fitted for business though reputed very wealthy, which there is no doubt he was, his whole property was seized and taken: and as he informed the writer himself, he did not know what for, as he had no debts that he knew of, until these suits were entered. Mr. Mechum was an energetic, industrious, persevering old gentleman—a baptist clergyman, and published a small pamphlet on the condition of the colored race. And although, it evinces great deficiency of literary qualifications, yet, does credit to the good old man, for the sound thoughts therein contained.

Also in the city of St. Louis, David Desara, who was a Mississippi pilot for many years. He made much money at his business, and owned at one time, a steamboat, which he piloted himself. Mr. Desara also failed, in consequence of having his business all in the hands of white men, as most of the slave state colored people have, entrusting to them entirely, without knowing anything of their own concerns.

Charles Moore, long and familiarly known as "Chancy Moore the Pilot," was for many years, one of the most popular pilots on the Ohio and Mississippi rivers. Mr. Moore made much money, and withdrew from his old business, purchasing a large tract of land in Mercer County, Ohio, where he has for the last ten or twelve years been farming.

Mr. Moore was an honest man, and we believe upon him originated the purely Western phrase, "Charley Moore the fair thing"; he always in his dealings saying "gentlemen, do the *fair* thing."

Abner H. Francis and James Garrett were formerly extensive clothes dealers in Buffalo, N.Y., doing business to the amount of sixty thousand dollars annually. They were energetic, industrious, persevering gentlemen, commencing business under very unfavorable circumstances, in fact, commencing on but *seventy-five* dollars, as the writer has been authentically informed by the parties.

They continued successfully for years, where their paper and endorsements were good for any amount they wanted —highly respected and esteemed; Mr. Francis sitting at one time as juryman in the court of quarter sessions. These gentlemen failed in business in 1849, but since then, have nearly adjusted the claims against them. Mr. Francis has since settled in Oregon Territory, Portland City, where he is again doing a fair mercantile business. They bid fair again to rank among the "merchant princes" of the times.

Robert Banks was for many years, a highly esteemed and extensive clothes dealer, on Jefferson Avenue, in Detroit, Mich. No man was more highly respected for unswerving integrity, and uprightness of purpose, than Robert Banks, of Detroit. Mr. Banks, had much enlarged his business, immediately succeeding a fire in which he was burnt out two years previous to closing, which ensued in July, 1851, being the second time he had lost his store by fire. He might have, had he done as merchants usually do under such circumstances, continued his business; but instead, he made an assignment, with few preferred creditors, rather as he expressed it, ruin his business, than wilfully wrong a creditor. What speaks volumes in his behalf, every person, even his greatest creditors say, "He is an honest man"; and while settling the business of the late concern, those to whom he was indebted, offered him assistance to commence business again. But this he thankfully declined, preferring to take his chance with others in the land of gold, California, where he now is, than commence again under the circumstances. Doubtless, if no special prevention ensue, Mr. Banks will be fully able to redeem his present obligations, and once more be found prospering and happy.

Henry Knight, of Chicago, commenced business in that city without capital; but by industry, soon gained the esteem and confidence of the public, making many friends. He fast rose in prosperity, until he became the proprietor of the most extensive livery establishment in the city, in which he had much capital invested. Determined to be equal to the times, the growing prosperity of the city, and the demands of the increasing pride of the place, he extended his possessions—erecting costly buildings, besides increasing his stock and livery extensively. He was burnt out—a pressure came upon him—he sold out his stock, staid suits against himself; went to California, returned in a year and a half—paid off old claims, saved his property—went back; opened a California hotel, returned in less than one year with several thousand dollars, and how stands entirely clear of all debt—and all this done in the space of two and a half years. Mr. Knight is a man of business, and will hold his position with others if he have but half a chance. With such a man, there is "no such a thing as fail"—he could not again, if he desired, because, his friends would not permit him.

XIV | LATE MEN OF LITERARY, PROFESSIONAL AND ARTISTIC NOTE

ATE Captain Frank Johnson, of Philadelphia, the most renowned band leader ever known in the United States, was a man of science, and master of his profession. In 1838, Captain Johnson went to England with his noble band of musicians, where he met with great success—played to Her Majesty Queen Victoria and His Royal Highness Prince Albert—Captain Johnson receiving a handsome French bugle, by order of her Majesty, valued at five hundred dollars—returning, lie held throughout the Eastern, Northern, and Western States, grand concerts, known as "Soirees Musicales." He was a great composer and teacher of music, and some of the finest Marches and Cotillions now extant, have been originally composed by Captain Frank Johnson. On his Western tour, by some awkwardness of management, he lost at Buffalo, original music in manuscript, which never had been published—as much of his composition had been; valued at one thousand dollars, which, although advertised, he never got. But his name was sufficient to give additional value to the prize; and there is no doubt, but the world is now being benefited by the labors of Captain Johnson, the credit being given to others than himself. This was an unfortunate circumstance, and had his amiable and excellent widow, Mrs. Helen Johnson of Philadelphia, now this composition, she could support herself in ease, by the sale of the published work. Captain Frank Johnson, died in Philadelphia in 1844, universally respected, and regretted as an irreparable loss to society. At his death the band divided, different members taking a leadership.

Andrew J. Conner, one of the members of Captain Johnson's band, also became a distinguished composer and teacher of music. Mr. Conner taught the piano forte in the best families in the city of Philadelphia—among merchants, bankers, and professional men. He contributed to the popular literary Magazines of the day, and very many who have read in Graham's and other literary issues, "Music composed by A. J. Conner," did not for a moment think that the author was a colored gentleman. Mr. Conner died in Philadelphia in 1850.

James Ulett, formerly of New York, became quite celebrated a few years since, as a comedian. He played several times in the old "Richmond Hill" Theatre, and quite successfully in Europe. Mr. Ulett was not well educated, and consequently, labored under considerable inconvenience in reading, frequently making grammatical blunders, as the writer noticed in a private rehearsal, in 1836, in the city of New York. He, however, possessed great intellectual powers, and his success depended more upon that, than his accuracy in reading. Of course, he was a great delineator of character, which being the principal feature in a comedian, his language was lost sight of in common conversation. Mr. Ulett died in New York a few years ago.

Doctor Lewis G. Wells was a most talented orator and man of literary qualifications. Residing in Baltimore, Maryland, he raised himself high in the estimation of all who knew him. He studied medicine, and was admitted into the Washington Medical College, attending the regular courses, and would have graduated, but for some misunderstanding between himself and the professors, which prevented it. He was a most successful practitioner, and effected more cures during the prevalence of the cholera in 1832, than any other physician in the city. Doctor Wells was also a most successful practical phrenologist, and lectured to large and fashionable houses of the first class ladies and gentlemen of Baltimore, and other cities. Being a great wit, he kept his audiences in uproars of laughter. Mr. Wells was also an ordained minister of the Gospel, belonging to the white Methodist connexion; and was author of several productions, among them, a large Methodist hymn book, containing several fine original poems. Dr. Wells died the same year of cholera, after successfully saving many others, because there was no physician at that time who understood the treatment of the disease.

XV | FARMERS AND HERDSMEN

L ITTLE need be said about farmers; there are hundreds of them in all parts of the country, especially in the Western States; still these may not be considered of a conspicuous or leading character—albeit, they are contributing largely to the wants of community, and wealth of the country at large. Ohio, Michigan, Wisconsin, Iowa, Illinois, and Indiana, all, are largely represented by the farming interests of colored men. We shall name but a sufficient number to show the character of their enterprise in this department of American industry.

Rev. William Watson, of Cincinnati, Ohio, is the owner of a fine farm in Mercer county, and six hundred acres of additional land.

Mr. Richard Phillips, of the same city, is owner of a fine farm in the same county, and three hundred and fifty additional acres of land.

Rev. Reuben P. Graham, of Cincinnati, owns a finely cultivated farm in Mercer county, three hundred acres of adjoining land; and one near Cincinnati.

Mr. John Woodson, of Jackson county, is one of the most successful farmers in the State of Ohio. Having a large tract of land, he has one of the best cultivated farms in the West, in a most productive state, raising grains, fruits, and livestock. In the year 1842, his farm produced that season, three thousand bushels of wheat, several hundred bushels of rye, eleven hundred bushels of oats, large crops of corn, potatoes, and other vegetables; large quantities of fruits, three hundred stacks of hay, with a large stock of several hundred heads of cattle on the place. Mr. Woodson has for many years, been a highly respectable man in his neighborhood, and continues his farming interests with unabated success.

Dr. Charles Henry Langston, of Columbus, Ohio, is also the proprietor of a very fine farm of eleven hundred acres, in Jackson county, upon which he has a white tenant. This gentleman is a surgeon-dentist by profession, educated at Oberlin College, making his home in Columbus.

Robert Purvis, Esq., a gentleman of collegiate education, is proprietor of one of the best improved farms in Philadelphia county, fifteen miles from Philadelphia. His cattle consist of the finest English breed.

Joseph Purvis, Esq., of Bucks county, Pennsylvania, a gentleman also of education and wealth, is an amateur stock farmer. Every animal on Mr. Purvis' farm is of the very best breed—Godolphin horses, Durham cattle, Leicestershire sheep, Berkshire swine, even English bull-terrier dogs, and whatever else pertains to the blooded breeds of brutes, may be found on the farm of Joseph Purvis. Mr. Purvis supplies a great many farmers with choice breeds of cattle, and it is said that he spends ten thousand dollars annually, in the improvement of his stocks.

Robert Briges Forten, also of Bucks county, Pennsylvania, is an amateur farmer. Mr. Forten is a gentleman of fine education, a pure, chaste poet, and attends to farming for the love of nature. He is a valuable member of the farming enterprise in the country.

If such evidence of industry and interest, as has been exhibited in the various chapters on the different pursuits and engagements of colored Americans, do not entitle them to equal rights and privileges in our common country, then indeed, is there nothing to justify the claims of any portion of the American people to the common inheritance of Liberty.

We proceed to another view of our condition in the United States.

XVI NATIONAL DISFRANCHISEMENT OF COLORED PEOPLE

W E give below the Act of Congress, known as the "Fugitive Slave Law," for the benefit of the reader, as there are thousands of the American people of all classes, who have never read the provisions of this enactment; and consequently, have no conception of its enormity. We had originally intended, also, to have inserted here, the Act of Congress of 1793, but since this Bill includes all the provisions of that Act, in fact, although called a "supplement," is a substitute, *de facto*, it would be superfluous; therefore, we insert the Bill alone, with explanations following:—

AN ACT

To Amend, and Supplementary to the Act, Entitled, "An Act Respecting Fugitives from Justice, and Persons Escaping from the Service of Their Masters," Approved February 12, 1793.

Be it enacted by the Senate and House of Representatives of the United States of America in Congress assembled, That the persons who have been, or may hereafter be, appointed commissioners, in virtue of any act of Congress, by the circuit courts of the United States, and who, in consequence of such appointment, are authorized to exercise the powers that any justice of the peace or other magistrate of any of the United States may exercise in respect to offenders for any crime or offence against the United States, by arresting, imprisoning, or bailing the same under and by virtue of the thirty-third section of the act of the twenty-fourth of September, seventeen hundred and eighty-nine, entitled "An act to establish the judicial courts of the United States," shall be, and are hereby authorized and required to exercise and discharge all the powers and duties conferred by this act.

SEC. 2. *And be it further enacted*, That the superior court of each organized territory of the United States shall have the same power to appoint commissioners to take acknowledgments of bail and affidavit, and to take depositions of witnesses in civil causes, which is now possessed by the circuit courts of the United States; and all commissioners who shall hereafter be appointed for such purposes by the superior court of any organized territory of the United States shall possess all the powers and exercise all the duties conferred by law upon the commissioners appointed by the circuit courts of the United States for similar purposes, and shall moreover exercise and discharge all the powers and duties conferred by this act.

SEC. 3. *And be it further enacted*, That the circuit courts of the United States, and the superior courts of each organized territory of the United States, shall from time to time enlarge the number of commissioners, with a view to afford reasonable facilities to reclaim fugitives from labor, and to the prompt discharge of the duties imposed by this act.

SEC. 4. *And be it further enacted*, That the commissioners above named shall have concurrent jurisdiction with the judges of the circuit and district courts of the United States, in their respective circuits and districts within the several States, and the judges of the superior courts of the Territories, severally and collectively, in term time and vacation; and shall grant certificates to such claimants, upon satisfactory proof being made, with authority to take and remove such fugitives from service or labor, under the restrictions herein contained, to the State or territory from which such persons may have escaped or fled.

SEC. 5. *And be it further enacted*, That it shall be the duty of all marshals and deputy marshals to obey and execute all warrants and precepts issued under the provisions of this act, when to them directed; and should any marshal or deputy marshal refuse to receive such warrant or other process, when tendered, or to use all proper means diligently to execute the same, he shall, on conviction thereof, be fined in the sum of one thousand dollars to the use of such claimant, on the motion of such claimant, by the circuit or district court for the district of such marshal; and after arrest of such fugitive by such marshal or his deputy, or whilst at any time in his custody, under the provisions of this act, should such fugitive escape, whether with or without the assent of such marshal or his deputy, such marshal shall be liable, on his official bond, to be prosecuted, for the benefit of such claimant for the full value of the service or labor of said fugitive in the State, Territory, or district whence he escaped; and the better to enable the said commissioners, when thus appointed, to execute their duties faithfully and efficiently, in conformity with the requirements of the constitution of the United States and of this art, they are hereby authorized and empowered, within their counties respectively, to appoint in writing under their hands, any one or more suitable persons, from time to time, to execute all such warrants and other process as may be issued by them in the lawful performance of their respective duties; with an authority to such commissioners, or the persons to be appointed by them, to execute process as aforesaid, to summon and call to their aid the bystanders, or *posse comitatus* of the proper county, when necessary to insure a faithful observance of the clause of the constitution referred to, in conformity with the provisions of this act: and all good citizens are hereby commanded to aid and assist in the prompt and efficient execution of this law, whenever their services may be required, as aforesaid, for that person; and said warrants shall run and be executed by said officers anywhere in the State within which they are issued.

SEC. 6. *And be it further enacted,* That when a person held to service or labor in any State or Territory of the United States has heretofore or shall hereafter escape into another State or Territory of the United States, the person or persons to whom such service or labor may be due, or his, her, or their agent or attorney, duly authorized, by power of attorney, in writing, acknowledged and certified under the seal of some legal office or court of the State or Territory in which the game may be executed, may pursue and reclaim such fugitive person, either by procuring a warrant from some one of the courts, judges, or commissioners aforesaid, of the proper circuit, district or county, for the apprehension of such fugitive from service or labor, or by seizing and arresting such fugitive, where the same can be done without process, and by taking and causing such person to be taken forthwith before such court, judge or commissioner, whose duty it shall be to hear and determine the case of such claimant in a summary manner; and upon satisfactory proof being made, by deposition or affidavit, in writing, to be taken and certified by such court, judge, or commissioner, or by other satisfactory testimony, duly taken and certified by some court, magistrate, justice of the peace, or other legal officer authorized to administer an oath, and take depositions under the laws of the State or Territory from which such person owing service or labor may have escaped, with a certificate of such magistracy or other authority, as aforesaid, with the seal of the proper court or officer thereto attached, which seal shall be sufficient to establish the competency of the proof, and with proof, also by affidavit, of the identity of the person whose service or labor is claimed to be due as aforesaid, that the person so arrested does in fact owe service or labor to the person or persons claiming him or her, in the State or Territory from which such fugitive may have escaped as aforesaid, and that said person escaped, to make out and deliver to such claimant, his or her agent or attorney, a certificate setting forth the substantial facts as to the service or labor due from such fugitive to the claimant, and of his or her escape from the State or Territory in which such service or labor was due to the State or Territory in which he or she was arrested, with authority to such claimant, or his or her agent or attorney to use such reasonable force and restraint as may be necessary under the circumstances of the case, to take and remove such fugitive person back to the State or Territory from whence he or she may have escaped as aforesaid. In no trial or hearing under this act shall the testimony of such alleged fugitive be admitted in evidence; and the certificates in this and the first section mentioned shall be conclusive of the right of the person or persons in whose favor granted to remove such fugitive to the State or Territory from which he escaped, and shall prevent all molestation of said person or persons by any process issued by any court, judge, magistrate, or other person whomsoever.

SEC. 7. *And be it further enacted*, That any person who shall knowingly and willingly obstruct, hinder, or prevent such claimant, his agent or attorney, or any person or persons lawfully assisting him, her, or them, from arresting such a fugitive from service or labor, either with or without process as aforesaid; or shall rescue, or attempt to rescue such fugitive from service or labor, from the custody of such claimant, his or her agent or attorney or other person or persons lawfully assisting as aforesaid, when so arrested, pursuant to the authority herein given and declared: or shall aid, abet, or assist such person, so owing service or labor as aforesaid, directly or indirectly, to escape from such claimant, his agent or attorney, or other person or persons, legally authorized as aforesaid; or shall harbor or conceal such fugitive, so as to prevent the discovery and arrest of such person, after notice or knowledge of the fact that such person was a fugitive from service or labor as aforesaid, shall, for either of said offences, be subject to a line not exceeding one thousand dollars, and imprisonment not exceeding six months, by indictment and conviction before the district court of the United States for the district in which such offence may have been committed, or before the proper court of criminal jurisdiction, if committed within any one of the organized territories of the United States; and shall moreover forfeit and pay, by way of civil damages to the party injured by such illegal conduct, the sum of one thousand dollars for each fugitive so lost as aforesaid, to be recovered by action of debt in any of the district or territorial courts aforesaid, within whose jurisdiction the said offence may have been committed.

SEC. 8. *And be it further enacted*, That the marshals, their deputies, and the clerks of the said district and territorial courts, shall be paid for their services the like fees as may be allowed to them for similar services in other cases; and where such services rendered exclusively in the arrest, custody, and delivery of the fugitive to the claimant, his or her agent or attorney, or where such supposed fugitive may be discharged out of custody for the want of sufficient proof as aforesaid, then such fees are to be paid in the whole by such claimant, his agent or attorney; and in all cases where the proceedings are before a commissioner, he shall be entitled to a fee of ten dollars in full for his services in each case, upon delivery of the said certificate to the claimant, his or her agent or attorney; or a fee of five dollars in cases where the proof shall not, in the opinion of such commissioner, warrant such certificate and delivery, inclusive of all services incident to such arrest and examination, to be paid in either case, by the claimant, his or her agent or attorney. The person or persons authorized to execute the process to be issued by such commissioners for the arrest and detention of fugitives from service or labor as aforesaid, shall also be entitled to a fee of five dollars each for each person he or they may arrest and take before any such commissioner as aforesaid at the instance and request of such claimant, with such other fees as may be deemed reasonable by such commissioner for such other additional services as may be necessarily performed by him or them: such as attending to the examination, keeping the fugitive in custody, and providing him with food and lodging during his detention, and until the final determination of such commissioner; and in general for performing such other duties as may be required by such claimant, his or her attorney or agent, or commissioner in the premises; such fees to be made up in conformity with the fees usually charged by the officers of the courts of justice within the proper district or county, as near as may be practicable, and paid by such claimants, their agents or attorneys, whether such supposed fugitive from service or labor be ordered to be delivered to such claimants by the final determination of such commissioners or not.

Sec. 9. *And be it further enacted*, That upon affidavit made by the claimant of such fugitive, his agent or attorney, after such certificate has been issued, that he has reason to apprehend that such fugitive will be rescued by force from his or their possession before he can be taken beyond the limits of the State in which the arrest is made, it shall be the duty of the officer making the arrest to retain such fugitive in his custody, and to remove him to the State whence he fled, and there to deliver him to said claimant, his agent or attorney. And to this end the officer aforesaid is hereby authorized and required to employ so many persons as he may deem necessary, to overcome such force, and to retain them in his service so long as circumstances may require; the said officer and his assistants, while so employed, to receive the same compensation, and to be allowed the same expenses as are now allowed by law for the transportation of criminals, to be certified by the judge of the district within which the arrest is made, and paid out of the treasury of the United States.

SEC. 10. *And be it further enacted*, That when any person held to service or labor in any State or Territory, or in the District of Columbia, shall escape therefrom, the party to whom such service or labor shall be due, his, her, or their agent or attorney may apply to any court of record therein, or judge thereof, in vacation, and make satisfactory proof to such court, or judge, in vacation, of the escape aforesaid, and that the person escaping owed service or labor to such party. Whereupon the court shall cause a record to be made of the matters so proved, and also a general description of the person so escaping, with such convenient certainty as may be; and a transcript of such record authenticated by the attestation of the clerk, and of the seal of the said court, being produced in any other State, Territory, or District in which the person so escaping may be found, and being exhibited to any judge, commissioner, or other officer, authorized by the law of the United States to cause persons escaping from service or labor to be delivered up, shall be held and taken to be full and conclusive evidence of the fact of escape, and that the service or labor of the person escaping is due to the party in such record mentioned. And upon the production by the said party of other and further evidence, if necessary, either oral or by affidavit, in addition to what is contained in the said record of the identity of the person escaping, he or she shall be delivered up to the claimant. And the said court, commissioner, judge or other person authorized by this act to grant certificates to claimants of fugitives, shall, upon the production of the record and other evidences aforesaid, grant to such claimant a certificate of his right to take any such person identified and proved to be owing service or labor as aforesaid, which certificate shall authorize such claimant to seize or arrest and transport such person to the State or Territory from which he escaped: *Provided*, That nothing herein contained shall be construed as requiring the production of a transcript of such record as evidence as aforesaid; but in its absence, the claim shall be heard and determined upon other satisfactory proofs competent in law.

HOWELL COBB,
Speaker of the House of Representatives.

WILLIAM R. KING,
President of the Senate, pro tempore.

Approved September 18, 1850.

MILLARD FILLMORE.

The most prominent provisions of the Constitution of the United States, and those which form the fundamental basis of personal security, are they which provide, that every person shall be secure in their person and property: that no person may be deprived of liberty without due process of law, and that for crime or misdemeanor; that there may be no process of law that shall work corruption of blood. By corruption of blood is meant, that process, by which a person is *degraded* and deprived of rights common to the enfranchised citizen—of the rights of an elector, and of eligibility to the office of a representative, of the people; in a word, that no person nor their posterity, may ever be debased beneath the level of the recognised basis of American citizenship. This debasement and degradation is "corruption of blood"; politically understood—a legal acknowledgement of inferiority of birth.

Heretofore, it ever has been denied, that the United States recognised or knew any difference between the people—that the Constitution makes no distinction, but includes in its provisions, all the people alike. This is not true, and certainly is blind absurdity in us at least, who have suffered the dread consequences of this delusion, not now to see it.

By the provisions of this bill, the colored people of the United States are positively degraded beneath the level of the whites—are made liable at any time, in any place, and under all circumstances, to be arrested—and upon the claim of any white person, without the privilege, even of making a defence, sent into endless bondage. Let no visionary nonsense about *habeas corpus*, or a *fair trial*, deceive us; there are no such rights granted in this bill, and except where the commissioner is too ignorant to understand when reading it, or too stupid to enforce it when he does understand, there is no earthly chance—no hope under heaven for the colored person who is brought before one of these officers of the law. Any leniency that may be expected, must proceed from the whims or caprice of the magistrate—in fact, it is optional with them; and *our* rights and liberty entirely at their disposal.

We are slaves in the midst of freedom, waiting patiently, and unconcernedly—indifferently and stupidly, for masters to come and lay claim to us, trusting to their generosity, whether or not they will own us and carry us into endless bondage.

The slave is more secure than we; he knows who holds the heel upon his bosom—we know not the wretch who may grasp us by the throat. His master may be a man of some conscientious scruples; ours may be unmerciful. Good or bad, mild or harsh, easy or hard, lenient or severe, saint or satan—whenever that master demands any one of us—even our affectionate wives and darling little children, *we must go into slavery*—there is *no alternative*. The *will* of the man who sits in judgment on our liberty, is the law. To him is given *all power* to say, whether or not we have a right to enjoy freedom. This is the power over the slave in the South—this is now extended to the North. The will of the man who sits in judgment over us is the law; because it is explicitly provided that the *decision* of the commissioner shall be final, from which there can be no appeal.

The freed man of the South is even more secure than the freeborn of the North; because such persons usually have their records in the slave states, bringing their "papers" with them; and the slaveholders will be faithful to their own acts. The Northern freeman knows no records; he despises the "papers."

Depend upon no promised protection of citizens in any quarter. Their own property and liberty are jeopardised, and they will not sacrifice them for us. This we may not expect them to do.

Besides, there are no people who ever lived, love their country and obey their laws as the Americans.

Their country is their Heaven—their Laws their Scriptures—and the decrees of their Magistrates obeyed as the fiat of God. It is the most consummate delusion and misdirected confidence to depend upon them for protection; and for a moment suppose even our children safe while walking in the streets among them.

A people capable of originating and sustaining such a law as this, are not the people to whom we are willing to entrust our liberty at discretion.

What can we do? What shall we do? This is the great and important question:—Shall we submit to be dragged like brutes before heartless men, and sent into degradation and bondage?—Shall we fly, or shall we resist? Ponder well and reflect.

A learned jurist in the United States, (Chief Justice John Gibson of Pennsylvania,) lays down this as a fundamental right in the United States: that "Every man's house is his castle, and he has the right to defend it unto the taking of life, against any attempt to enter it against his will, except for crime," by well authenticated process.

But we have no such right. It was not intended for us, any more than any other provision of the law, intended for the protection of Americans. The policy is against us—it is useless to contend against it.

This is the law of the land and must be obeyed; and we candidly advise that it is useless for us to contend against it. To suppose its repeal, is to anticipate an overthrow of the Confederative Union; and we must be allowed an expression of opinion, when we say, that candidly we believe, the existence of the Fugitive Slave Law *necessary* to the continuance of the National Compact. This Law is the foundation of the Compromise—remove it, and the consequences are easily determined. We say necessary to the continuance of the National Compact: certainly we will not be understood as meaning that the enactment of such a Law was *really* necessary, or as favoring in the least this political monstrosity of the THIRTY-FIRST CONGRESS of the UNITED STATES OF

AMERICA—surely not at all; but we speak logically and politically, leaving morality and right out of the question—taking our position on the acknowledged popular, basis of American Policy; arguing from premise to conclusion. We must abandon all vague theory, and look at *facts* as they really are; viewing ourselves in our true political position in the body politic. To imagine ourselves to be included in the body politic, except by express legislation, is at war with common sense, and contrary to fact. Legislation, the administration of the laws of the country, and the exercise of rights by the people, all prove to the contrary. We are politically, not of them, but aliens to the laws and political privileges of the country. These are truths—fixed facts, that quaint theory and exhausted moralising, are impregnable to, and fall harmlessly before.

It is useless to talk about our rights in individual States: we can have no rights here as citizens, not recognised in our common country; as the citizens of one State, are entitled to all the rights and privileges of an American citizen in all the States—the nullity of the one necessarily implying the nullity of the other. These provisions then do not include the colored people of the United States; since there is no power left in them, whereby they may protect us as their own citizens. Our descent, by the laws of the country, stamps us with inferiority—upon us has this law worked *corruption of blood*. We are in the hands of the General Government, and no State can rescue us. The Army and Navy stand at the service of our enslavers, the whole force of which, may at any moment—even in the dead of night, as has been done —when sunk in the depth of slumber, called out for the purpose of forcing our mothers, sisters, wives, and children, or ourselves, into hopeless servitude, there to weary out a miserable life, a relief from which, death would be hailed with joy. Heaven and earth—God and Humanity!—are not these sufficient to arouse the most worthless among mankind, of whatever descent, to a sense of their true position? These laws apply to us—shall we not be aroused?

What then shall we do?—what is the remedy—is the important question to be answered?

This important inquiry we shall answer, and find a remedy in when treating of the emigration of the colored people.

THAT there have been people in all ages under certain circumstances, that may be benefited by emigration, will be admitted; and that there are circumstances under which emigration is absolutely necessary to their political elevation, cannot be disputed.

This we see in the Exodus of the Jews from Egypt to the land of Judea; in the expedition of Dido and her followers from Tyro to Mauritania; and not to dwell upon hundreds of modern European examples—also in the ever memorable emigration of the Puritans, in 1620, from Great Britain, the land of their birth, to the wilderness of the New World, at which may be fixed the beginning of emigration to this continent as a permanent residence.

This may be acknowledged; but to advocate the emigration of the colored people of the United States from their native homes, is a new feature in our history, and at first view, may be considered objectionable, as pernicious to our interests. This objection is at once removed, when reflecting on our condition as incontrovertibly shown in a foregoing part of this work. And we shall proceed at once to give the advantages to be derived from emigration, to us as a people, in preference to any other policy that we may adopt. This granted, the question will then be, Where shall we go? This we conceive to be all important—of paramount consideration, and shall endeavor to show the most advantageous locality; and premise the recommendation, with the strictest advice against any countenance whatever, to the emigration scheme of the so called Republic of Liberia.

XVIII "REPUBLIC OF LIBERIA"

THAT we desire the civilization and enlightenment of Africa—the high and elevated position of Liberia among the nations of the earth, may not be doubted, as the writer was among the first, seven or eight years ago, to make the suggestion and call upon the Liberians to hold up their heads like men; take courage, having confidence in their own capacity to govern themselves, and come out from their disparaging position, by formally declaring their Independence.

As our desire is to impart information, and enlighten the minds of our readers on the various subjects herein contained, we present below a large extract from the "First Annual Report of the Trustees of Donations for Education in Liberia." This Extract will make a convenient statistic reference for matters concerning Liberia. We could only wish that many of our readers possessed more historical and geographical information of the world, and there could be little fears of their going anywhere that might be incongenial and unfavorable to their success. We certainly do intend to deal fairly with Liberia, and give the reader every information that may tend to enlighten them. What the colored people most need, is *intelligence*; give them this, and there is no danger of them being duped into anything they do not desire. This Board was incorporated by the Legislature of

Massachusetts, March 19th, 1850—Ensign H. Kellogg, Speaker of the House, Marshall P. Wilder, President of the Senate. Trustees of the Board—Hon. George N. Briggs, LL.D., Hon. Simon Greenleaf, LL.D., Hon. Stephen Fairbanks, Hon. William J. Hubbard, Hon. Joel Giles, Hon. Albert Fearing, Amos A. Lawrence, Esq. Officers of the Board—Hon. G. N. Briggs, President; Hon. S. Fairbanks, Treasurer; Rev. J. Tracy, Secretary. The conclusion of the Report says:—"In view of such considerations, the Trustees cannot doubt the patrons of learning will sustain them in their attempt to plant the FIRST COLLEGE on the *only* continent which yet remains *without* one." In this, the learned Trustees have fallen into a statistical and geographical error, which we design to correct. The *continent* is *not without* a College. There are now in Egypt, erected under the patronage of that singularly wonderful man, Mehemet Ahi, four colleges conducted on the European principle—Scientific, Medical, Legal, and Military.★ These are in successful operation; the Military College having an average of eleven hundred students annually. The continent of Africa then, is not without a college, but though benighted enough, even to an apparent hopeless degeneration, she is still the seat of learning, and must some day rise, in the majesty of ancient grandeur, and vindicate the rights and claims of her own children, against the incalculable wrongs perpetrated through the period of sixty ages by professedly enlightened Christians, against them.

A glance at the map will show a sharp bend in this coast at Cape Palmas, from which it extends, on time one side,

---

★It may be, that the Medical and Legal Schools, are adjunct departments of the Scientific College, which would make the number of Colleges in Egypt but two: as we are certain that the Military is separate entirely from the Scientific School, and spoken of by travelers as a splendid College.

about 1,100 miles north-west and north, and on the other, about 1,200 or 1,300 almost directly east. In this bend is the Maryland Colony of Cape Palmas, with a jurisdiction extending nearly 100 miles eastward. This Colony is bounded on the north-west by the Republic of Liberia, which extends along the coast about 400 miles to Sherbro. These two governments will ultimately be united in one Republic, and may be considered as one, for all the purposes of this inquiry. The extent of their united sea-coast is about 520 miles. The jurisdiction of the Republic over the four hundred miles or more which it claims, has been formally acknowledged by several of the leading powers of Europe, and is questioned by none. To almost the whole of it, the native title has been extinguished; the natives, however, still occupying, as citizens, such portions of it as they need.

The civilized population of these governments, judging from the census of 1843, and other information, is some 7,000 or 8,000. Of the heathen population, no census has ever been taken; but it probably exceeds 300,000.

The grade of Liberian civilization may be estimated from the fact, that the people have formed a republican government, and so administer it, as to secure the confidence of European governments in its stability. The native tribes who have merged themselves in the Republic, have all bound themselves to receive and encourage teachers; and some of them have insisted on the insertion, in their treaties of annexation, of pledges that teachers and other means of civilization shall be furnished.

Our accounts of churches, clergy and schools are defective, but show the following significant facts:

The clergy of the Methodist Episcopal Church in Liberia are nearly all Liberian citizens, serving as missionaries of the Methodist Missionary Society in the

United States. The last Report of that Society gives the
names of fifteen missionaries, having in charge nine circuits, in which are 882 members in full communion, and
235 probationers; total, 1,117. They have 20 Sabbath
Schools, with 114 officers and teachers, 810 scholars, and
507 volumes in their libraries. They have a Manual Labor
School and Female Academy. The number of Day
Schools is not reported; but seven of the missionaries are
reported as superintendents of schools, and the same
number have under their charge several "native towns,"
in some of which there are schools. The late superinten-
dent of the missions writes:—

"It appears plain to my mind, that nothing can now
retard the progress of our missions in this land, unless it
be the want of a good high school, in which to rear up
an abundant supply of well qualified teachers, to supply,
as they shall rapidly increase in number, all your schools."

The Baptists are next in number to the Methodists.
The Northern Baptist Board, having its seat in Boston, has
in Liberia one mission, two out-stations, one boarding
school, and two day schools, with about twenty scholars
each, one native preacher, and four native assistants. The
whole mission is in the hands of converted natives. The
Southern Board operates more extensively. More than a
year since, the Rev. John Day, its principal agent there,
reported to the Rev. R. R. Gurley, United States
Commissioner to Liberia, as follows:

"In our schools are taught, say, 330 children, 92 of
whom are natives. To more than 10,000 natives, the Word
of Life is statedly preached; and in every settlement in
these colonies, we have a church, to whom the means of
grace are administered; and in every village we have an
interesting Sunday school, where natives as well as colonists are taught the truths of God's word. Say, in our
Sunday schools, are taught 400 colonists, and 200 natives.
. . . We have this year baptized 18 natives and 7 colonists,

besides what have been baptized by Messrs. Murray and Drayton, from whom I have had no report."

The missionaries are all, or nearly all, Liberian citizens.

The Board of Missions of the Presbyterian Church in the United States has five missionaries at four stations in Liberia. The first is at Monrovia, under the care of the Rev. Harrison W. Ellis, well known as "the Learned Black Blacksmith." While a slave in Alabama, and working at his trade as a blacksmith, he acquired all the education, in English, Latin, Greek, Hebrew, and Theology, which is required for ordination as a Presbyterian minister. The Presbyterians of that region then bought him, and sent him out as a missionary. His assistant, Mr. B. V. R. James, a colored man, was for some years a printer in the service of the American Board at their mission at Cape Palmas and the Gaboon River. He first went to Liberia as a teacher, supported by a society of ladies in New York. In the Presbyterian Church under the care of Mr. Ellis are 39 communicants. During the year, 24 had been added, and 8 had been dismissed to form a new church in another place. Mr. Ellis also has charge of the "Alexander High School," which is intended mainly for teaching the rudiments of a classical education. This institution has an excellent iron school-house, given by a wealthy citizen of New York, at the cost of one thousand dollars, and a library and philosophical apparatus, which cost six hundred dollars, given by a gentleman in one of the southern States. The library contains a supply of classical works, probably equal to the wants of the school for some years. The land needed for the accommodation of the school was given by the government of Liberia. The number of scholars appears to be between twenty and thirty, a part of whom support themselves by their daily labor. The English High School under the care of Mr. James, had, according to the last Annual Report, 52 scholars. At a later date, the number in both schools was 78. Mr. James has also a large Sabbath school; but the number of pupils is not given.

The second station is at the new settlement of Kentucky, on the right or north bank of the St. Paul's, about fifteen miles from Monrovia, and six miles below Millsburgh. The missionary is a Liberian, Mr. H. W. Erskine. On a lot of ten acres, given by the government, buildings on an economical scale have been erected, in which is a school of twenty scholars. A church was organized in November, 1849, with eight members from the church in Monrovia. They have since increased to fourteen. Here, too, is a flourishing Sabbath school. The citizens, and especially the poor natives in the neighbourhood, are extremely anxious that a boarding school should be established. To this the Committee having charge of this mission objects, as the expense for buildings and for the support of pupils would be great, and would absorb funds that can be more profitably expended on day schools.

The third station is on the Sinou river, 150 miles down the coast from Monrovia, where, at the mouth of the river, is the town of Greenville, and a few miles higher up, the newer settlements of Readville and Rossville. It is under the care of the Rev. James M. Priest. The number of communicants, at the latest date, was thirty, and the field of labor was rapidly enlarging by immigration. The station is new, and it does not appear that any mission school had yet been organized.

The fourth station is at Settra Kroo, where there are five or six miles of coast, to which the native title has not yet been extinguished. This station has been maintained for some years, at a lamentable expense of the lives and health of white missionaries. About 200 boys and a few girls have been taught to read. The station is now under the care of Mr. Washington McDonogh, formerly a slave of the late John McDonogh, of Louisiana, so well known for the immense estate which he has bequeathed to benevolent purposes. He was well educated, and with more than eighty others, sent out some years since at his master's expense. He has a school of fifteen scholars, with the prospect of a large increase.

The mission of the Protestant Episcopal Church is located in the Maryland Colony at Cape Palmas. Its last Report specifies seven schools, and alludes to several others, in actual operation; all containing from 200 to 300 scholars, of whom about 100 are in one Sabbath school. Five other schools had been projected, and have probably gone into operation since that time. The greater part of the pupils are from native families. The Report states the number of communicants at sixty-seven, of whom forty are natives. A High school was opened January 1, 1850.

The laws of the Republic of Liberia provide for a common school in every town. It is supposed, however, that where there is a mission school, accessible to all children of suitable age, no other school exists; so that, in fact, nearly all the common schools in Liberia are connected with the different missions, the missionaries have the superintendence of their studies, and the Missionary Societies defray a large portion of the expense. Yet it must be remembered that a large majority of the missionaries are citizens of the Republic, and some of them native Africans; so that the immediate control of the schools is not generally in foreign hands. A portion, also, of the missionary funds, is contributed in Liberia; and something is paid by parents for the tuition of their children. Yet the Republic evidently needs an educational system more independent of missionary aid and control; and for that purpose, needs a supply of teachers who are not raised up in mission schools. And we have it in testimony, that the missions themselves might be more efficient for good, if well supplied with teachers of higher qualifications.

Here, then, we have a Republic of some 300,000 inhabitants, of whom 7,000 or 8,000 may be regarded as civilized, and the remainder as having a right to expect, and a large part of them actually expecting and demanding the means of civilization and Christianity. We have,—supplying as well as we can by estimate, the numbers not definitely given,—more than 2,000 communicants in Christian churches, and more than 1,500 children in Sabbath Schools; some 40 day schools containing, exclusive of the Methodists, who are the most numerous, and of whose numbers in school we have no report, about 635 scholars. The whole number in day schools, therefore, is probably not less than 1,200. We have the Alexander High School at Monrovia, where instruction is given to some extent in the classics; the English High School, at the same place, under Mr. James; the Methodist Manual Labor School and Female Academy at Millsburg; the Baptist Boarding School at Bexley; and the Protestant Episcopal High School at Cape Palmas. These institutions must furnish some students for a higher seminary, such as we propose to establish; and such a population must need their labors when educated.

However foreign to the designs of the writer of ever making that country or any other out of America, his home; had this been done, and honorably maintained, the Republic of Liberia would have met with words of encouragement, not only from himself, an humble individual, but we dare assert, from the leading spirits among, if not from the whole colored population of the United States. Because they would have been willing to overlook the circumstances under which they went there, so that in the end, they were willing to take their stand as men, and thereby throw off the degradation of slaves, still under the control of American slave-holders, and American slave-ships. But in this, we were disappointed—grievously disappointed, and proceed to show in short, our objections to Liberia.

Its geographical position, in the first place, is objectionable, being located in the *sixth degree* of latitude North of the equator, in a district signally unhealthy, rendering it objectionable as a place of destination for the colored people of the United States. We shall say nothing about other parts of the African coast, and the reasons for its location where it is: it is enough for us to know the facts as they are, to justify an unqualified objection to Liberia.

In the second place, it originated in a deep laid scheme of the slaveholders of the country, to *exterminate* the free colored of the American continent; the origin being sufficient to justify us in impugning the motives.

Thirdly and lastly—Liberia is not an Independent Republic: in fact, *it is not* an independent nation at all; but a poor *miserable mockery*—a *burlesque* on a government—a pitiful dependency on the American Colonizationists, the Colonization Board at Washington city, in the District of Columbia, being the Executive and Government, and the principal man, called President, in Liberia, being the echo—a mere parrot of Rev. Robert R. Gurley, Elliot Cresson, Esq., Governor Pinney, and other leaders of the Colonization scheme—to do as they bid, and say what they tell him. This we see in all of his doings.

Does he go to France and England, and enter into solemn treaties of an honorable recognition of the independence of his country; before his own nation has any knowledge of the result, this man called President, dispatches an official report to the Colonizationists of the United States, asking their gracious approval? Does king Grando, or a party of fishermen besiege a village and murder some of the inhabitants, this same "President," dispatches an official report to the American Colonization Board, asking for instructions—who call an Executive Session of the Board, and immediately decide that war must be waged against the enemy, placing ten thousand dollars at his disposal—and war *actually declared in Liberia*, by virtue of the *instructions* of the *American Colonization Society*. A mockery of a government— a disgrace to the office pretended to be held—a parody on the position assumed. Liberia in Africa, is a mere dependency of Southern slaveholders, and American Colonizationists, and unworthy of any respectful consideration from us.

What would be thought of the people of Hayti, and their heads of government, if their instructions emanated from the American Anti-Slavery Society, or the British Foreign Missionary Board? Should they be respected at all as a nation? Would they be worthy of it? Certainly not. We do not expect Liberia to be all that Hayti is; but we ask and expect of her, to have a decent respect for herself—to endeavor to be freemen instead of voluntary slaves. Liberia is no place for the colored freemen of the United States; and we dismiss the subject with a single remark of caution against any advice contained in a pamphlet, which we have not seen, written by Hon. James G. Birney, in favor of Liberian emigration. Mr. Birney is like the generality of white Americans, who suppose that we are too ignorant to understand what we want; whenever they wish to get rid of us, would drive us any where, so that we left them. Don't adhere to a word therein contained; we will think for ourselves. Let Mr. Birney go his way, and we will go ours. This is one of those confounded gratuities that is forced in our faces at every turn we make. We dismiss it without further comment—and with it Colonization *in toto*—and Mr. Birney *de facto*.

But to return to emigration: Where shall we go? We must not leave this continent; America is our destination and our home.

That the continent of America seems to have been designed by Providence as an asylum for all the various nations of the earth, is very apparent. From the earliest discovery, various nations sent a representation here, either as adventurers and speculators, or employed seamen and soldiers, hired to do the work of their employers. And among the earliest and most numerous class who found their way to the New World, were those of the African race. And it is now ascertained to our mind, beyond a peradventure, that when the continent was discovered, there were found in Central America, a tribe of the black race, of fine looking people, having characteristics of color and hair, identifying them originally of the African race—no doubt being a remnant of the Africans who, with the Carthaginian expedition, were adventitiously cast upon this continent, in their memorable excursion to the "Great Island," after sailing many miles distant to the West of the Pillars of Hercules.

We are not inclined to be superstitious, but say, that we can see the "finger of God" in all this; and if the European race may with propriety, boast and claim, that this continent is better adapted to their development, than their own father-land; surely, it does not necessarily detract from our father-land, to claim the superior advantages to the African race, to be derived from this continent. But be that as it may, the world belongs to mankind—his common Father created it for his common good—his temporal destiny is here; and our present warfare, is not upon European rights, nor for European countries; but for the common rights of man, based upon the great principles of common humanity—taking our chance in the world of rights, and claiming to have originally more right to this continent, than the European race. And had we no other claims than those set forth in a former part of this work, they are sufficient to cause every colored man on the continent, to stand upon the soil unshaken and unmoved. The aboriginee of the continent, is more closely allied to us by consanguinity, than to the European—being descended from the Asiatic, whose alliance in matrimony with the African is very common —therefore, we have even greater claims to this continent on that account, and should unite and make common cause in elevation, with our similarly oppressed brother, the Indian.

The advantages of this continent are superior, because it presents every variety of climate, soil, and production of the earth, with every variety of mineral production, with all kinds of water privileges, arid ocean coast on all sides, presenting every commercial advantage. Upon the American continent we are determined to stay, in spite of every odds against us. What part of the great continent shall our destination be—shall we emigrate to the North or South?

XIX | THE CANADAS

T HIS is one of the most beautiful portions of North America. Canada East, formerly known as Lower Canada, is not quite so favorable, the climate being cold and severe in winter, the springs being late, the summers rather short, and the soil not so productive. But Canada West, formerly called Upper Canada, is equal to any portion of the Northern States. The climate being milder than that of the Northern portions of New York, Ohio, Michigan, Indiana, Illinois, or any of the States bordering on the lakes, the soil is prolific in productions of every description. Grains, vegetables, fruits, and cattle, are of the very best kind; from a short tour by the writer, in that country in the fall, 1851, one year ago, he prefers Canada West to any part of North America, as a destination for the colored people. But there is a serious objection to the Canadas—a political objection. The Canadians are descended from the same common parentage as the Americans on this side of the Lakes—and there is a manifest tendency on the part of the Canadians generally, to Americanism. That the Americans are determined to, and will have the Canadas, to a close observer, there is not a shadow of doubt; and our brethren should know this in time. This there would be no fear of, were not the Canadian people in favor of the project, neither would the Americans attempt an attack upon the provinces, without the move being favored by the people of those places.

Every act of the Americans, ostensibly as courtesy and friendship, tend to that end. This is seen in the policy pursued during the last two or three years, in the continual invitations, frequently reciprocated, that pass from the Americans to their "Canadian brethren"—always couched in affectionate language—to join them in their various celebrations, in different parts of the States. They have got them as far as Boston, and we may expect to hear of them going to New York, Philadelphia, Baltimore—and instead of the merrymaking over the beginning or ending of internal improvements, we may expect to see them ere long, wending their way to the seat of the federal government—it may be with William McKenzie, the memorable *patriot* and present member of the Colonial parliament, bearing in his hand the stars and stripes as their ensign—there to blend their voices in the loud shout of jubilee, in honor of the "bloodless victory," of Canadian annexation. This we forewarn the colored people, in time, is the inevitable and not far distant destiny of the Canadas. And let them come into the American Republic when they may, the fate of the colored man, however free before, is doomed, doomed, forever doomed. Disfranchisement, degradation, and a delivery up to slave catchers and kidnappers, are their only fate, let Canadian annexation take place when it will. The odious infamous fugitive slave law, will then be in full force with all of its terrors; and we have no doubt that fully in anticipation of this event, was the despicable law created.

Let not colored people be deceived and gulled by any visionary argument about original rights, or those of the people remaining the same as they were previous to cecession of the territory. The people can claim no rights than such as are known to exist previous to their annexation. This is manifestly the case with a large class of the former inhabitants of Mexico, who though citizens before, in the full exercise of their rights as such, so soon as the cession of the territory took place, lost them entirely, as they could claim only such as were enjoyed by the people of a similar class, in the country to which they made their union. The laudatories heaped upon the Americans, within the hearing of the writer, while traveling the provinces the last fall, by one of the Canadian officiaries, in comparing their superior intelligence to what he termed the "stupid aristocracy," then returning from the Boston celebration, where there was a fair opportunity of comparing the intellect of their chief magistrate, his excellency, Lord Elgin, governor-general of the Canadas, and Sir Allen Napier McNab, knight baronet with that of some of the "plain republicans" who were present on the occasion, were extravagant. The Canadians generally were perfectly carried away with delight at their reception. They reminded us of some of our poor brethren, who had just made their escape from Southern bondage, and for the first time in their life, had been taken by the hand by a white man, who acknowledged them as equals. They don't know when to stop talking about it, they really annoy one with extravagant praises of them. This was the way with those gentlemen; and we dare predict, that from what we heard on that occasion, that Mr. McKenzie nor Big Bill Johnson, hero of the Forty Islands, are no greater *patriots* than these Canadian visitors to the Boston husa! We are satisfied that the Canadas are no place of safety for the colored people of the United States; otherwise we should have no objection to them.

But to the fugitive—our enslaved brethren flying from Southern despotism—we say, until we have a more preferable place—go on to Canada. Freedom, always; liberty any place and ever—before slavery. Continue to fly to the

Canadas, and swell the number of the twenty-five thousand already there. Surely the British cannot, they will not look with indifference upon such a powerful auxiliary as these brave, bold, daring men—the very flower of the South, who have hazarded every consequence, many of whom have come from Arkansas and Florida in search of freedom. Worthy surely to be free, when gained at such a venture. Go on to the North, till the South is ready to receive you—for surely, he who can make his way from Arkansas to Canada, can find his way from Kentucky to Mexico. The moment his foot touches this land South, he is free. Let the bondman but be assured that he can find the same freedom South that there is in the North; the same liberty in Mexico, as in Canada, and he will prefer going South to going North. His risk is no greater in getting there. Go either way, and he in the majority of instances must run the gauntlet of the slave states.

CENTRAL AND SOUTH AMERICA AND THE WEST INDIES

XX

ENTRAL and South America, are evidently the ultimate destination and future home of the colored race on this continent; the advantages of which in preference to all others, will be apparent when once pointed out.★

Geographically, from the Northern extremity of Yucatan, down through Central and South America, to Cape Horn, there is a variation of climate from the twenty-second degree of North latitude, passing through the equatorial region; nowhere as warm as it is in the same latitude in Africa; to the *fifty-fifth degree* of South latitude, including a climate as cold as that of the Hudson Bay country in British America, colder than that of Maine, or any part known to the United States of North America; so that there is every variety of climate in South, as well as North America.

★The native language of these countries, as well as the greater part of South America, is *Spanish*, which is the easiest of all foreign languages to learn. It is very remarkable and worthy of note, that with a view of going to Mexico or South America, the writer several years ago paid some attention to the Spanish language; and now, a most singular coincidence, without preunderstanding, in almost every town, where there is any intelligence among them, there are some *colored persons* of both sexes, who are studying the Spanish language. Even the Methodist and other clergymen, among them. And we earnestly entreat all colored persons who can, to study, and have their children taught Spanish. No foreign language will be of such *import* to colored people, in a very short time, as the Spanish. Mexico, Central and South America, importune us to speak their language; and if nothing else, the silent indications of Cuba, urge us to learn the Spanish tongue.

In the productions of grains, fruits, and vegetables, Central and South America are also prolific; and the best of herds are here raised. Indeed, the finest Merino sheep, as well as the principal trade in rice, sugar, cotton, and wheat, which is now preferred in California to any produced in the United States— the Chilian flour—might be carried on by the people of this most favored portion of God's legacy to man. The mineral productions excel all other parts of this continent; the rivers present the greatest internal advantages, and the commercial prospects, are without a parallel on the coast of the new world.

The advantages to the colored people of the United States, to be derived from emigration to Central, South America, and the West Indies, are incomparably greater than that of any other parts of the world at present.

In the first place, there never have existed in the policy of any of the nations of Central or South America, an inequality on account of race or color, and any prohibition of rights, has generally been to the white, and not to the colored races.★ To the whites, not because they were white, not

---

★The Brazilians have formed a Colonization Society, for the purpose of colonizing free blacks to Africa. The Brazilians are Portuguese, the only nation that can be termed white, and the only one that is a real slave holding nation in South America. Even the black and colored men have equal privileges with whites; and the action of this society will probably extend only to the sending back of such captives as may be taken from piratical slavers. Colonization in Brazil, has doubtless been got up under the influence of United States slave holders and their abettors, such as the consuls and envoys, who are sent out to South America, by the government. Chevalier Niteroi, *charge de affaires* from Brazil near the government of Liberia, received by the President on the 28th of last January, is also charged with the mission of establishing a colony of free blacks in Liberia. The Chevalier was once a Captain in the Brazilian navy on the coast of Africa; and no doubt is conversant with the sentiments of Roberts, who was charged with the slave trade at one time. The scheme of United States slaveholders and President J. J. Roberts, their agent of Liberia, will not succeed, in establishing prejudice against the *black* race; not even in slaveholding Brazil.

We have no confidence in President Roberts of Liberia, believing him to be wholly without principle—seeking only self-aggrandizement; even should it be done, over the ruined prospects of his staggering infant country. The people of Liberia, should beware of this man. His *privy councillors* are to be found among *slaveholders* in the United States.

on account of their color, but because of the policy pursued by them towards the people of other races than themselves. The population of Central and South America, consist of fifteen millions two hundred and forty thousand, adding the ten millions of Mexico; twenty-five millions two hundred and forty thousand, of which vast population, but *one-seventh* are whites, or the pure European race. Allowing a deduction of one-seventh of this population for the European race that may chance to be in those countries, and we have in South and Central America alone, the vast colored population of *thirteen millions one hundred and seventy-seven thousand*; and including Mexico, a *colored* population on this glorious continent of *twenty-one millions, six hundred and forty thousand.*

This vast number of people, our brethren—because they are precisely the same people as ourselves and share the same fate with us, as the case of numbers of them have proven, who have been adventitiously thrown among us—stand ready and willing to take us by the hand—nay, are anxiously waiting, and earnestly importuning us to come, that they may make common cause with us, and we all share the same fate. There is nothing under heaven in our way—the people stand with open arms ready to receive us. The climate, soil, and productions—the vast rivers and beautiful sea-coast —the scenery of the landscape, and beauty of the starry heavens above—the song of the birds—the voice of the people say come—and God our Father bids us go.—Will we go? Go we must, and go we will, as there is no alternative. To remain here in North America, and be crushed to the earth in vassalage and degradation, we never will.

Talk not about religious biases—we have but one reply to make. We had rather be a Heathen *freeman*, than a Christian *slave*.

There need be no fear of annexation in these countries—the prejudices of the people are all against it, and with our influences infused among them, the aversion would be ten-fold greater. Neither need there be any fears of an attempt on the part of the United States, at a subjugation, of these countries. Policy is against it, because the United States has too many colored slaves in their midst, to desire to bring under their government, twenty-one millions of disfranchised people, whom it would cost them more to keep under subjection, than ten-fold the worth of the countries they gained. Besides, let us go to whatever parts of Central and South America we may, we shall make common cause with the people, and shall hope, by one judicious and signal effort, to assemble one day—and a glorious day it will be— in a great representative convention, and form a glorious union of South American States, "inseparably connected one and forever."

This can be done, easily done, if the proper course be pursued, and necessity will hold them together as it holds together the United States of North America—self-preservation. As the British nation serves to keep in check the Americans; so would the United States serve to keep in Union the South American States.

We should also enter into solemn treaties with Great Britain, and like other free and independent nations, take our chance, and risk consequences. Talk not of consequences; we are now in chains; shall we shake them off and go to a land of liberty? shall our wives and children be protected, secure, and affectionately cherished, or shall they be debased and degraded as our mothers and fathers were? By the light of heaven, no! By the instincts of nature, no!

Talk not about consequences. White men seek responsibilities; shall we shun them? They brave dangers and risk consequences; shall we shrink from them? What are consequences, compared in the scale of value, with liberty and freedom; the rights and privileges of our wives and children? In defence of our liberty—the rights of my wife and children; had we the power, we would command the vault of a volcano, charged with the wrath of heaven, and blast out of existence, every thing that dared obstruct our way.

The time has now fully arrived, when the colored race is called upon by all the ties of common humanity, and all the claims of consummate justice, to go forward and take their position, and do battle in the struggle now being made for the redemption of the world. Our cause is a just one; the greatest at present that elicits the attention of the world. For it there is a remedy; that remedy is how at hand. God himself as assuredly as he rules the destinies of nations, and entereth measures into the "hearts of men," has presented these measures to us. Our race is to be redeemed; it is a great and glorious work, and we are the instrumentalities by which it is to be done. But we must go from among our oppressors; it never can be done by staying among them. God has, as certain as he has ever designed any thing, has designed this great portion of the New World, for us, the colored races; and as certain as we stubborn our hearts, and stiffen our necks against it, his protecting arm and fostering care will be withdrawn from us.

Shall we be told that we can live nowhere, but under the will of our North American oppressors; that this (the United States,) is the country most favorable to our improvement and progress? Are we incapable of self-government, and making such improvements for ourselves as we delight to enjoy after American white men have made them for themselves? No, it is not true. Neither is it true that the United States is the best country for our improvement. That country is the best, in which our manhood can be best developed; and that is Central and South America, and the West Indies—all belonging to this glorious Continent.

Whatever may be our pretended objections to any place, whenever and wherever our oppressors go, there will our people be found in proportionate numbers. Even now could they get possession of the equatorial region of South America, there would colored men be found living on their boats and in their houses to do their menial services; but talk to them about going there and becoming men, and a thousand excuses and objections are at once raised against the climate or whatever else.

The writer, within the past few years, and as early as seventeen years ago, then being quite young, and flushed with geographical and historical speculations, introduced in a Literary Institution of Young Men, the subject of Mexican, Californian, and South American Emigration. He was always hooted at, and various objections raised: one on account of distance, and another that of climate.

He has since seen some of the same persons engage themselves to their white American oppressors—officers in the war against Mexico, exposing themselves to the chances of the heat of day and the damp of night—risking the dangers of the battle-field, in the capacity of servants. And had the Americans taken Mexico, no people would have flocked there faster than the colored people from the United States. The same is observed of California.

In conversation, in the city of New York, a few weeks ago, with a colored lady of intelligence, one of the "first families," the conversation being the elevation of the colored people, we introduced emigration as a remedy, and Central America as the place. We were somewhat surprised, and certainly unprepared to receive the rebuking reply—"Do you suppose that I would go in the woods to live for the sake of freedom? no, indeed! if you wish to do so, go and do it. I am free enough here!" Remarking at the same time, that her husband was in San Francisco, and she was going to him, as she learned that that city was quite a large and handsome place.

We reminded her, that the industry of white men and women, in four years' time, had made San Francisco what it is. That in 1846, before the American emigration, the city contained about seven hundred people, surrounded by a dense wilderness; and that we regretted to contrast her conduct or disposition with that of the lady of Col. Fremont, a daughter of Senator Benton, who tenderly and indulgently raised, in the spring after his arduous adventure across the mountains, and almost miraculous escape, while the country was yet a wilderness, left her comfortable home in Missouri, and braved the dangers of the ocean, to join her husband and settle in the wilderness. That she was going now to San Francisco, because it was a populous and "fine city"—that Mrs. Fremont went, when it was a wilderness, to help to *make* a populous and fine city.

About two hours previous to the writing of the following fact, two respectable colored ladies in conversation, pleasantly disputing about the superiority of the two places, Philadelphia and New York, when one spoke of the uniform cleanliness of the streets of Philadelphia, and the dirtiness of those of New York; when the other triumphantly replied.—"The reason that our streets are so dirty is, that we do more business in one day, than you do in a month." The other acknowledged the fact with some degree of reluctance, and explained, with many "buts" as an excuse in extenuation. Here was a seeming appreciation of business and enterprise; but the query flashed through our mind in an instant, as to whether they thought for a moment, of the fact, that *they* had no interest in either city, nor its *business*. It brought forcibly to our mind, the scene of two of our oppressed brethren South, fighting each other, to prove his *master* the greatest gentleman of the two.

Let no objections be made to emigration on the ground of the difficulty of the fugitive slave, in reaching us; it is only necessary for him to know, that he has safety South, and he will find means of reaching the South, as easily as he now does the North. Have no fears about that—his redemption draws nigh, the nearer we draw to him. Central and South America, *must be our future homes.* Our oppressors will not want us to go there. They will move heaven and earth to prevent us—they will talk about us getting our rights, and offer us a territory here, and all that. It is of no use. They have pressed us to the last retreat—the die is cast—the Rubicon must be crossed—go we will, in defiance of all the slave-power in the Union. And we shall not go there, to be idle—passive spectators to an invasion of South American rights. No—go when we will, and where we may, we shall hold ourselves amenable to defend and protect the country that embraces us. We are fully able to defend ourselves, once concentrated, against any odds—and by the help of God, we will do it. We do not go, without counting the cost, cost what it may; all that it may cost, it is worth to be free.

In going, let us have but one object—to become elevated men and women, worthy of freedom—the worthy citizens of an adopted country. What to us will be adopted—to our children will be legitimate. Go not with an anxiety of political aspirations; but go with the fixed intention—as Europeans come to the United States—of cultivating the soil, entering into the mechanical operations, keeping of shops, carrying on merchandise, trading on land and water, improving property—in a word, to become the producers of the country, instead of the consumers.

Let young men who go, have a high object in view; and not go with a view of becoming servants to wealthy gentlemen there; for be assured, that they place themselves beneath all respectful consideration.

XXI NICARAGUA AND NEW GRENADA

As it is not reasonable to suppose, that all who read this volume—especially those whom it is intended most to benefit—understand geography; it is deemed advisable, to name some particular places, as locality of destination.

We consequently, to begin with, select NICARAGUA, in Central America, North, and NEW GRENADA, the Northern part of South America, South of Nicaragua, as the most favorable points at present, in every particular, for us to emigrate to.

In the first place, they are the nearest points to be reached, and countries at which the California adventurers are now touching, on their route to that distant land, and not half the distance of California.

In the second place, the advantages for all kinds of enterprise, are equal if not superior, to almost any other points—the climate being healthy and highly favorable.

In the third place, and by no means the least point of importance, the British nation is bound by solemn treaty, to protect both of those nations from foreign imposition, until they are able to stand alone.

Then there is nothing in the way, but every thing in favor, and opportunities for us to rise to the full stature of manhood. Remember this fact, that in these countries, colored men now fill the highest places in the country: and colored people have the same chances there, that white people have in the United States. All that is necessary to do, is to go, and the moment your foot touches the soil, you have all the opportunities for elevating yourselves as the highest, according to your industry and merits.

Nicaragua and New Grenada, are both Republics, having a President, Senate, and Representatives of the people. The municipal affairs are well conducted; and remember, however much the customs of the country may differ, and appear strange to those you have left behind— remember that you are free; and that many who, at first sight, might think that they could not become reconciled to the new order of things, should recollect, that they were once in a situation in the United States, (in *slavery*,) where they were compelled to be content with customs infinitely more averse to their feelings and desires. And that customs become modified, just in proportion as people of different customs from different parts, settle in the same communities together. All we ask is Liberty—the rest follows as a matter of course.

XXII | THINGS AS THEY ARE

"And if thou boast TRUTH to utter,
SPEAK, and leave the rest to God."

I N presenting this work, we have but a single object in
view, and that is, to inform the minds of the colored
people at large, upon many things pertaining to their elevation, that but few among us are acquainted with. Unfortunately for us, as a body, we have been taught to believe, that
we must have some person to think for us, instead of
thinking for ourselves. So accustomed are we to submission
and this kind of training, that it is with difficulty, even
among the most intelligent of the colored people, an audience may be elicited for any purpose whatever, if the
expounder is to be a colored person; and the introduction
of any subject is treated with indifference, if not contempt,
when the originator is a colored person. Indeed, the most
ordinary white person, is almost revered, while the most
qualified colored person is totally neglected. Nothing from
them is appreciated.

We have been standing comparatively still for years, following in the footsteps of our friends, believing that what
they promise us can be accomplished, just because they say
so, although our own knowledge should long since, have
satisfied us to the contrary. Because even were it possible,

with the present hate and jealousy that the whites have towards us in this country, for us to gain equality of rights with
them; we never could have an equality of the exercise and
enjoyment of those rights—because, the great odds of numbers are against us. We might indeed, as some at present, have
the right of the elective franchise—nay, it is not the elective
franchise, because the *elective franchise* makes the enfranchised, *eligible* to any position attainable; but we may exercise the right of *voting* only, which to us, is but poor satisfaction; and we by no means care to cherish the privilege of
voting somebody into office, to help to make laws to
degrade us.

In religion—because they are both *translators* and *com-
mentators*, we must believe nothing, however absurd, but
what our oppressors tell us. In Politics, nothing but such as
they promulge; in Anti-Slavery, nothing but what our white
brethren and friends say we must; in the mode and manner
of our elevation, we must do nothing, but that which may
be laid down to be done by our white brethren from some
quarter or other; and now, even on the subject of emigration, there are some colored people to be found, so lost to
their own interest and self-respect, as to be gulled by slave
owners and colonizationists, who are led to believe there is
no other place in which they can become elevated, but
Liberia, a government of American slave-holders, as we have
shown—simply, because white men have told them so.

Upon the possibility, means, mode and manner, of our
Elevation in the United States—Our Original Rights and
Claims as Citizens—Our Determination not to be Driven
from our Native Country—the Difficulties in the Way of
our Elevation—Our Position in Relation to our Anti-
Slavery Brethren—the Wicked Design and Injurious Tendency of the American Colonization Society—Objections

to Liberia—Objections to Canada—Preferences to South America, &c., &c., all of which we have treated without reserve; expressing our mind freely, and with candor, as we are determined that as far as we can at present do so, the minds of our readers shall be enlightened. The custom of concealing information upon vital and important subjects, in which the interest of the people is involved, we do not agree with, nor favor in the least; we have therefore, laid this cursory treatise before our readers, with the hope that it may prove instrumental in directing the attention of our people in the right way, that leads to their Elevation. Go or stay—of course each is free to do as he pleases—one thing is certain; our Elevation is the work of our own hands. And Mexico, Central America, the West Indies, and South America, all present now, opportunities for the individual enterprise of our young men, who prefer to remain in the United States, in preference to going where they can enjoy real freedom, and equality of rights. Freedom of Religion, as well as of politics, being tolerated in all of these places.

Let our young men and women, prepare themselves for usefulness and business; that the men may enter into merchandise, trading, and other things of importance; the young women may become teachers of various kinds, and otherwise fill places of usefulness. Parents must turn their attention more to the education of their children. We mean, to educate them for useful practical business purposes. Educate them for the Store and the Counting House—to do everyday practical business. Consult the children's propensities, and direct their education according to their inclinations. It may be, that there is too great a desire on the part of parents, to give their children a professional education, before the body of the people, are ready for it. A people must be a business people, and have more to depend upon than mere help in people's houses and Hotels, before they are either able to support, or capable of properly appreciating the services of professional men among them. This has been one of our great mistakes—we have gone in advance of ourselves. We have commenced at the superstructure of the building, instead of the foundation—at the top instead of the bottom. We should first be mechanics and common tradesmen, and professions as a matter of course would grow out of the wealth made thereby. Young men and women, must now prepare for usefulness—the day of our Elevation is at hand —all the world now gazes at us—and Central and South America, and the West Indies, bid us come and be men and women, protected, secure, beloved and Free.

The branches of Education most desirable for the preparation of youth, for practical useful every-day life, are Arithmetic and good Penmanship, in order to be Accountants; and a good rudimental knowledge of Geography—which has ever been neglected, and under estimated—and of Political Economy; which without the knowledge of the first, no people can ever become adventurous—nor of the second, never will be an enterprising people. Geography, teaches a knowledge of the world, and Political Economy, a knowledge of the wealth of nations; or how to make money. These are not abstruse sciences, or learning not easily acquired or understood; but simply, common School Primer learning, that every body may get. And, although it is the very key to prosperity and success in common life, but few know any thing about it. Unfortunately for our people, so soon as their children learn to read a Chapter in the New Testament, and scribble a miserable hand, they are pronounced to have "Learning enough"; and taken away from School, no use to themselves, nor community. This is apparent in our Public Meetings, and Official Church Meetings; of the great number of men present, there are but few capable of filling a Secretaryship. Some of the large cities may be an exception to this. Of the multitudes of Merchants, and Businessmen throughout this country, Europe, and the world, few are qualified, beyond the branches here laid down by us as necessary for business. What did John Jacob Astor, Stephen Girard, or do the millionaires and the greater part of the merchant princes, and mariners, know about Latin and Greek, and the Classics? Precious few of them know any thing. In proof of this, in 1841, during the Administration of President Tyler, when the mutiny was detected on board of the American Man of War Brig Somers, the names of the Mutineers, were recorded by young S—a Midshipman in Greek. Captain Alexander Slidell McKenzie, Commanding, was unable to read them; and in his despatches to the Government, in justification of his policy in executing the criminals, said that he "discovered some curious characters which he was unable to read," &c.; showing thereby, that that high functionary, did not understand even the Greek Alphabet, which was only necessary, to have been able to read proper names written in Greek.

What we most need then, is a good business practical Education; because, the Classical and Professional education of so many of our young men, before their parents are able to support them, and community ready to patronize them, only serves to lull their energy, and cripple the otherwise, praiseworthy efforts they would make in life. A Classical education, is only suited to the wealthy, or those who have a prospect of gaining a livelihood by it. The writer does not wish to be understood, as underrating a Classical and Professional education; this is not his intention; he fully appreciates them, having had some such advantages himself; but he desires to give a proper guide, and put a check to the extravagant idea that is fast obtaining, among our people especially, that a Classical, or as it is termed, a "finished education," is necessary to prepare one for usefulness in life. Let us have an education, that shall practically develope our thinking faculties and manhood; and then, and not until then, shall we be able to vie with our oppressors, go where we may. We as heretofore, have been on the extreme; either no qualification at all, or a Collegiate education. We jumped too far; taking a leap from the deepest abyss to the highest summit; rising from the ridiculous to the sublime; without medium or intermission.

Let our young women have an education; let their minds be well informed; well stored with useful information and practical proficiency, rather than the light superficial acquirements, popularly and fashionably called accomplishments. We desire accomplishments, but they must be *useful*.

Our females must be qualified, because they are to be the mothers of our children. As mothers are the first nurses and instructors of children; from them children consequently, get their first impressions, which being always the most lasting, should be the most correct. Raise the mothers above the level of degradation, and the offspring is elevated with them. In a word, instead of our young men, transcribing in their blank books, recipes for *Cooking*; we desire to see them making the transfer of *Invoices of Merchandise*. Come to our aid then; the *morning* of our *Redemption* from degradation, adorns the horizon.

In our selection of individuals, it will be observed, that we have confined ourself entirely to those who occupy or have occupied positions among the whites, consequently having a more general bearing as useful contributors to society at large. While we do not pretend to give all such worthy cases, we gave such as we possessed information of, and desire it to be understood, that a large number of our most intelligent and worthy men and women, have not been named, because from their more private position in community, it was foreign to the object and design of this work. If we have said aught to offend, "take the will for the deed," and be assured, that it was given with the purest of motives, and best intention, from a true hearted man and brother; deeply lamenting the sad fate of his race in this country, and sincerely desiring the elevation of man, and submitted to the serious consideration of all, who favor the promotion of the cause of God and humanity.

XXIII
A GLANCE AT OURSELVES—CONCLUSION

With broken hopes—sad devastation;
A race *resigned* to DEGRADATION!

WE have said much to our young men and women, about their vocation and calling; we have dwelt much upon the menial position of our people in this country. Upon this point we cannot say too much, because there is a seeming satisfaction and seeking after such positions manifested on their part, unknown to any other people. There appears to be, a want of a sense of propriety or *self-respect*, altogether inexplicable; because young men and women among us, many of whom have good trades and homes, adequate to their support, voluntarily leave them, and seek positions, such as servants, waiting maids, coachmen, nurses, cooks in gentlemens' kitchen, or such like occupations, when they can gain a livelihood at something more respectable, or elevating in character. And the worse part of the whole matter is, that they have become so accustomed to it, it has become so "fashionable," that it seems to have become second nature, and they really become offended, when it is spoken against.

Among the German, Irish, and other European peasantry who come to this country, it matters not what they were employed at before and after they come; just so soon

as they can better their condition by keeping shops, cultivating the soil, the young men and women going to night-
schools, qualifying themselves for usefulness, and learning
trades—they do so. Their first and last care, object and aim
is, to better their condition by raising themselves above the
condition that necessity places them in. We do not say too
much, when we say, as an evidence of the deep degradation
of our race, in the United States, that there are those among
us, the wives and daughters, some of the *first ladies*, (and who
dare say they are not the "first," because they belong to the
"first class" and associate where any body among us can?)
whose husbands are industrious, able and willing to support
them, who voluntarily leave home, and become chamber-
maids, and stewardesses, upon vessels and steamboats, in all
probability, to enable them to obtain some more fine or
costly article of dress or furniture.

We have nothing to say against those whom *necessity*
compels to do these things, those who can do no better; we
have only to do with those who can, and will not, or do not
do better. The whites are always in the advance, and we
either standing still or retrograding; as that which does not
go forward, must either stand in one place or go back. The
father in all probability is a farmer, mechanic, or man of
some independent business; and the wife, sons and daughters, are chamber-maids, on vessels, nurses and waiting-
maids, or coachmen and cooks in families. This is retrogra-
dation. The wife, sons, and daughters should be elevated
above this condition as a necessary consequence.

If we did not love our race superior to others, we would
not concern ourself about their degradation; for the greatest
desire of our heart is, to see them stand on a level with the
most elevated of mankind. No people are ever elevated
above the condition of their *females*; hence, the condition of

the *mother* determines the condition of the child. To know the position of a people, it is only necessary to know the *condition* of their *females*; and despite themselves, they cannot rise above their level. Then what is our condition? Our *best ladies* being washerwomen, chambermaids, children's traveling nurses, and common house servants, and menials, we are all a degraded, miserable people, inferior to any other people as a whole, on the face of the globe.

These great truths, however unpleasant, must be brought before the minds of our people in its true and proper light, as we have been too delicate about them, and too long concealed them for fear of giving offence. It would have been infinitely better for our race, if these facts had been presented before us half a century ago—we would have been now proportionably benefitted by it.

As an evidence of the degradation to which we have been reduced, we dare premise, that this chapter will give offence to many, very many, and why? Because they may say, "He dared to say that the occupation of a *servant* is a degradation." It is not necessarily degrading; it would not be, to one or a few people of a kind; but a *whole race of servants* are a degradation to that people.

Efforts made by men of qualifications for the toiling and degraded millions among the whites, neither gives offence to that class, nor is it taken unkindly by them; but received with manifestations of gratitude; to know that they are thought to be, equally worthy of, and entitled to stand on a level with the elevated classes; and they have only got to be informed of the way to raise themselves, to make the effort and do so as far as they can. But how different with us. Speak of our position in society, and it at once gives insult. Though we are servants; among ourselves we claim to be *ladies* and *gentlemen*, equal in standing, and as the popular expression goes, "Just as good as any body"—and so believing, we make no efforts to raise above the common level of menials; because the *best* being in that capacity, all are content with the position. We cannot at the same time, be domestic and lady; servant and gentleman. We must be the one or the other. Sad, sad indeed, is the thought, that hangs drooping in our mind, when contemplating the picture drawn before us. Young men and women, "we write these things unto you, because ye are strong," because the writer, a few years ago, gave unpardonable offence to many of the young people of Philadelphia and other places, because he dared tell them, that he thought too much of them, to be content with seeing them the servants of other people. Surely, she that could be the mistress, would not be the maid; neither would he that could be the master, be content with being the servant; then why be offended, when we point out to you, the way that leads from the menial to the mistress or the master. All this we seem to reject with fixed determination, repelling with anger, every effort on the part of our intelligent men and women to elevate us, with true Israelitish degradation, in reply to any suggestion or proposition that may be offered, "Who made thee a ruler and judge?"

The writer is no "Public Man," in the sense in which this is understood among our people, but simply an humble individual, endeavoring to seek a livelihood by a profession obtained entirely by his own efforts, without relatives and friends able to assist him; except such friends as he gained by the merit of his course and conduct, which he here gratefully acknowledges; and whatever he has accomplished, other young men may, by making corresponding efforts, also accomplish.

We have advised an emigration to Central and South

America, and even to Mexico and the West Indies, to those who prefer either of the last named places, all of which are free countries, Brazil being the only real slave-holding State in South America—there being nominal slavery in Dutch Guiana, Peru, Buenos Ayres, Paraguay, and Uraguay, in all of which places colored people have equality in social, civil, political, and religious privileges; Brazil making it punishable with death to import slaves into the empire.

Our oppressors, when urging us to go to Africa, tell us that we are better adapted to the climate than they—that the physical condition of the constitution of colored people better endures the heat of warm climates than that of the whites; this we are willing to *admit*, without argument, without adducing the physiological reason why, that colored people can and do stand warm climates better than whites; and find an answer fully to the point in the fact, that they also stand *all other* climates, cold, temperate, and modified, that white people can stand; therefore, according to our oppressors' own showing, we are a *superior race*, being endowed with properties fitting us for *all parts* of the earth, while they are only adapted to *certain* parts. Of course, this proves our right and duty to live wherever we may *choose*; while the white race may only live where they *can*. We are content with the fact, and have ever claimed it. Upon this rock, they and we shall ever agree.

Of the West India Islands, Santa Cruz, belonging to Denmark; Porto Rico, and Cuba with its little adjuncts, belonging to Spain, are the only slaveholding Islands among them—three-fifths of the whole population of Cuba being colored people, who cannot and will not much longer endure the burden and the yoke. They only want intelligent leaders of their own color, when they are ready at any moment to charge to the conflict—to liberty or death. The remembrance of the noble mulatto, PLACIDO, the gentleman, scholar, poet, and intended Chief Engineer of the Army of Liberty and Freedom in Cuba; and the equally noble black, CHARLES BLAIR, who was to have been Commander-in-Chief, who were shamefully put to death in 1844, by that living monster, Captain General O'Donnell, is still fresh and indelible to the mind of every bondman of Cuba.

In our own country, the United States, there are *three million five hundred thousand slaves*; and we, the nominally free colored people, are *six hundred thousand* in number; estimating one-sixth to be men, we have *one hundred thousand* able bodied freemen, which will make a powerful auxiliary in any country to which we may become adopted—an ally not to be despised by any power on earth. We love our country, dearly love her, but she don't love us—she despises us, and bids us begone, driving us from her embraces; but we shall not go where she desires us; but when we do go, whatever love we have for her, we shall love the country none the less that receives us as her adopted children.

For the want of business habits and training, our energies have become paralyzed; our young men never think of business, any more than if they were so many bondmen, without the right to pursue any calling they may think most advisable. With our people in this country, dress and good appearances have been made the only test of gentleman and ladyship, and that vocation which offers the best opportunity to dress and appear well, has generally been preferred, however menial and degrading, by our young people, without even, in the majority of cases, an effort to do better; indeed, in many instances, refusing situations equally lucrative, and superior in position; but which would not allow as much display of dress and personal appearance. This, if we ever expect to rise, must be discarded from among us, and a high and respectable position assumed.

One of our great temporal curses is our consummate poverty. We are the poorest people, as a class, in the world of civilized mankind—abjectly, miserably poor, no one scarcely being able to assist the other. To this, of course, there are noble exceptions; but that which is common to, and the very process by which white men exist, and succeed in life, is unknown to colored men in general. In any and every considerable community may be found, some one of our white fellow-citizens, who is worth more than all the colored people in that community put together. We consequently have little or no efficiency. We must have means to be practically efficient in all the undertakings of life; and to obtain them, it is necessary that we should be engaged in lucrative pursuits, trades, and general business transactions. In order to be thus engaged, it is necessary that we should occupy positions that afford the facilities for such pursuits. To compete now with the mighty odds of wealth, social and religious preferences, and political influences of this country, at this advanced stage of its national existence, we never may expect. A new country, and new beginning, is the only true, rational, politic remedy for our disadvantageous position; and that country we have already pointed out, with triple golden advantages, all things considered, to that of any country to which it has been the province of man to embark.

Every other than we, have at various periods of necessity, been a migratory people; and all when oppressed, shown a greater abhorrence of oppression, if not a greater love of liberty, than we. We cling to our oppressors, as the objects of our love. It is true that our enslaved brethren are here, and we have been led to believe that it is necessary for us to remain, on that account. Is it true, that all should remain in degradation, because a part are degraded? We believe no such thing. We believe it to be the duty of the Free, to elevate themselves in the most speedy and effective manner possible; as the redemption of the bondman depends entirely upon the elevation of the freeman; therefore, to elevate the free colored people of America, anywhere upon this continent; forebodes the speedy redemption of the slaves. We shall hope to hear no more of so fallacious a doctrine—the necessity of the free remaining in degradation, for the sake of the oppressed. Let us apply, first, the lever to ourselves; and the force that elevates us to the position of manhood's considerations and honors, will cleft the manacle of every slave in the land.

When such great worth and talents—for want of a better sphere—of men like Rev. Jonathan Robinson, Robert Douglass, Frederick A. Hinton, and a hundred others that might be named, were permitted to expire in a barber-shop; and such living men as may be found in Boston, New York, Philadelphia, Baltimore, Richmond, Washington City, Charleston, (S. C.) New Orleans, Cincinnati, Louisville, St. Louis, Pittsburg, Buffalo, Rochester, Albany, Utica, Cleveland, Detroit, Milwaukie, Chicago, Columbus, Zanesville, Wheeling, and a hundred other places, confining themselves to Barber-shops and waiterships in Hotels; certainly the necessity of such a course as we have pointed out, must be cordially acknowledged; appreciated by every brother and sister of oppression; and not rejected as heretofore, as though they preferred inferiority to equality. These minds must become "unfettered," and have "space to rise." This cannot be in their present positions. A continuance in any position, becomes what is termed "Second Nature"; it begets an *adaptation*, and *reconciliation* of *mind* to such condition. It changes the whole physiological condition of the system, and adapts man and woman to a higher or lower sphere in the pursuits of life. The offsprings of slaves and peasantry, have the general characteristics of their parents; and nothing but a different course of training and education, will change the character.

The slave may become a lover of his master, and learn to forgive him for continual deeds of maltreatment and abuse; just as the Spaniel would couch and fondle at the feet that kick him; because he has been taught to reverence them, and consequently, becomes adapted in body and mind to his condition. Even the shrubbery-loving Canary, and lofty-soaring Eagle, may be tamed to the cage, and learn to love it from habit of confinement. It has been so with us in our position among our oppressors; we have been so prone to such positions; that we have learned to love them. When reflecting upon this all important, and to us, all absorbing subject; we feel in the agony and anxiety of the moment, as though we could cry out in the language of a Prophet of old: "Oh that my head were waters, and mine eyes a fountain of tears, that I might weep day and night for the" degradation "of my people! Oh that I had in the wilderness a lodging place of way-faring men; that I might leave my people, and go from them!"

The Irishman and German in the United States, are very different persons to what they were when in Ireland and Germany, the countries of their nativity. There their spirits were depressed and downcast; but the instant they set their foot upon unrestricted soil; free to act and untrammeled to move; their physical condition undergoes a change, which in time becomes physiological, which is transmitted to the off-spring, who when born under such circumstances, is a decidedly different being to what it would have been, had it been born under different circumstances.

A child born under oppression, has all the elements of

servility in its constitution; who when born under favorable circumstances, has to the contrary, all the elements of freedom and independence of feeling. Our children then, may not be expected, to maintain that position and manly bearing; born under the unfavorable circumstances with which we are surrounded in this country; that we so much desire. To use the language of the talented Mr. Whipper, "they cannot be raised in this country, without being stoop shouldered." Heaven's pathway stands unobstructed, which will lead us into a Paradise of bliss. Let us go on and possess the land, and the God of Israel will be our God.

The lessons of every school book, the pages of every history, and columns of every newspaper, are so replete with stimuli to nerve us on to manly aspirations, that those of our young people, who will now refuse to enter upon this great theatre of Polynesian adventure, and take their position on the stage of Central and South America, where a brilliant engagement, of certain and most triumphant success, in the drama of human equality awaits them; then, with the blood of *slaves*, write upon the lintel of every door in sterling Capitals, to be gazed and hissed at by every passer by—

> Doomed by the Creator
> To servility and degradation;
> The SERVANT of the *white man*,
> And despised of every nation!

A PROJECT FOR AN EXPEDITION OF ADVENTURE, TO THE EASTERN COAST OF AFRICA

E VERY people should be the originators of their own designs, the projector of their own schemes, and creators of the events that lead to their destiny—the consummation of their desires.

Situated as we are, in the United States, many, and almost insurmountable obstacles present themselves. We are four-and-a-half millions in numbers, free and bond; six hundred thousand free, and three-and-a-half millions bond.

We have native hearts and virtues, just as other nations; which in their pristine purity are noble, potent, and worthy of example. We are a nation within a nation;—as the Poles in Russia, the Hungarians in Austria, the Welsh, Irish, and Scotch in the British dominions.

But we have been, by our oppressors, despoiled of our purity, and corrupted in our native characteristics, so that we have inherited their vices, and but few of their virtues, leaving us in character, really a *broken people*.

Being distinguished by complexion, we are still singled out—although having merged in the habits and customs of our oppressors—as a distinct nation of people; as the Poles, Hungarians, Irish, and others, who still retain their native peculiarities, of language, habits, and various other traits. The claims of no people, according to established policy and usage, are respected by any nation, until they are presented in a national capacity.

To accomplish so great and desirable an end, there should be held, a great representative gathering of the colored people of the United States; not what is termed a National Convention, represented en masse, such as have been, for the last few years, held at various times and places; but a true representation of the intelligence and wisdom of the colored freemen; because it will be futile and an utter failure, to attempt such a project without the highest grade of intelligence.

No great project was ever devised without the consultation of the most mature intelligence, and discreet discernment and precaution.

To effect this, and prevent intrusion and improper representation, there should be a CONFIDENTIAL COUNCIL held; and circulars issued, only to such persons as shall be *known* to the projectors to be equal to the desired object.

The authority from whence the call should originate, to be in this wise:—The originator of the scheme, to impart the contemplated Confidential Council, to a limited number of known, worthy gentlemen, who agreeing with the project, endorse at once the scheme, when becoming joint proprietors in interest, issue a *Confidential Circular,* leaving blanks for *date, time,* and *place* of *holding* the Council; sending them to trusty, worthy, and suitable colored freemen, in all parts of the United States, and the Canadas, inviting them to attend; who when met in Council, have the right to project any scheme they may think proper for the general good of the whole people—provided, that the project is laid before them after its maturity.

By this Council to be appointed, a Board of Commissioners, to consist of three, five, or such reasonable number as may be decided upon, one of whom shall be chosen as Principal or Conductor of the Board, whose duty and business shall be, to go on an expedition to the EASTERN COAST of AFRICA, to make researches for a suitable location on that section of the coast, for the settlement of colored adventurers from the United States, and elsewhere. Their mission should be to all such places as might meet the approbation of the people; as South America, Mexico, the West Indies, &c.

The Commissioners all to be men of decided qualifications; to embody among them, the qualifications of physician, botanist, chemist, geologist, geographer, and surveyor, —having a sufficient knowledge of these sciences, for practical purposes.

Their business shall be, to make a topographical, geographical, geological, and botanical examination, into such part or parts as they may select, with all other useful information that may be obtained; to be recorded in a journal kept for that purpose.

The Council shall appoint a permanent Board of Directors, to manage and supervise the doings of the Commissioners, and to whom they shall be amenable for their doings, who shall hold their office until successors shall be appointed.

A National Confidential Council, to be held once in three years; and sooner, if necessity or emergency should demand it; the Board of Directors giving at least three months' notice, by circulars and newspapers. And should they fail to perform their duty, twenty-five of the representatives from any six States, of the former Council, may issue a call, authentically bearing their names, as sufficient authority for such a call. But when the Council is held for the reception of the report of the Commissioners, a general mass convention should then take place, by popular representation.

MANNER OF RAISING FUNDS.

The National Council shall appoint one or two Special Commissioners, to England and France, to solicit, in the name of the Representatives of a Broken Nation, of four-and-a-half millions, the necessary outfit and support, for any period not exceeding three years, of such an expedition. Certainly, what England and France would do, for a little nation—mere nominal nation, of five thousand civilized Liberians, they would be willing and ready to do, for five millions; if they be but authentically represented, in a national capacity. What was due to Greece, enveloped by Turkey, should be due to US, enveloped by the United States; and we believe would be respected, if properly presented. To England and France, we should look for sustenance, and the people of those two nations—as they would have every thing to gain from such an adventure and eventual settlement on the EASTERN COAST OF AFRICA—the opening of an immense trade being the consequence. The whole Continent is rich in minerals, and the most precious metals, as but a superficial notice of the topographical and geological reports from that country, plainly show to any mind versed in the least, in the science of the earth.

The Eastern Coast of Africa has long been neglected, and never but little known, even to the ancients; but has ever been our choice part of the Continent. Bounded by the Red Sea, Arabian Sea, and Indian Ocean, it presents the greatest facilities for an immense trade, with China, Japan, Siam, Hindoostan, in short, all the East Indies—of any other country in the world. With a settlement of enlightened freemen, who with the immense facilities, must soon grow into a powerful nation. In the Province of Berbera, south of the Strait of Babelmandel, or the great pass, from the Arabian to the Red Sea, the whole commerce of the East must touch this point.

Also, a great rail road could be constructed from here, running with the Mountains of the Moon, clearing them entirely, except making one mountain pass, at the western extremity of the Mountains of the Moon, and the southeastern terminus of the Kong Mountains; entering the Province of Dahomey, and terminating on the Atlantic Ocean West; which would make the GREAT THOROUGHFARE for all the trade with the East Indies and Eastern Coast of Africa, and the Continent of America. All the world would pass through Africa upon this rail road, which would yield a revenue infinitely greater than any other investment in the world.

The means for prosecuting such a project—as stupendous as it may appear—will be fully realised in the prosecution of the work. Every mile of the road, will thrice pay for itself, in the development of the rich treasures that now lie hidden in the bowels of the earth. There is no doubt, that in some one section of twenty-five miles, the developments of gold would more than pay the expenses of any one thousand miles of the work. This calculation may, to those who have never given this subject a thought, appear extravagant, and visionary; but to one who has had his attention in this direction for years, it is clear enough.

But a few years will witness a development of gold, precious metals, and minerals in Eastern Africa, the Moon and Kong Mountains, ten-fold greater than all the rich productions of California.

There is one great physiological fact in regard to the colored race—which, while it may not apply to all colored persons, is true of those having black skins—that they can bear *more different* climates than the white race. They bear *all* the temperates and extremes, while the other can only bear the temperates and *one* of the extremes. The black race is endowed with natural properties, that adapt and fit them for temperate, cold, and hot climates; while the white race is only endowed with properties that adapt them to temperate and cold climates; being unable to stand the warmer climates; in them, the white race cannot work, but become perfectly indolent, requiring somebody to work for them—and these, are always people of the black race.

The black race may be found, inhabiting in healthful improvement, every part of the globe where the white race reside; while there are parts of the globe where the black race reside, that the white race cannot live in health.

What part of mankind is the "denizen of every soil, and the lord of terrestrial creation," if it be not the black race? The Creator has indisputably adapted us for the "denizens of *every soil*," all that is left for us to do, is to *make* ourselves the "*lords* of terrestrial creation." The land is ours—there it lies with inexhaustible resources; let us go and possess it. In Eastern Africa must rise up a nation, to whom all the world must pay commercial tribute.

OFFICIAL REPORT OF THE NIGER VALLEY EXPLORING PARTY

O N or about the latter part of July, 1853, the following document was sent on, and shortly
appeared in the columns of "FREDERICK DOUGLASS'
PAPER," Rochester, N.Y., and the "ALIENED AMERICAN,"
published and edited by William Howard Day, Esq., M.A.,
at Cleveland, Ohio, U.S., which continued in those papers
every issue, until the meeting of the Convention:

CALL FOR A NATIONAL EMIGRATION
CONVENTION OF COLORED MEN
*To be held in Cleveland, Ohio, on the 24th, 25th, and
26th of August, 1854*

MEN AND BRETHREN: The time has fully come when we,
as an oppressed people, should do something effectively,
and use those means adequate to the attainment of the
great and long desired end—do something to meet the
actual demands of the present and prospective necessities
of the rising generation of our people in this country. To
do this, we must occupy a position of entire *equality*, of
unrestricted rights, composing in fact, an acknowledged *necessary* part of the *ruling element* of society in which we live.
The policy *necessary* to the *preservation* of this *element* must
be *in our favor*, if ever we expect the enjoyment, freedom,
sovereignty, and equality of rights anywhere. For this pur-

pose, and to this end, then, all colored men in favor of Emigration out of the United States, and *opposed* to the American Colonization scheme of leaving the Western Hemisphere, are requested to meet in CLEVELAND, OHIO, TUESDAY, the 24th day of AUGUST, 1854, in a great NATIONAL CONVENTION, then and there to consider and decide upon the great and important subject of Emigration from the United States.

No person will be admitted to a seat in the Convention, who would introduce the subject of Emigration to the Eastern Hemisphere—either to Asia, Africa, or Europe—as our object and determination are to consider our claims to the West Indies, Central and South America, and the Canadas. This restriction has no reference to *personal* preference, or *individual* enterprise; but to the great question of national claims to come before the Convention.

All persons coming to the Convention must bring credentials properly authenticated, or bring verbal assurance to the Committee on Credentials—appointed for the purpose—of their fidelity to the measures and objects set forth in this call, as the Convention is specifically by and for the friends of Emigration, and none others—and no opposition to them will be entertained.

The question is not whether our condition can be bettered by emigration, but whether it can be made worse. If not, then, there is no part of the wide spread universe, where our social and political condition are not better than here in our native country, and nowhere in the world as here, proscribed on account of color.

We are friends to, and ever will stand shoulder to shoulder by our brethren, and all our friends in all good measures adopted by them for the bettering of our condition in this country, and surrender no rights but with our last breath; but as the subject of Emigration is of vital importance, and has ever been shunned by all delegated assemblages of our people as heretofore met, we cannot longer delay, and will not be farther baffled; and deny the right of our most sanguine friend or dearest brother, to prevent an intelligent inquiry into, and the carrying out of these measures, when this can be done, to our entire advantage, as we propose to show in Convention—as the West Indies, Central and South America—the majority of which are peopled our brethren, or those identified with us in race, and what is more, *destiny*, on this continent—all stand with open arms and yearning hearts, importuning us in the name of suffering humanity to come—to make common cause, and share one common fate on the continent.

The Convention will meet without fail at the time fixed for assembling, as none but those favorable to Emigration are admissible; therefore no other gathering may prevent it. The number of delegates will not be restricted—except in the town where the Convention may be held—and there the number will be decided by the Convention when assembled, that they may not too far exceed the other delegations.

The time and place fixed for holding the Conventions are ample; affording sufficient time, and a leisure season generally—and as Cleveland is now the centre of all directions—a good and favorable opportunity to all who desire to attend. Therefore, it may reasonably be the greatest gathering of the colored people ever before assembled in a Convention in the United States.

Colonizationists are advised, that no favors will be shown to them or their expatriating scheme, as we have no sympathy with the enemies of our race.

All colored men, East, West, North, and South, favorable to the measures set forth in this Call will send in their names (post-paid) to M. R. DELANY, or REV. WM. WEBB, Pittsburgh, Pa., that there may be arranged and attached to the Call, *five* names from each State.

We must make an issue, create an event, and establish a position *for ourselves*. It is glorious to think of, but far more glorious to carry out.

REV. WM. WEBB, M. R. DELANY, H. G. WEBB, THOS. A. BROWN, JOHN JONES, R. L. HAWKINS, SAMUEL VENERABLE, JOHN WILLIAMS, A. F. HAWKINS, S. W. SANDERS, JEFFERSON MILLER, *Pittsburgh, Pa.*; REV. A. R. GREEN, P. L. JACKSON, J. H. MAHONEY, G. HARPER, JONATHAN GREEN, H. A. JACKSON, E. R. PARKER, SAMUEL BRUCE, *Allegheny City*; J. J. GOULD BIAS, M.D., REV. M. M. CLARK, A. M. SUMNER, JOHNSON WOODLIN, *Philadelphia*; JAMES M. WHITFIELD, JOHN N. STILL, STANLEY MATTHEWS, *New York*.

This Call was readily responded to by the addition of names from other States, which appeared in subsequent issues.

At the Convention, which according to the Call sat in Cleveland successively on Thursday, 24th, Friday, 25th, and Saturday, 26th of August, 1854, the following States were represented: Rhode Island, New York, Pennsylvania, Ohio, Michigan, Wisconsin, Indiana, Missouri, Kentucky, Tennessee, Louisiana, Virginia, and the Canadas; the great body consisting of nearly sixteen hundred persons. W. H. DAY, Esq., editor of the *Aliened American*, entered the Convention, and the Chairman invited him forward, offering him the privileges of the Convention, stating that wherever colored people were, William Howard Day was free—whether or not he altogether agreed in sentiment on minor points; and the Convention unanimously concurred in the invitation given.

Mr. Day subsequently proffered to the Convention any books or documents at his command for the use of that body.

The following permanent Institution was established:

ORGANIZATION OF THE
NATIONAL BOARD OF COMMISSIONERS

Central Commissioners, Pittsburgh, Pennsylvania—M. R. DELANY, President; WM. WEBB, Vice-President; THOS. A. BROWN, Treasurer; EDW. R. PARKER, Auditor; CHAS. W. NIGHTEN, Secretary; PROFESSOR M. H. FREEMAN, A.M., Special For. Sec.; SAMUEL VENERABLE, ALFRED H. JOHNS, SAMUEL BRUCE, PARKER SORRELL.

DEPARTMENTS

Committee on Domestic Relations.—SAMUEL BRUCE, Chairman; SAMUEL VENERABLE, CHARLES W. NIGHTEN. *Financial Relations.*—THOMAS A. BROWN, Chairman; PARKER SORRELL, ALFRED H. JOHNS. *Foreign Relations.*—REV. WM. WEBB, Chairman; M. R. DELANY, EDW. R. PARKER. *Special Foreign Secretary.* PROF. MARTIN H. FREEMAN, A. M. *State Commissioners.*—*Massachusetts*—WM. C. NELL, Boston; C. L. REMOND, Salem. *New York, Buffalo.*—JAMES M. WHITFIELD, J. THEODORE HOLLY. *Ohio, Cincinnati.*—AUGUSTUS R. GREEN, PHILLIP TOLIVAR, Jun. *Michigan, Detroit.*—WILLIAM C. MUNROE, WILLIAM LAMBERT. *Kentucky, Louisville.*—CONAWAY BARBOUR, JAMES H. GIPSON. *Missouri, St. Louis.*—REV RICH'D ANDERSON, REV. JORDAN BROWN. *Virginia, Richmond.*—RICHARD HENDERSON, JOHN E. FERGUSON. *Tennessee, Nashville.*—ELDER PETER A. H. LOWRY, CHARLES BARRATT. *Louisiana, New Orleans.*—JORDAN B. NOBLE, REV. JOHN GARROW. *California, San Francisco.*—HENRY M. COLLINS, ORANGE LEWIS.

THE Second Convention, pursuant to a call, was held in Cleveland, in August, 1856, when some modification and amendments were made in the Constitution, and some changes in the officers of the Board; but the president was unanimously re-elected, and continued in office until the close of the of the Third Convention, which met pursuant to a call in the town of Chatham, Canada West, in August, 1858, when, resigning his position in the Board, the following officers succeeded to the

GENERAL BOARD OF COMMISSIONERS

CENTRAL COMMISSIONERS—CHATHAM, CANADA
WILLIAM HOWARD DAY, President
MATISON F. BAILEY Vice-President
GEORGE WASH. BRODIE, Secretary
JAMES MADISON BELL, Treasurer
ALFRED WHIPPER, Auditor
MARTIN R. DELANY, Foreign Secretary

NOTE.—The names only of the Central Commissioners are here given, the others being re-elected as chosen in 1856, at Cleveland.

OTHER MEMBERS

ABRAM D. SHADD
J. HENRY HARRIS
ISAAC D. SHADD

At an Executive Council Meeting of the Board, September 1st, 1858, the following resolution, as taken from the Minutes, was adopted: That Dr. Martin R. Delany, of Chatham, Kent Country, Canada West, be a Commissioner to explore in Africa, with full power to choose his own colleagues.

III | HISTORY OF THE PROJECT

I N the winter of 1831–32, being then but a youth, I formed the design of going to Africa, the land of my ancestry; when in the succeeding winter of 1832–33, having then fully commenced to study, I entered into a solemn promise with the Rev. Molliston Madison Clark, then a student in Jefferson College, at Cannonsburg, Washington County, Pennsylvania, being but seventeen miles from Pittsburgh, where I resided (his vacations being spent in the latter place), to complete an education, and go on an independent and voluntary mission—to travel in Africa—I as a physician and he as a clergyman, for which he was then preparing.

During these vacations of about seven weeks each, Mr. Clark was of great advantage to me in my studies, he being then a man of probably thirty years of age, or more, and in his senior year (I think) at college.

This design I never abandoned, although in common with my race in America, I espoused the cause, and contended for our political and moral elevation on equality with the whites, believing then, as I do now, that merit alone should be the test of individual claims in the body politic. This cause I never have nor will abandon; believing that no man should hesitate or put off any duty for another time or place, but "act, act in the *living present*, act," *now* or *then*. This has been the rule of my life, and I hope ever shall be.

In 1850, I had fully matured a plan for an adventure, and to a number of select intelligent gentlemen (of African descent, of course) fully committed myself in favor of it. They all agreed that the scheme was good; and although neither of them entered personally into it, all fully sanctioned it, bidding me God-speed in my new adventure, as a powerful handmaid to their efforts in contending for our rights in America.

In 1854, at the great Emigration Convention in Cleveland, my paper, read and adopted as a "Report on the Political Destiny of the Colored Race on the American Continent," set forth fully my views on the advantages of Emigration.

Although the Call itself strictly prohibits the introduction of the question of emigration from the American Continent or Western Hemisphere, the qualification which directly follows—"This restriction has no reference to *personal* preference, or *individual* enterprise"—may readily be understood. It was a mere policy on the part of the authors of those documents, to confine their scheme to America (including the West Indies), whilst they were the leading advocates of the regeneration of Africa, lest they compromised themselves and their people to the avowed enemies of the race.

The Convention (at Cleveland, 1854), in its Secret Sessions made, Africa, with its rich, inexhaustible productions, and great facilities for checking the abominable Slave Trade, its most important point of dependence, though each individual was left to take the direction which in his judgment best suited him. Though our great gun was leveled, and the first shell thrown at the American Continent, driving a slaveholding faction into despair, and a political confusion from which they have been utterly unable to extricate themselves, but become more and more complicated every year, *Africa was held in reserve, until by the help of an All-wise Providence we could effect what has just been accomplished with signal success*—a work which the most sanguine friend of the cause believed would require at least the half of a century.

It is a curious, and not less singular historical fact, that a leading political journal, and the first newspaper which nominated Mr. James Buchanan, many years ago, for the Presidency of the United States; and at a time whilst he was yet at the court of St. James (1854), as Envoy Extraordinary, this paper was strongly urging his claims as such, thus expresses itself, which gives a fair idea of the political pro-slavery press generally, especially in Pennsylvania, Mr. Buchanan's native State. I intended to give the article entire, as alarm will be seen even at the commencement; but pressure for space will prevent my quoting but a few sentences. It is from the Pittsburgh *Daily Morning Post*, Wednesday, October 18th, 1854:

A GRAND SCHEME FOR THE COLORED RACE

In August last, a National Convention of colored people was held at Cleveland, Ohio. It was composed of delegates from most of the States. It was called the 'National Emigration Convention,' and its objects were to consider the political destinies of the black race; and recommend a plan of Emigration to countries where they can enjoy political liberty, and form nations 'free and independent.'

The Committee then proceeds to mark out a grand scheme by which the Negro race may be regenerated, and formed into free, intelligent, and prosperous nations.

The West India Islands, Central America, and all the Northern and middle portions of South America, including the whole of Brazil, are designated as the regions desired; and that can be obtained as the seat of Negro civilization and empire. These regions and islands together are represented as containing twenty-four and a half millions of population; but one-seventh of which, some three and a half millions, are whites of pure European extraction; and the remainder, nearly twenty-one millions, are colored people of African and Indian origin. This immense preponderance of the colored races in those regions, it is supposed, will enable them, with the aid of Emigration from the United States, to take possession of all those countries and islands, and become the ruling race in the empires to be formed out of those wide and fruitful realms. The Committee expresses full confidence in the practicability of this great undertaking; and that nothing is wanting to its success at no distant day but unanimity of sentiment and action among the masses of the colored people. The climate of those regions is represented as entirely congenial to the colored race, while to the European races it is enervating and destructive; and this fact, added to the present immense superiority of numbers on the part of the negroes, is relied on as a sure guarantee of the success of the great enterprise; and that their race could forever maintain the possession and control of those regions.

Other great events, it is supposed, will follow in the train of this mighty movement. With the West India Islands, and Central and South America, composing free negro nations, slavery in the United States would, they suppose, soon be at an end. The facility of escape, the near neighborhood of friends and aid, it is urged, would rapidly drain off from the Southern States all the most intelligent, robust, and bold of their slaves.

Dr. M. R. Delany, of Pittsburgh, was the chairman of

the committee that made this report to the convention. It was, of course, adopted.

If Dr. D. drafted this report, it certainly does him much credit for learning and ability; and cannot fail to establish for him a reputation for vigor and brilliancy of imagination never yet surpassed. It is a vast conception of impossible birth. The Committee seem to have entirely overlooked the strength of the 'powers on earth' that would oppose the Africanization of more than half the Western Hemisphere.

We have no motive in noticing this gorgeous dream of 'the Committee,' except to show its fallacy—its impracticability, in fact, its absurdity. No sensible man, whatever his color, should be for a moment deceived by such impracticable theories.

On the African coast already exists a thriving and prosperous Republic. It is the native home of the African race; and there he can enjoy the dignity of manhood, the rights of citizenship, and all the advantages of civilization and freedom. Every colored man in this country will he welcomed there as a free citizen; and there he can not only prosper, and secure his own comfort and happiness, but become a teacher and benefactor of his kindred races; and become an agent in carrying civilization and Christianity to a benighted continent. That any one will be turned aside from so noble a mission by the delusive dream of conquest and empire in the Western Hemisphere is an absurdity too monstrous and mischievous to be believed. Yet 'the Committee's Report' was accepted, and adopted, and endorsed by a 'National Convention;' and is published and sent forth to the world.

In July, 1855, Rev. James Theodore Holly, an accomplished black gentleman, now rector of St. Luke's Church, New Haven, Connecticut, U.S., was commissioned to

Faustin Soulouque, Emperor of Hayti, where he was received at court with much attention, interchanging many official notes during a month's residence there, with favorable inducements to laborers to settle.

During the interval from the first convention, 1854 to 1858, as President of the Council, I was actively engaged corresponding in every direction, among which were several States of Central and South America, as well as Jamaica and Cuba; the Rev. J. T. Holly, who, during two years of the time, filled the office of Foreign Secretary, contributing no small share in its accomplishment.

Immediately after the convention of 1856, from which I was absent by sickness, I commenced a general correspondence with individuals, imparting to each the basis of my adventure to Africa to obtain intelligent colleagues. During this time (the Spring of 1857), "Bowen's Central Africa" was published, giving an interesting and intelligent account of that extensive portion of Africa known on the large missionary map of that continent as Yoruba. Still more encouraged to carry out my scheme at this juncture, Livingstone's great work on Africa made its appearance, which seemed to have stimulated the Africo-Americans in many directions, among others, those of Wisconsin, from whom Mr. Jonathan J. Myers, a very respectable grocer, was delegated as their Chairman to counsel me on the subject. In the several councils held between Mr. Myers and myself, it was agreed and understood that I was to embody their cause and interests in my mission to Africa, they accepting of the policy of my scheme.

At this time, I made vigorous efforts to accomplish my design, and for this purpose, among others, endeavored to obtain goods in Philadelphia to embark for Loando de St. Paul, the Portuguese colony in Loango, South Africa, where the prospect seemed fair for a good trade in beeswax and ivory, though Lagos, West Central Africa, was my choice and destination. Robert Douglass, Esq., artist, an accomplished literary gentleman (landscape, portrait painter, and photographer) of Philadelphia with whom I was in correspondence, sent me the following note:

MR. M. R. DELANY:—   PHILADELPHIA, June 17, 1858

DEAR SIR—I think very highly of the intended Expedition to the 'Valley of the Niger.' I would be pleased to accompany it professionally, if I were to receive a proper outfit and salary. Dr. Wilson declines; but Mr. Robert Campbell, of the 'Institute for Colored Youth,' a very accomplished Chemist, &c., &c., &c., says he will gladly accompany the Expedition, if a proper support for his family in his absence were assured. Rev. William Douglass, in conversation with me, has expressed very favorable views. Hoping you may be very successful, I remain in expectation of receiving more detailed accounts of the plan, its prospects and progress,

Your friend and well-wisher,
661, N. Thirteenth St., Phil.   ROBERT DOUGLASS

Up to this time, I had never before known or heard of Mr. Campbell, who is a West India gentleman, native bred in Jamaica, but the recommendation of Mr. Douglass, an old acquaintance and gentleman of unsullied integrity, accompanied as it was by the following note from Dr. Wilson, also an accomplished gentleman of equal integrity, a physician, surgeon, and chemist, who, being selected by me as Surgeon and Naturalist of the party, also recommended Mr. Campbell in a detached note which has been mislaid, was sufficient at the time:

Dr. Delany:—   PHILADELPHIA, June 7th, 1858

DEAR SIR—I received your note of May 25th, through the kindness of R. Douglass, Jr., and can truly say, I am highly gratified to learn of so laudable an enterprise and expedition; and would be happy and proud to be numbered with the noble hearts and brilliant minds, identified with it. Yet, whilst I acknowledge (and feel myself flattered by) the honor conferred upon me in being selected for so important and honorable position, I regret to inform you, that it will be wholly out of my power to accept.

Very respectfully,
838, Lombard Street.   JAMES H. WILSON

I have been the more induced to give the letters of Mr. Douglass and Dr. Wilson in favor of Mr. Campbell, because some of my friends were disposed to think that I "went out of the way to make choice of an entire stranger, unknown to us, instead of old and tried acquaintances," as they were pleased to express it. I had but one object in view—the Moral, Social, and Political Elevation of Ourselves, and the Regeneration of Africa, for which I desired, as a *preference*, and indeed the only *adequate* and *essential* means by which it is to be accomplished, men of African descent, properly qualified and of pure and fixed principles. These I endeavored to select by corresponding only with such of my acquaintances.

At the Council which appointed me Commissioner to Africa, having presented the names of Messrs. Douglass and Campbell, asking that they also might be chosen; at a subsequent meeting the following action took place:

Whereas, Dr. Martin R. Delany, Commissioner to Africa, having presented the names of Messrs. Robert Douglas and

Robert Campbell of Philadelphia, Pa., U.S., requesting that they be appointed Commissioners, the Board having made him Chief Commissioner with full power to appoint his own Assistants, do hereby sanction the appointment of these gentlemen as Assistant Commissioners.

A paper was then laid before the Council, presenting the name and scheme of the party, which was received and adopted.

Dr. Amos Aray, surgeon, a highly intelligent gentleman, and Mr. James W. Purnell, also an intelligent young gentleman, bred to mercantile pursuits, having subsequently sent in their names and received appointments by the Chief Commissioner, the following document was made out:

AFRICAN COMMISSION

The President and Officers of the General Board of Commissioners, viz: William H. Day, A.M., President; Matison F. Bailey, Vice-President; George W. Brodie, Secretary; James Madison Bell, Treasurer; Alfred Whipper, Auditor; Dr. Martin R. Delany, Special Foreign Secretary; Abram D. Shadd, James Henry Harris, and Isaac D. Shadd, the Executive Council in behalf of the organization for the promotion of the political and other interests of the Colored Inhabitants of North America, particularly the United States and Canada.

To all, unto whom these letters may come, greeting: The said General Board of Commissioners, in Executive Council assembled, have this day chosen, and by these presents do hereby appoint and authorize Dr. Martin Robison Delany, of Chatham, County of Kent, Province of Canada, Chief Commissioner; and Robert Douglass, Esq., Artist, and Prof. Robert Campbell, Naturalist, both of Philadelphia, Pennsylvania, one of the United States of America, to be Assistant Commissioners; Amos Aray, Surgeon; and James W. Purnell, Secretary and Commercial

Reporter, both of Kent County, Canada West, of a Scientific Corps, to be known by the name of

THE NIGER VALLEY EXPLORING PARTY

The object of this Expedition is to make a Topographical, Geological and Geographical Examination of the Valley of the River Niger, in Africa, and an inquiry into the state and condition of the people of that Valley, and other parts of Africa, together with such other scientific inquiries as may by them be deemed expedient, for the purposes of science and for general information; and without any reference to, and with the Board being entirely opposed to any Emigration there as such. Provided, however, that nothing in this Instrument be so construed as to interfere with the right of the Commissioners to negotiate in their own behalf, or that of any other parties, or organization for territory.

The Chief-Commissioner is hereby authorized to add one or more competent Commissioners to their number; it being agreed and understood that this organization is, and is to be exempted from the pecuniary responsibility of sending out this Expedition.

Dated at the Office of the Executive Council, Chatham, county of Kent, Province of Canada, this Thirtieth day of August, in the year of our Lord, One Thousand Eight Hundred and Fifty-eight.

By the President,
WILLIAM HOWARD DAY
ISAAC D. SHADD, Vice-President★
GEORGE W. BRODIE, Secretary

★Mr. Shadd was elected Vice-President in the place of Mr. Bailey, who left the Province for New Caledonia.

So soon as these names with their destined mission were officially published, there arose at once from mistaken persons (*white*) in Philadelphia, a torrent of opposition, who presuming to know more about us (the blacks) and our own business than we did ourselves, went even so far as to speak to one of our party, and tell him that we were *not ready* for any such *important* undertaking, nor could be in *three years yet to come!* Of course, as necessary to sustain this, it was followed up with a dissertation on the *disqualification* of the Chief of the Party, mentally and physically, *external* appearances and all. So effectually was this opposition prosecuted, that colored people in many directions in the United States and the Canadas, were not only affected by it, but a "Party" of three had already been chosen and appointed to supersede us! Even without any knowledge on my part, claims were made in England in behalf of the "Niger Valley Exploring Party," solely through the instrumentality of these Philadelphians.

Such were the effects of this, that our preparatory progress was not only seriously retarded (I having to spend eight months in New York city to counteract the influence, where six weeks only would have been required), but three years originally intended to be spent in exploring had to be reduced to one, and the number of Commissioners from five to two, thereby depriving Mr. Robert Douglass from going, an old friend and most excellent gentleman, whose life, as well as that of his father before him, had been spent in efforts, not only of self-elevation, but the elevation also of his people. Many years ago, the accomplished articles of "Robert Douglass, Jun," to the *United States Gazette*, and other public journals, forced those negro-hating periodicals to respect at least the writer, if not his race. Dr. Aray, also an excellent gentleman who had given up business to join the party, was doomed to disappointment. And of Mr. Jas. W. Purnell—who met me in New York two weeks after my arrival, and through the whole eight months of adversity and doubtful progress, stood by me, performing the duty of Secretary, writing in every direction, copying, and from dictation for hours at a time—I cannot say too much. For a young gentleman inexperienced in such matters, he has no superior; and for integrity, true heartedness, and trustworthiness, in my estimation, he has few if any rivals. To his great and good uncle, under whom he was brought up, much of his character is to be credited.

As an expression of the feelings of the most intelligent emigrationists with whom I corresponded generally in America, I give below two extracts from letters of Professor Freeman. The Professor is now as he then was, the Principal of Avery College.

ALLEGHANY CITY, April 14, 1858

My DEAR FRIEND—Your letter of condolence was duly received, for which we tender you our warmest thanks.

I have read Bowen's work, and shall to-day purchase Livingstone's. I am more and more convinced that Africa is the country to which all colored men who wish to attain the full stature of manhood, and bring up their children to be men and not creeping things, should turn their steps; and I feel more and more every day, that I made a great mistake in not going there, when I was untrammelled by family ties, and had the opportunity.

Respectfully yours,
M. H. FREEMAN

Again the Professor says:

I see that Emigration has broken out in the East, and that ＿＿＿＿＿＿ can notice one now without scoffing at, which he could not in 1854. Well, people can grow wondrously wise in four years. But it will take several more *Olympiads* to bring the leaders among us up to the old Cleveland Platform of 1854.

All the fault of that movement was this, that it was at least one generation ahead of the colored heads of our people. We may, if we please, refuse to emigrate, and crouch like spaniels, to lick the hand that beats us; but children's children at the farthest, will have outgrown such pitiful meanness, and will dare to do all that others have dared and done for the sake of freedom and independence. Then all this cowardly cant about the unhealthy climate, the voracious beasts, and venomous reptiles of Africa, will be at a discount, instead of passing current as now for wisdom and prudence.

Mr. Campbell, who finally agreed voluntarily to be one of the "Niger Valley Exploring Party," spent some time with us in New York and some time in Philadelphia, but finally, in consequence of the doubtful prospects of my success, left, it would seem, at the suggestion and with the advice and recommendation of parties in Philadelphia, disconnected with and unknown to me, from whom he received letters of introduction for England. In justice to myself and party as organized, as well as the great cause and people whom I represent, I here simply remark, that this was no arrangement of mine nor our party, as such at the time; and whatever of success the visit was attended with, and benefit thereby accrued mutually to us in Africa, I as frankly decline any authority in the matter and credit to myself, as I should had the result proved what it might have done otherwise. I am only willing to claim that which is legitimately mine, and be responsible for my own doings whether good or bad; but this act the integrity of the Party was forced to acknowledge, as the following circular published in England will show:

EXPEDITION TO AFRICA
To Promote the Cultivation of Cotton and Other Products of Slave-Labor by Emigrants from America

A party, consisting of Martin R. Delany, M.D., Robert Campbell, J. W. Purnell, Robert Douglass, and Amos Aray, M.D., (the last two subsequently omitted) has been commissioned by a Convention of Colored Persons, held at Chatham, C.W., to proceed to Africa, and select a location for the establishment of an Industrial Colony.

While such an enterprise is of importance in the Evangelization and Civilization of Africa, and in affording an asylum in which the oppressed descendants of that country may find the means of developing their mental and moral faculties unimpeded by unjust restrictions, it is regarded as of still greater importance in facilitating the production of those staples, particularly Cotton, which now are supplied to the world chiefly by Slave Labor. The effect of this would be to lessen the profits of Slavery, to render in time the slave a burden to his owner, and thus furnish an irresistible motive to Emancipation Africa possesses resources which, properly developed, must doubtless render her eventually a great, if not the greatest, producer of all the products of Slave Labor. And how would all good men rejoice to see the blow which shall effectually prostrate the giant Slavery, struck by the Black Man's arm! It is necessary, however, that civilized influences be diffused in her midst or, at least, that facilities for rendering available her products, be supplied equal to the demand for them.

It is the purpose of the party to proceed to Lagos,

thence through Abbeokuta to Rabba, on the Niger, about 350 miles from the coast; to study the Agricultural and Commercial facilities of the country, and the disposition of the Natives towards strangers as settlers; also to negotiate for the grant or purchase of land, and to ascertain the conditions on which we might be protected in the usages of civilized life.

These objects being accomplished, the party will return and report the result of their labors, when a considerable number of intelligent and enterprising persons from the United States and Canada, many of them intimately acquainted with the production of Cotton, and its preparation for market, will be prepared to emigrate.

Towards defraying the expenses of this undertaking, £500 has been subscribed in America. This amount has been expended in providing for the families of two of the party in their absence; in paying the passage of Martin R. Delany and J. W. Purnell to Africa, direct from America, and providing them a few articles of outfit; in defraying the current expenses of the party since the 1st December ult., while engaged in soliciting subscriptions and otherwise forwarding the objects of the Expedition; and in providing the Subscriber with the means of coming hither.

It is desired to raise in this country, in time to enable the Subscriber to depart for Africa in June by the steamer from Liverpool, an additional sum of £250, with which to provide other articles of outfit, and goods for trading with the natives for the means of subsistence, as well as to provide for other necessary and contingent expenses.

The Subscriber will take the liberty of calling upon you personally, at an early day, to solicit your aid in this enterprise.

MANCHESTER, May 13th, 1859   ROBERT CAMPBELL

Grant, for charity's sake, that it was done with the best of motives, it was flagrantly and fatally at variance with every principle of intelligent—to say nothing of enlightened—organizations among civilized men, and in perfect harmony with that mischievous interference by which the enemies of our race have ever sought to sow discord among us, to prove a natural contempt for the Negro and repugnance to his leadership, then taunt us with incapacity for self-government. These flambeaus and rockets directed with unerring precision, taking effect in the very centre of our magazine, did not cause, in those for whom it was intended, a falter nor a wince in their course, but steadily and determinedly they pressed their way to the completion of their object under prosecution. In this design the enemy was thwarted.

I drop every reflection and feeling of unpleasantness towards my young brother Campbell, who, being a West Indian, probably did not understand those *white Americans*, and formed his opinion of American *blacks* and their capacity to "lead," from the estimate they set upon them. I owe it to posterity, the destiny of my race, the great adventure into which I am embarked and the position I sustain to it, to make this record with all Christian (or *African*, if you please) forgiveness, against this most glaring and determined act of theirs to blast the negro's prospects in this his first effort in the Christian Era, to work out his own moral and political salvation, by the regeneration of his Fatherland, through the medium of a self-projected scheme; and thereby take the credit to themselves. It was too great an undertaking for negroes to have the credit of, and therefore they *must* go *under* the auspices of some white American Christians. To be black, it would seem, was necessarily to be "ungodly"; and to be white was necessarily to be "godly," or Christian, in the estimation of some.

With a grateful heart, I here as freely record as an equal duty I owe to posterity, my unfeigned thanks to all those gentlemen who took an active part and in any way aided the mission on my behalf, either from the pulpit, by the contribution of books, stationery, charts, instruments, or otherwise, especially those who made each the *one hundred dollar contribution*, and the two in New York, through whose instrumentality and influence these were obtained. Those disinterested and voluntary acts of kindness I never shall forget whilst reason occupies her throne, and would here willingly record their names, had I their consent to do so.

I sailed from New York May 24th, in the fine *barque Mendi*—Captain M'Intyre—vessel and cargo owned by Johnson, Turpin and Dunbar, three enterprising colored gentlemen of Monrovia, Liberia, all formerly of New York, U.S. In the name of the General Board of Commissioners for the promotion of the political and other interest of the colored people of the United States and the Canadas, by self-exertion, I thank them.

I cannot close this section without expressing my obligations to Captain M'Intyre for his personal kindness to me; and also to his first officer, Captain Vernon Locke, (himself a ship-master, who took the position of first officer for the voyage, and who had been, for the last three or four years, collecting scientific information by astronomical, meteorological, and other observations, for Lieutenant Maury, Director of the Observatory at Washington, D.C., U.S.,) I am greatly indebted for many acts of kindness in facilitating my microscopic and other examinations and inquiries, during the voyage. Concerning the *nautilus and whale*, I learned more through this accomplished seaman than I had ever learned before. The first by examination of the mollusca, which were frequently caught by Captain L. for my accommodation—and of the latter, by oral information received from him (who had been a great whaler) on frequently observing those huge monsters (during the voyage.*

---

*On the 16th day of June, lat 35 deg. 35 min., long. 38 deg. 39 min., a very large school (the largest Captain Locke said that he had ever seen or read of), probably *five hundred*, of sperm whales made their appearance in the segment of a circle to windward and leeward of the vessel about noon, continuing in sight, blowing and spouting, filling the air with spray for a long time, to our amusement and delight. The captain said, though an old whaler, he had never known (of sperm whales in that latitude before; and from the immense number, and as they were frequently seen as we approached Africa many times on different days afterwards, that he thought a new whaling point had been discovered. Other whales were also seen frequently in these latitudes—lazy, shy, "old bulls," which floated with their huge backs and part of their heads out of water, so as to expose their eyes, when they would suddenly disappear and as quickly appear again; but the great quantity of *squid spawn*, the peculiar *mollusca* upon which the sperm whale feeds, made it ominous, according to the opinion of Captain Locke, that a great new sperm whale fishery had been discovered, the spawn being seen during several days' sail before and after observing the great school.

NOTE.—I should not close this part of my report without stating that, during the year 1858, Mr. Myers wrote to the Royal Geographical Society, London; Thomas Clegg, Esq., Manchester; Dr. Livingstone, and perhaps others, all over *my name* as secretary and himself chairman. The letters referred to were written (without my knowledge) by a son of Mr. Myers; and I only mention the fact here because I am unwilling to claim the honor of the authorship of correspondence carried on through a lad of sixteen years of age.

Arrival in Africa

SATURDAY, July 10th.—I landed on the beach at Grand Cape Mount, Robertsport, in company with Messrs. the Hon. John D. Johnson, Joseph Turpin, Dr. Dunbar, and Ellis A. Potter, amid the joyous acclamations of the numerous natives who stood along the beautiful shore, and a number of Liberians, among whom was Reverend Samuel Williams, who gave us a hearty reception. Here we passed through the town (over the side of the hill), returning to the vessel after night.

Monrovia

Monday, July 12th.—The roadstead of Monrovia was made about noon, when I, in company with B. E. Castendyk, Esq., a young German gentleman traveling for pleasure, took lodgings at Widow Moore's, the residence of Rev. John Seys, the United States consular agent, and commissioner for recaptured Africans.

On the day after my arrival, the following correspondence took place:

Residence of the United States Consular Agent
Monrovia, Liberia, July 12th, 1859

To His Excellency, the President of the Republic of Liberia: SIR—By a Convention of Colored People of the United States and the Canadas, Martin R. Delany, Robert Douglass, Robert Campbell, Amos Aray, and James W. Purnell, were appointed as Commissioners under the name of the 'Niger Valley Exploring Party,' to make an Exploration through different parts of Africa.

I have arrived, Sir, near your Government, and expect soon to meet other members of the party. Any aid, orally, documentary, or in the person of an Official Commissioner, which you may please to give to facilitate the mission in Liberia will be gratefully and highly appreciated. I ask the favor of an interview with your Excellency, either privately or in Cabinet Council, or with any other gentlemen that the occasion may suggest, at such time as may be designated.

I am happy, Sir, of the opportunity of giving your Excellency assurance of my most distinguished consideration.

M. R. DELANY

His Excellency, President Benson.

Government House, Monrovia, July 13, 1859
SIR—I have the honor to acknowledge the receipt of your note of the 12th instant, conveying to me the information of your appointment (in connection with colleagues expected soon to arrive), by a Convention of the colored people of the United States and the Canadas, 'Commissioners,' under the name of 'The Niger Valley Exploring Party'; and of your arrival near this Government. You have also been pleased to signify, that you will duly appreciate any aid, oral, documentary or in the form of an official Commissioner this Government may feel disposed to afford you, in facilitation of the enterprise.

In reply, I have to express my deep regret, that the receipt of your very interesting note is on the very eve of my leaving this city on an official visit to the leeward counties, which will, for the present, deprive me of the pleasure I had anticipated of an interview with you on the very interesting and highly important objects of your mission.

The Hon. John N. Lewis, Secretary of State, with whom I will converse on the subject matter of your note before leaving, will be pleased to grant you an audience; and will, with pleasure, meet your wishes, so far as he can consistently.

Please be reassured of the deep interest I feel in your very laudable enterprise; and that, if it were not for very important despatches received last week from the county of Maryland, which make it absolutely necessary that I should delay no time in reaching there, I would defer my departure a couple of days for the express purpose of consultation with you in person.

I have the honor to be most respectfully,

Your very obedient servant,

To M. R. Delany, Esq., &c.   STEPHEN A. BENSON

Monrovia, July 13, 1859

Martin R. Delany, Esq.:

DEAR SIR—The undersigned, citizens of the city of Monrovia, having long heard of you and your efforts in the United States to elevate our down-trodden race, though those efforts were not infrequently directed against Liberia, are glad to welcome you, in behalf of the community to these shores; recognizing, as they do in you, an ardent and devoted lover of the African race, and an industrious agent in promoting their interests. And they take this opportunity of expressing to you their most cordial sympathy with the enterprise which has brought you to these shores, sincerely praying that your endeavors may be crowned with complete success.

The undersigned, further, in the name and behalf of the members of this community, respectfully request that you would favor the citizens with a lecture to-morrow evening, or on any other evening you may choose to appoint, at half-past seven o'clock, on any subject you may be pleased to select.

On receiving your reply notices will be issued accordingly.

B. P. YATES   H. W. DENNIS
D. B. WARNER   URIAS A. MCGILL
SAML. F. MCGILL   H. A. JOHNSON
B. V. R. JAMES   EDW. W. BLYDEN
SAML. MATTHEWS

Residence of the United States Consular Agent,
Monrovia, July 13th, 1859

GENTLEMEN—Your note of to-day has been received, for the honor of which I thank you, and beg to say that numerous engagements prevent me from complying with your request on to-morrow evening.

You are mistaken, gentlemen, in supposing that I have ever spoken directly 'against Liberia,' as wherever I have been I have always acknowledged a unity of interests in our race wherever located; and any seeming opposition to Liberia could only be constructively such, for which I am not responsible.

Should it be your pleasure, I will do myself the honor serving you on Monday evening next, or any other evening during the week, by a discourse on the 'Political Destiny of the African Race,' and assure you of the pleasure with which I have the honor to be,

Your most obedient servant,

M. R. Delany

Col. B. P. Yates; Hon. D. B. Warner; S. F. McGill, M.D.; Hon. B.V. R. James; Rev. Saml. Matthews; Urias McGill, Esq.; Rev. Edw. W. Blyden; H. W. Dennis, Esq.; H. A. Johnson, Esq., District Attorney.

———————————

M. R. Delany, Esq.:   Monrovia, July 14, 1859

Sir—We have the honor to acknowledge your note of to-day in reply to an invitation of yesterday from us requesting that you would favor us, with many others, with an address on tomorrow evening, or at any other time agreeable to yourself. Having signified to us that next Monday evening you would be pleased to comply with the request, we tender you our thanks and will be happy to listen to a discourse on the 'Political destiny of the African Race.'

We have the honor to be, very respectfully, &c., yours,

B. V. R. James
Saml. Matthews
And others

Reception

On Monday evening, the 19th of July, having addressed a crowded audience in the Methodist Episcopal Church, Ex-Governor McGill in the chair, T. M. Chester, Esq., Secretary; Ex-President Roberts rose and in a short speech, in the name of the Liberians, welcomed me to Africa. By a vote of thanks and request to continue the discourse on a subsequent evening, this request was complied with on the following Tuesday evening.

Dr. M. R. Delany,   Monrovia, July 28, 1859

DEAR SIR—The undersigned citizens of Monrovia having been much edified by listening to two very interesting lectures delivered by you in the Methodist church, avail themselves of this method to express their appreciation of the same, and to respectfully request that you will favor the community with a popular lecture on 'Physiology' on Friday evening, the 29th inst.

> HENRY J. ROBERTS
> SAML. F. MCGILL
> B. P. YATES
> HENRY W. DENNIS
> EDWD. W. BLYDEN

Public Lecture

The reply to this polite invitation of Doctors Roberts and McGill, and others, having been mislaid, I simply remark here that the request was complied with on the evening of August 3d, in the Methodist Church, to a crowded house of the most intelligent citizens of Monrovia, of both sexes and all ages.

Departure from Monrovia.
Coasting, Cape Palmas

On the evening of August 5th, I left Monrovia in the bark Mendi, stopping at Junk, Little Bassa, Grand Bassa mouth of

St. John's River, Sinou, arriving at Cape Palmas Sabbath noon, August 20th.

Missionary Greeting

Half an hour after my arrival, I was called upon by the Rev. Mr. Hoffman, Principal of the Female Orphan Asylum, at the residence of John Marshall, Esq., whose hospitality I was then receiving, and in the name of the white Missionaries welcomed to that part of Liberia. Before Mr. Hoffman left I was honored by a visit also from Rev. Alexander Crummell, Principal of Mount Vaughan High School, where, after partaking of the hospitality of Mr. Marshall during that day and evening, I took up my residence during a month's stay in this part of Liberia.

Correspondence

Having taken the *acclimating fever* on the 5th of the month, the day I left Monrovia, and besides regularly a dessert spoonful of a solution of the sulphate of *quinia* three times a day, and the night of my arrival two eight grain doses of Dover's Powder, the reference to "the state of my health" in the following correspondence, will be understood:

To Dr. M. R. Delany:

DEAR SIR—We, the undersigned citizens of the county of Maryland, Liberia, beg to tender you a heartfelt welcome to our neighborhood, and to assure you of our warmest interest in the important mission which has called you to the coast of Africa. Perhaps you will consent, should your health permit, to favor us with a public interview before you leave. We would be most happy to hear your views concerning the interest of our race in general, and of your mission in particular. Moreover, by so doing, you will afford us an opportunity of paying you that respect which your reputation, talents, and noble mission command, and which it is our sincere desire to pay you.

If Thursday or Friday will suit your convenience it will be agreeable to us; but we leave the character of the meeting to be designated by yourself.

Aug. 23, 1859   ALEX CRUMMEL

D. R. FLETCHER   THOS. FULLER
B. J. DRAYTON   RICHD. W. KNIGHT
J. T. GIBSON   JOHN MARSHALL
C. H. HARMON   GILES ELEM
S. B. D'LYLON   T. S. DENT
L. R. HAMILTON   A. WOOD
BENJAMIN COOK   J. W. WILLIAMS
H. W. MOULTON   WM. W. PEARCE
ANSBURN TUBMAN   R. A. GRAY
JAMES M. MOULTON   JAS. ADAMS
N. JACKSON, JUN.   J. W. COOPER
JNO. E. MOULTON

Mount Vaughan, near Harper, Cape Palmas
August 27th, 1859

Gentlemen—Your note of the 23rd inst., requesting me, should my health permit, to appear before the citizens of your county, is before me, and for the sentiments therein expressed I thank you most kindly.

As I have reason to believe that I am now convalescent from my second attack of native fever, should my health continue to improve I shall start on an exploration for the head of Kavalla river on Monday next ensuing, to return on Friday evening.

Should it be your pleasure, gentlemen, and my health will permit, I will meet you on Monday, the 5th of September, the place and hour to be hereafter named according to circumstances.

I assure you of the pleasure, Gentlemen, with which I have the honor to be,

Your most obedient servant,
M. R. Delany

Gen. Wood; Judge Drayton; Rev. Alex. Crummell; John Marshall, Esq.; Hon. J. T. Gibson; C. H. Harmon, Esq.; J. W. Cooper, Esq.; Dr. Fletcher; Giles Elem, Esq.; Jas. M. Moulton, Esq.; Benjamin Cook, Esq.; S. B. D'Lyon, M.D., and others, Committee, &c., &c.

Reception Meeting at Palmas

On the evening of the 14th this request was complied with in the Methodist Church at Latrobe, an out-village of Harper, by addressing a crowded assemblage of both sexes and all ages of the most respectable people of the Cape, on the part of whom I was most cordially welcomed by Rev. Alexander Crummell.

LIBERIA— CLIMATE, SOIL, PRODUCTIONS, ETC.

Territory, Climate

LIBERIA extends from a point north of Grand Cape Mount, about 7 deg. 30 min. north lat., on sea shore, northeasterly to the western extremity of the most southern range of the Kong Mountains, lat. 4 deg. 30 min. The climate is generally salubrious, and quite moderate. But it is frequently somewhat oppressive, though mild and genial, and the high hills and mountain ranges sometimes enervating to strangers or foreigners from temperate climates, in consequence of the "air being freighted with *fragrance*" from the *flowers* and *aroma* of the exuberant, rich, rank growth of vegetable matter, as trees, shrubbery, and other herbage.

Temperature

The temperature is seldom or never great, the average being 85 deg. Fahr.★ This, it will be perceived, is but 5 deg. above

---

★This day, August 2, 1861, while revising this Report, the thermometer Fahr. stands in the most favorable shade in the town of Chatham, Kent county, C. W., 96 deg. (98 is the general test of this day) and in the sun 113—being one degree above *fever heat*. A fact to which my attention was called by an intelligent Liberian—and which science may hereafter account for—that the nearer the approach to the equator, the more mod-

summer temperature in the temperate *zone* of America, according to Fahrenheit's scale.

Comparative Temperature Bees

It is worthy of observation that, by a natural law, we are enabled to compare the temperature in many parts of Africa satisfactorily with that of some other countries. There are parts of India, and also Central and South America, where it is said that *bees* cannot propagate, in consequence of their inability to build their cells because of the heat, the cera or wax melting in their hive or habitation. While in Africa such is not the case, there being no part known to civilized travelers where bees are not seen ever busy on every blossom, gathering their store, leaving laden with the rich delicacies of the blooming flowers; and Doctor Livingstone not only speaks most frequently of the profusion of honey in the extensive country through which he traveled, but says that, while near the coast in Loango, he encountered many persons laden with "tons of *beeswax*," carried on their heads exposed to the sun, on their way to the trading posts. And during our stay at Abbeokuta, Mr. Campbell my colleague, had two swarms of bees; the first taken by him when in *transitu* (swarmed) and hived, which bred a new swarm in the hive at the Mission House where we resided.

---

erate is the heat. Has the sun the same effect upon the general bulk of the earth that it has upon particular locations—the greater the elevation the cooler—or is it because of the superior velocity of this part, that a *current* is kept up by its passage through the *atmosphere* surrounding it? It is a settled fact that the earth is "elevated at the equator and depressed at the poles," and hills are cool, while valleys and plains are hot, because of their peculiar property of attracting and reflecting heat.

Soil, Stone, Minerals, Productions

The soil is very rich, which, like that of other parts of Africa through which I traveled, rates from a sandy loam to a rich alluvial, resting on strata of granite, limestone, and quartz with a large percentage of mica, profusely incorporated with iron, and doubtless other rich minerals not yet discovered. Palm oil and camwood are abundant, comprising the principal articles of native products for exportation; a good deal of ivory from tile interior through the Golah country, but not so much as formerly; palm nuts, which principally go to France; ginger, arrowroot, pepper, coffee, sugar and molasses, to which three latter articles (as well as pepper, ginger and arrowroot,) the industrious citizens of Liberia have, during the last six years, turned their attention.

Domestic Animals, Fowls, Goats, Sheep, Swine, Cattle

The stock consists of fowls of various kinds—as chickens, ducks, common and Muscovy; Guinea fowls in abundance; turkeys, and on one farm—the *Gaudilla farm* of William Spencer Anderson, Esq., sugar planter, on the St. Paul River—geese. Neither are the cows so small as supposed to be from the general account given of them by travelers. Those which are common to, and natives of this part of Africa, which I shall classify as the *Bassa* (pronounced *Bassaw*) cattle, are handsome and well-built, comparing favorably in size (though neither so long-legged nor long-bodied) with the small cattle in the interior counties of Pennsylvania, U.S., where no attention is paid scientifically to the breeding of cattle; though the Liberia or Bassa are much the heaviest, and handsomely made like the *Golah*, or *Fulatah*, hereafter to be described, resembling the Durham cattle of England in form. Also swine, goats, and sheep are plentiful.

Horses, None. Why?

I saw but one horse in Liberia, and that on the Gaudillla farm of Mr. Anderson; and though, as the Liberians themselves informed me, they have been taken there by the Mandingo and Golah traders, they never lived. And why—if they live in other parts of Africa, on the western coast, which they do, even near the *Mangrove swamps*, as will hereafter be shown—do they not live in Liberia, the civilized settlements of which as yet, except on the St. Paul and at Careysburg, are confined to the coast? There are certainly causes for this, which I will proceed to show.

Horse Feed, Pasturage, Hay

In the first place, horses, like all other animals, must have feed naturally adapted to their sustenance. This consists mainly of grass, herbage, and grains, especially the latter when the animal is domesticated. Secondly, adequate shelter from sun and weather, as in the wild state by instinct they obtain these necessary comforts for themselves.

No Cultivated Farms—
No Shelter for Horses

Up to the time, then, when the Liberians ceased the experiment of keeping horses, they had not commenced in any extensive manner to cultivate farms, consequently did not produce either maize (Indian corn), Guinea corn (an excellent article for horses in Africa, resembling the American broom corn both in the stock, blade, and grain, the latter being larger and browner than those of the broom corn, and more nutritious than oats); peas, nor any other grain upon which those animals are fed, and the great, heavy, rich, rank, pseudo reed-grass of tile country was totally unfit for them, there being no grass suited either for pasturage or hay. Again, I was informed by intelligent, respectable Liberians, that to their knowledge there never had been a stable or proper shelter prepared for a horse, but that they had, in one or more instances, known horses to be kept standing in the sun the entire day, and in the open air and weather during the entire night, while their owners had them.

No Horses; Why, and Why Not

It is very evident from this, that horses could not live in Liberia, and since the *tsetse* fly introduced to the notice of the scientific world recently by Doctor Livingstone the African Explorer, has never been seen nor heard of in this part of the continent, nor any other insect that tormented them, those must have been the prime causes of fatality to these noble and most useful domestic creatures. I have been thus explicit in justice to Liberia, even in opposition to the opinion of some very intelligent and highly qualified gentlemen in that country (among whom is my excellent friend, Doctor Roberts, I think,) because I believe that horses can live there as well as in other parts of Africa, when fairly and scientifically inquired into and tested. Proper feed and care, I have no doubt, will verify my opinion; and should I but be instrumental, by calling the attention of my brethren in Liberia to these facts, in causing them *successfully* to test the matter, it will be but another evidence of the fact, that the black race should take their affairs in their own hands, instead of placing them in the hands of others.

Exploration. Farms, Sugar, Coffee

My explorations in Liberia extended to every civilized settlement in the Republic except Careysburg, and much beyond these limits up the Kavalla River. There is much improvement recently up the St. Paul River, by the opening up of fine, and in some cases, extensive farms of coffee and sugar; also producing rice, ginger, arrowroot, and pepper, many of which have erected upon them handsome and well-constructed dwellings; also sugar mills and machinery for the manufacture of sugar and molasses, which articles manufactured, compare favorably with the best produced in other countries. There has, as yet, been no improvement introduced in the hulling and drying of coffee, there being probably not enough produced to induce the introduction of machinery. I am informed that there have also been commenced several good farms on the Junk River, which district, farther than the settlement at the mouth, I did not visit. The people are willing and anxious for improvement, and on introducing to many of the farmers the utility of cutting off the centre of each young coffee-tree so soon as it grew above the reach of a man of ordinary height, I had the satisfaction of seeing them immediately commence the execution of the work. The branches of the tree spread, in proportion to the checking of the height; hence, instead of eight feet apart, as some of the farmers have done, the trees should be planted at least twenty feet apart, thus leaving ample space between for the spreading of the branches. The tree should never be permitted to grow too high to admit of the berry being picked from the ground, or at least from a stand which may be stepped upon without climbing.

Schools

The schools are generally good, every settlement being amply accommodated with them; and in Monrovia and at Cape Palmas the classics are being rigidly prosecuted.★

Churches Missionaries

Churches are many and commodious, of every Christian denomination—except, I believe, the Roman Catholic. The Missionaries seem to be doing a good work, there being many earnest and faithful laborers among them of both sexes, black and white, and many native catechists and teachers, as well as some few preachers.

★The "Liberia College" has been fully established since my visit there, by the erection of a fine stone edifice, and the choice of the Hon. Ex-President Joseph Jenkins Roberts, President and Professor of Jurisprudence and International Law; Rev. Alexander Crummell, A.B., Professor of Intellectual and Moral Philosophy and English Literature; Rev. Edward Welmot Blydon, Professor of Greek and Latin Languages and Literature. This is a grand stride in the march of African Regeneration and Negro Nationality.

Business, Professions, Theology, Medicine, Law

The principal business carried on in Liberia is that of trading in native and foreign produce, the greater part being at the Capital. The greater part of merchants here are Liberians; but there are also three white houses—two German and one American. And along the coast there are a number of native trading-posts, the proprietors of which are white foreigners, with black agents. Many of the Liberian Clergy of all denominations are well educated gentlemen; and the Medical Profession is well represented by highly accomplished Physicians; but of all the professions, the Law is the most poorly represented—there being, as I learnt when there, but one young gentlemen at the bar who had been bred to the profession; and not a Judge on the bench who was learned in the law. This I do not mention in disparagement of the gentlemen who fill those honorable positions of presiding over the legal investigations of their country, as many—indeed, I believe the majority of them—are clergymen, who from necessity have accepted those positions, and fill their own legitimate callings with credit. I sincerely hope that the day is not far distant when Liberia will have her learned counsellors and jurists—dispensing law, disseminating legal opinions, and framing digests as well as other countries, for the benefit of nations.

Council

At Grand Bassa I held a Council with some of the most eminent Liberians, among whom were several members of the National Legislature—the venerable Judge Hanson in the chair. Several able speeches were made—the objects of my mission and policy approved; and I shall never forget the profound sensation produced at that ever-memorable Council, and one of the most happy hours of my life. When the honored old judge and sage, sanctioning my adventure, declared that, rather than it should fail, he would join it himself, and with emotion rose to his feet; the effect was inexpressible, each person being as motionless as a statue.

Public Affairs, Municipal and Public Improvements

The laws of Liberia seem to be well constructed, and framed to suit the wants of the people, and their public affairs are quite well and creditably conducted. But there is a great deficiency in public improvements, and, as I learned—and facts from actual observation verified until comparatively recent—also in public spirit. There are no public buildings of note, or respectable architectural designs; no harbor improvements, except a lighthouse each on the beautiful summit rock-peaks of Cape Messurado and Cape Palmas—not even a buoy to indicate the shoal; no pier, except a little one at Palmas; nor an attempt at a respectable wharfage for canoes and lighters (the large keels owned by every trading vessel, home and foreign, which touches there.) And, with the exception of a handsome wagon-road, three and a half miles out from Harper, Cape Palmas, beyond Mount Vaughan, there is not a public or municipal road in all Liberia. Neither have I seen a town which has a paved street in it, although the facilities for paving in almost all the towns are very great, owing to the large quantities of stone everywhere to be had.

The Capital No City

And what is surprising, Monrovia, although the capital, has not a city municipality to give it respectability as such; hence, there is neither mayor nor council (city council I mean) to give character to any public occasion, but His Excellency the President, the Chief Executive of the nation, must always be dragged down from his reserved and elevated position, and made as common as a common policeman to head every little petty affair among the people. The town was once, by the wisdom of some legislators, chartered into a city, and Dr. T. F. M'Gill (ex-governor) chosen mayor, who, by his high intelligence and fitness for the office, had commenced the most useful and commendable improvements; but the wisdom of other legislators, after a year's duration, in consequence of the heavy expenses incurred to "make Monrovia, where big folks lived, a fine place," repealed the act, degrading their Capital to a town. That is the same as declaring that a court shall not have a judge—the nation a President or Executive, or there shall be no head at all; hence, to reduce the judge to the grade of a lawyer, the lawyer to that of the clerk of the court, the President of the nation to that of the county magistrate, and the county magistrate to that of a constable. How much respect would a people be entitled to who would act thus? They must understand that nothing is greater than its head, and the people of a nation cannot rise above the level of the head of their nation any more than the body of the individual in its natural position can be raised above the head. It is just so with a town population. A villager is a villager, a citizen is a citizen, and a metropolitan is a metropolitan—each of which is always expected to have a standing commensurate with his opportunities.

Self-Reliance, Ways and Means

One word as a suggestion in political economy to the young politician of Liberia: Always bear in mind, that the fundamental principle of every nation is *self-reliance*, with the *ability to create their own ways and means*: without this, there is no capacity for *self-government*. In this short review of public affairs, it is done neither to disparage nor under-rate the gentlemen of Liberia with whom, from the acquaintance I have made with them in the great stride for black nationality, I can make common cause, and hesitate not to regard them, in unison with ourselves, a noble band of brothers.

Executive Munificence

There has been much progress made in the various industrial vocations within a few years past by the munificence of President Benson, aided by the wisdom of the Legislature, through the agency of a national agricultural fair, with liberal premiums on samples exhibited in a spacious receptacle prepared each season for the purpose, in the Public Square in front of the President's mansion, called Palm Palace. Like his predecessor President Roberts, in pressing the claims of his country before the nations of Europe, President Benson has spared no authority which he possessed in developing the agricultural resources of his country. Every man has his *forte*, and in his turn probably becomes a *necessity* for the time being, according to his faculty. Consequently my opinion is, that the *forte* and mission of President Roberts for the time being were the establishment of a Nationality, and that of President Benson the development of its resources, especially the agricultural. Neither of these gentlemen, therefore, might be under-rated, as each may have been the instrument which God in his wisdom appointed to a certain work.

Official and Personal Favors

To John Moore, Esq., Government Surveyor; the Hon. B. P. Yates, ex-Vice-President of the Republic; Hon. John Seys, U.S. Agent for Re-captured Africans, and Consular Agent, I am much indebted for acts of kindness in facilitating my Explorations in Liberia. The Hon. Mr. Seys and Mr. Moore, for personally accompanying me up the St. Paul River; and Colonel Yates, for the loan of his fine canvas-covered boat for my use. Also to Dr. Henry J. Roberts, for remedies and medicines for my own use; Dr. Thomas F. M'Gill, for offering to make advances on articles of merchandise which I took out on trade to bear expenses, much beyond the market price; and to those excellent gentlemen, Messrs. Johnson, Turpin, and Dunbar, also for large advances made above market price in cash for my commodity, as well as other favors, especially on the part of Mr. Johnson, who, having for years been a resident in Monrovia, did everything to advance my mission and make my duty an agreeable one.

To the Rev. Alexander Crummell, who accompanied me up the Kavalla, above the Falls, making my task an easy one; to Drs. Fletcher and D'Lyon, who rendered me professional aid, and also to our excellent, faithful, and reliable guide, Spear Mehia is, a native civilized Christian Prince, the son of the old friend of the missionaries, Nmehia, the deceased King of Kavalla, I here make acknowledgments. And I cannot close this section without an acknowledgment that, wherever I went, the people of the country generally did everything to make me happy—Esquire Wright at Junk, Dr. Smith at Grand Bassa, and the Hon. Mr. Priest at Sinou whose guest I was, all here will receive my thanks for their aid in facilitating my mission.

Settlement and Sites of Towns

I conclude this section by remarking, that Monrovia is one of the handsomest and most eligible sites for a city that I ever saw, and only lacks the population and will of the people to make it a most beautiful place; and how much it is to be regretted that the charter was repealed, and Mayor M'Gill and the City Council cut off in the beginning of the first steps towards a national pride, which was to have a Capital City in reality as well as name.★ How unsightly to a stranger, as he steps from the boat at the mouth of Stockton Creek, on the Messurado River, is the rude and rugged steep, leading by simple pathways in true native style, from the warehouses up to the town, which, if improved as it might and should be, would be one of the most pleasing as well as attractive approaches to any city in the world. Not even is there a respectable public market-house or market space in town. But wisdom decreed it otherwise, and for the present it must be so. "Wisdom" in this case "hath" *not* "built her house" neither "hath she hewn out" the stone "pillars" leading from the beach.

Another good site for a city is Edina, on the northeast

★I am happy to learn by advices recently received from Liberia, that Monrovia has again been created and organized a City Municipality, ex-Judge James Mayor; and I should have named in connection with the public spirit of Liberia, three newspapers—the *Liberia Herald*, *Star of Liberia*, and *Christian Advocate*—the last, a religious journal, under the auspices of that excellent Christian gentleman, Bishop Burns the Methodist Missionary-Bishop of Liberia.

side of the St. John River, opposite Buchanan, Grand Bassa, which doubtless in time Buchanan will include. This is also a handsome place, from the gradually rising elevation. Edina is the residence of that great-hearted, good old gentleman, Judge Hanson. Junk, Little Bassa, and Sinou, are also good, but each of these are low, and consequently not so imposing.

Next to Monrovia is Cape Palmas for beauty of location and scenery, and a stranger will more readily be pleased at first sight with Harper than the Capital. A beautiful city will in time occupy the extensive Cape for several miles back, including Mount Vaughan and the country around; and it may be remarked, that this place presents greater evidences of public improvement than any town in Liberia, and the only place in the country which has a regular wagon road with ox-teams running upon it.

Buildings

The private buildings in Liberia are generally good and substantial, and especially those of Monrovia, built of brick. Many of them are handsome and quite extensive mansions, the warehouses mostly being built of stone. The wooden houses generally are well-built frames, and "weatherboarded," and not, as some romancers and wonder-vendors would have it, being either log, bamboo, or mud huts. To take the settlers generally, there cannot be much fault found with their style of living, except perhaps in some instances, rather a little too much extravagance. Caldwell, Clay-Ashland, and Millsburg on the St. Paul, are pleasant and prospectively promising villages, and deserve a notice in this place. Clay-Ashland is the residence of Judge Moore, to whom I am indebted for personal favors and much useful information when examining the land over his extensive sugar and coffee farms. And to my excellent friend Dr. Daniel Laing, of the same place, for similar acts of courtesy and kindness, I am much indebted.

Public Meeting

I addressed the citizens in a very long political meeting in the Methodist church, on the evening of my visit there.

VI DISEASES—CAUSE—REMEDY

First Symptoms

THE first sight and impressions of the coast of Africa are always inspiring, producing the most pleasant emotions. These pleasing sensations continue for several days, more or less, until they gradually merge into feelings of almost intense excitement, not only mentally, but the entire physical system share largely in it, so that it might be termed a hilarity of feeling almost akin to approaching intoxication; or as I imagine, like the sensation produced by the beverage of champagne wine. Never having enjoyed the taste for it, I cannot say from experience.

Second Stage of Symptoms

The first symptoms are succeeded by a relaxity of feelings, in which there is a disposition to stretch, gape, and yawn, with fatigue.

Third Stage of Symptoms

The second may or may not be succeeded by actual febrile attacks, with nausea, chills, or violent headache; but whether or not such symptoms ensue, there is one most remarkable, as almost (and I think quite) a necessary affection, attendant upon the acclimation at this incipient stage: *a feeling of regret that you left your native country for a strange one; an almost frantic desire to see friends and nativity; a despondency and loss of the hope of ever seeing those you love at home again.*

These feelings, of course, must be resisted, and *regarded as a mere morbid affection of the mind* at the time, arising from an approaching disease, which is not necessarily serious, and may soon pass off; which is really the case.

Its Effects

It is generally while laboring under this last-described symptom, that persons send from Africa such despairing accounts of their disappointments and sufferings, with horrible feelings of dread for the worst to come.

Recovery

When an entire recovery takes place, the love of the country is most ardent and abiding. I have given the symptoms *first*, to make a proper impression first.

Diseases

I have thought it proper to give a section in my Report entirely to the diseases of Liberia, which are the same as those in other parts of Africa, with their complication with diseases carried from America by the settlers.

Native Diseases,
Peculiar Character in Liberia

The native diseases are mainly the native fever, which is nothing but the *intermittent fever* of America, known in different parts as *ague, chills and fever, fever and ague*, with its varied forms of *bilious, intermittent, remittent, continued*, and it is worst form of *inflammatory* when it most generally assumes the *congestive* type of the American Southern States. In this condition, the typhoid symptoms with *coma*, give unmistakable evidence of the character of the malady. The native fever which is common to all parts of Africa, in Liberia while to my judgment not necessarily fatal (and in by far the greater percentage of cases in the hands of an intelligent, skilful physician, quite manageable), is generally much worse in its character there than in the Yoruba country, where I have been. The symptoms appear to be much more aggravated and the patient to suffer more intensely.

Causes

The density and rankness of the vegetable growth, the saturation of the air continually with fragrance, and other *miasma*, and the *malaria* from the mangrove swamps, I assign as the cause of difference in the character of the same disease in different parts of the continent. The habits also of the settlers, have much to do with the character of the disease. A free indulgence in improper food and drink, which doubtless is the case in many instances, are exciting causes to take the malady, and aggravating when suffering under it.

Complication

There are several other diseases that might be named, which I reserve for a section on another part of Africa, and confine my remarks simply to the complication of the native with foreign. All *scorbutic*, *scrofulous*, or *syphilitic* persons, where the affection has not been fully suppressed, may become easy victims to the fever in Liberia, or lingering sufferers from *ulcers*, *acute rheumatism*, or *elephantiasis*—a frightful enlargement of the limbs. *Ulcerated opthalmia* is another horrible type, that disease in such chronically affected persons may assume. But any chronic affection—especially lung, liver, kidney, and rheumatic—when not too deeply seated, may, by favorable acclimation, become eliminated, and the ailing person entirely recover from the disease.

Remedies, Natural and Artificial

The natural remedy for the permanent decrease of the native fever, is the clearing up and cultivation of the land, which will be for some time yet to come, tardy; as emigration to Liberia is very slow, and the natives very unlike those of Yoruba—cultivate little or nothing but rice, cassaba, and yams, and these in comparative small patches, so that there is very little need for clearing off the forest. Neither have they in this part of Africa any large towns of substantial houses, all of which would necessitate a great deal of clearing; but instead, they consist of small clusters of reed or bamboo huts in a circle, always in the densest of the forest, which can scarcely ever be seen (except they be situated on a high hill) until you are right upon them. The clearing away of the mangrove swamps—which is practicable—will add greatly to the sanitary condition of Liberia; but this also will take time, as it must be the work of a general improvement in the country, brought about by populating and civilizing progress.

Treatment

The treatment of the native fever must be active and prudential. But the remedies are simple and easily obtained, being such as may be had at any well-kept apothecary's shop. The *sulphate of quinia*, in moderate doses, three or four times a day, with the usual attention to the febrile changes, gentle *aperients*, *effervescent* and *acidulous* drinks, taking care to prevent acridness in the stomach. In my advice to persons going to Africa, I shall speak more pointedly of the domestic or social customs to be avoided.

Locality

I observed that all elevated places, as Monrovia and Freetown, subject to severe visitations of disease, are situated near mangrove swamps; consequently, from the *rising* of the *malaria*, they are much more unhealthy than those in low plains, such as Lagos and many other places, *above* which the *miasma* generally rises for the most part passing off harmlessly.

I left Cape Palmas, Liberia, on Thursday, 2 P.M. the 15TH

of Sept., on the British Royal Mail African steamer, "Armenian," Captain Walker, to whom and his officers, I make acknowledgments for acts of kindness.

VII | THE INTERIOR— YORUBA

Coasting. Cape Coast Castle, Bight of Benin

THURSDAY, the 20th of September, about noon, after stopping at Cape-Coast Castle for twelve hours, on the Coast of Benin, the steamer made her moorings in the roadstead, Bight of Benin, Gulf of Guinea, off Lagos. I disembarked, going ashore with the mail-boat managed by natives; from whence, by the politeness of the gentlemanly young clerk (a native gentleman) of Captain Davies', a native merchant, I was taken in a sail-boat, also manned by natives, up the bay, and landed at the British Consulate; whence I was met by Mr. Carew, the native agent of the Rev. J. M. Harden, a most excellent man, Missionary, and conducted to the Baptist Mission House.

After a stay of five weeks, visiting almost everything and place worthy of note, being called upon by many of the most noted persons, among whom were several chiefs, having several interviews with the authorities, and meeting the most active, intelligent, Christian young men, in several of their associated gatherings, I was waited on by the messenger of the king; when after several interchanges of "words" between us, the following instrument of writing was "duly executed, signed, sealed, and delivered," I, and Mr.

Harden being present, and witnessing the measurement of the land, according to the present custom in that place:

TITLE DEED
DR. M. R. DELANY

Lagos, October 25th, 1859

Know all Men by these Presents:

That I DOCEMO, King of Lagos and the Territories thereunto belonging, have this day granted, assigned, and made over, unto Doctor Martin R. Delany, for his use and the use of his Heirs and Assigns forever, All that Piece of Ground, situated on the South of the Premises and Ground occupied by Fernando, in the field at Okai Po, Po, measuring as follows, Three Hundred and Thirty Feet square.

Witness my Stamp hereunto affixed, and the Day and Year above written.

KING
DOCEMO
OF LAGOS.

BRITISH CONSULATE,
Lagos, October 28th, 1859

I CERTIFY that the Circular Stamp, as above, with KING DOCEMO, of LAGOS in the centre, is the Official Stamp of Docemo, King of Lagos, and is used by him as his signature to all Letters, Deeds, and Documents.

{SEAL}   EDWD. F. LODDER
                          Acting Consul.

The Deed of Land above, granted to Doctor Martin R. Delany, by King Docemo of Lagos, has this 18th day of

October, 1859, been registered in the Registry Book of the British Consulate, and numbered.

JOHN P. BOYLE, Clerk

On the 30th of October, I left Lagos, proceeding *via* Ogun river, to Abbeokuta, which I reached on Saturday, the 5th of November.

Explorations. Abbeokuta

Here I met for the first time with my colleague and Assistant Commissioner, Mr. Robert Campbell, from whom, at Lagos, I found a letter waiting for my arrival in the hands of Acting Consul, Lieut. Edward F. Lodder, of Her Majesty's war vessel "Brun," which continually lies in the harbor, directly opposite and near to the Consulate. Consul Campbell (since deceased), had paid an official visit to England, and Lieut. Lodder was supplying his place.

Towns from Abbeokuta

From Abbeokuta, population 110,000, we proceeded to Ijaye, population 78,000, reckoned by the white missionaries and officers of the Niger Expedition of Her Majesty's service, who passed through once, at 80,000; Oyo, population, 75,000; Ogbomoso, population 70,000; Illorin, population 120,000; returning back, *via* Ogbomoso to Oyo: when by arrangement, Mr. Campbell leaving me at Oyo, returned to Abbeokuta by a new route through Isen and Biolorin–Pellu, small places: whence I, a week later, also by another strange route, returned, passing through Iwo, population 75,000; and Ibaddan, population 150,000 an immense city, the estimated number of inhabitants by the Civil Corps who passed through, being 250,000. It will be seen that I have made a liberal deduction of two-fifths, or 100,000 from this estimate; still, the population is immense and the city extensive, the walls embracing an outline of at least twenty-three miles.

Return to Lagos

From Abbeokuta, the water being very low, it was thought advisable that Mr. Campbell take charge of all our luggage, and proceed by way of the Ogun to Lagos, (he having disposed of his horse at Abbeokuta) whilst I, on horseback, with William Johnson our cook, the only servant we retained—a civilized native—as guide and attendant, proceeded by land, both reaching Lagos three days after, in the same hour of the same day.

VIII   TOPOGRAPHY, CLIMATE, ETC.

Topography, Climate

T HE whole face of the country extending through the Aku region or Yoruba, as it is laid down on the large missionary map of Africa, is most beautifully diversified with plains, hills, dales, mountains, and valleys, interlined with numerous streams, some of which are merely temporary or great drains; whilst the greater part are perennial, and more or less irrigating the whole year, supplying well the numerous stocks of cattle and horses with which that country is so well everywhere provided. The climate is most delightful.

First Plateau and Second Plateau, or Table Lands

The first plateau or low land from Lagos, extends about thirty-five or forty miles interiorly, with but occasionally, small rugged or rocky elevations breaking the surface, when it almost abruptly rises into elevated lands, undulating and frequently craggy, broken often by deep declivities of glens and dales.

Soil

The soil of the first plateau, for ten or fifteen miles, is moist and sandy, more or less, gradually incorporating with a dark rich earth, which, extending quite through the second plateau, continually varies in quality, consistence, and color, from a sandy loam and clay-red iron pyrite appearance to a potter's-clay, and rich alluvial color and quality, the whole being exceedingly fertile and productive; as no district through which we traveled was without cultivation more or less, and that always in a high degree, whatever the extent of ground under cultivation or the produce cultivated.

Stone Formation

The stone formation throughout these regions consist of primitive dark-gray granite, quartz, and conglomerates, with, occasionally, strata of felspar and mica, which are found mainly in the beautiful mountain regions (which are detailed extensions of the great mountains of Kong), having in these sections always beautiful gaps or passes of delightful valleys.

Minerals, Iron, Copper, Zinc

The minerals consist of iron in the greatest abundance, which at present is smelted by the natives from the clay, and every town of any note or size has not only its blacksmiths' shops, but the largest all have iron smelting works. At Ijaye there is quite an extensive and interesting establishment of the kind. And, as they manufacture *brass*, there must be also zinc and copper found there—indications of the last-named metal being often seen by the color of certain little water surfaces. The stone formation bears the usual indications of aqueous and igneous deposits, but more of the former than the latter.

Productions Timber

The timber is numerous, and for the following classification I am indebted to my learned friend the Rev. Alexander Crummell, Episcopal missionary and Principal of the Mount Vaughn High School at Cape Palmas: Teak, ebony, lignum vitae, mahogany, brimstone, rosewood, walnut, hickory, oak, cedar, unevah, and mangrove.

Medical Productions

Gum Yoruba (the same as gum Arabic), acacia or senna, castor oil, croton oil, rhubarb root, colomba-root, ipecacuanha, quasia, nux-vomica, cubebs, tobacco, and many others.

Fruits

All the fruits common to the tropics are found in these regions; in fact, so redundant is Africa with these productions, that she combines the whole within herself; that is, there are some fruits found in the tropical parts of Asia, South America, the Asiatic and West India Islands, common or peculiar to one which may not be found in the other, but all of which, it may safely be said, can be found in Africa. Pineapples the most delicious in flavor and taste conceivable oranges the same, bananas the finest, plantains equally so, mangrove plums (a peculiar but delightful and wholesome fruit, said by the natives to be a *febrifuge*), guavas, and "soursops," a delightful *febrifuge* of pure *citric acid*, without the least acridness, as well as a hundred others which I cannot now name. The papaw or tree-melon also grows very finely here, and is a very useful and wholesome fruit. When green, "stewed and mashed," and well-flavored with the usual culinary spices, it cannot be distinguished from the best green apple-sauce—for which reason it makes excellent pies. When fully ripe, it cannot be told from the finest muskmelon or cantelope.

Agricultural Products

The Agricultural labor of this part of Africa is certainly very great, and merits the attention of every intelligent inquirer; from the simple fact that, so far as it exhibits the industry of the inhabitants, it shows the means which may be depended upon for a development of the commercial resources of the country.

Palm Oil

Palm oil is produced in great abundance, as a staple commodity among themselves, as well as for exportation since the common light for houses consists of palm oil burnt in native manufactured lamps, some constructed of iron and others of earthenware. The oil of the nut is the most general in use among the natives, both for light and cooking, because it is the richest, being the most unctuous. This use of the nut-oil is certainly an antiquated custom among the people of this region, whilst those contiguous to Liberia have recently learned that the kernels could be put to commercial use, by the discovery or rather practical application by Mr. Herron, of Grand Bassa, Liberia, and subsequent demand by the French traders. The fact that the Yorubas generally produce their charcoal from the hull of the palm nut, is an evidence of the long-continued and abundant use of the latter article for the manufacture of oil. They have regular establishments for the manufacture of the palm oil, with vats and apparatus (simple though they be), places and persons for each process: as bruising the fruit from the nut, boiling, carrying the pulp to a vat, where it is pressed and washed to extract the oil; one to skim it off from the top of the liquid—another to carry off the fiber of the pulp or bruised fruit, which fiber is also appropriated to kindling and other uses. There is no such method of extracting the oil, as the mistaken idea so frequently reported by African traders from Europe and America, that the natives bruise the nut with stones in holes made in the ground, thereby losing a large percentage of the oil. Even among the crudest they know better than this, and many use shallow troughs, made of wood in some parts of Africa, as the Grebo, Golah, and some other peoples on the western coast, adjacent to Liberia.

Palm Trees Cultivated. Camwood. Ivory

All through the Yoruba country the palm tree is cultivated, being regularly trimmed and pruned, and never cut down in clearing a farm, except when from age the tree has ceased to bear, or is of the male species, when it is cut clown for the wine, which is the sap, extracted from the trunk, in a horizontal position, by boring a hole near the top and catching it in a vessel, when it is drunk either before, during, or after fermentation.

Camwood is also very plentiful, but owing to its great weight and the inconvenience at present of transportation, it does not enter extensively into the commerce of these parts, except as dyestuffs in the native markets. Gum elastic or India rubber is plentiful.

Ivory enters largely into commerce, being brought by "middle men" from the distant interior.

Indian Corn or Maize, Peas, Beans, Ginger, Pepper, Arrowroot, &c

Indian corn, the finest in the world (usually white), is here raised in the greatest quantities, we having frequently passed through hundreds of acres in unbroken tracts of cultivated land, which is beginning to enter into foreign commerce; Guinea corn in great abundance—an excellent article for horses, spoken of in another place; also peas, such as are raised for horse and cattle feed in Canada and other parts of America; white beans in great quantities, as well as those of all colors; black-eye peas; horse beans; in fact, all of the pulse vegetables; also ginger, arrowroot, red pepper in pods (the cayenne of commerce), and black pepper, all of which are articles of commerce; indigo; they also produce salt, and pea-nuts.

Kitchen Vegetables

Yams, cassaba, sweet potatoes, onions, cucumbers, and many other culinary roots and vegetables; and I am certain that beets, parsnips, and carrots, which we did not see under cultivation, could be successfully raised, if desired. Cabbage grows freely in all parts of Africa, if planted in the right season.

Potatoes, None

Whether or not the common potato of America and Europe can be propagated here has not been tested, but such is the excellence of the yam, that served up in the same manner, there is little or no difference between them and potatoes; and I am certain that when well cooked, "mashed" and seasoned, the best judge could not tell them from good potatoes. I mean good yams, because they differ in quality like potatoes.

Manufactories Iron, Brass, Glass

Crockeryware is manufactured very extensively, of almost every conceivable size and kind of vessel, for various purposes. Some of them are quite handsome, and all nearly of the ancient oriental mould. The largest earthen vessels I ever saw are made by these people, some of them being large enough for small cisterns. Iron implements for agricultural and military, as well as other domestic purposes, are made by them in every large city. They make excellent razors, which shave quite well, as also other steel-bladed knives, which prove that they have the art of tempering iron. Brass as well as glass ornaments and trinkets are made in considerable quantities.

Inhabitants

The people are of fine physical structure and anatomical conformation, well and regularly featured; not varying more in this particular from the best specimen of their own race than the Caucasian or Anglo-Saxon from that of theirs. They are very polite—their language abounding in vowels, and consequently euphonious and agreeable—affable, sociable, and tractable, seeking information with readiness, and evincing willingness to be taught. They are shrewd, intelligent, and industrious, with high conceptions of the Supreme Being, only using their images generally as mediators. "So soon," said all intelligent missionary, "as you can convince them that there is a mediator to whom you *may talk, but cannot see,* just so soon can you make Christians of them"; their idea being that God is too great to be directly approached; therefore there must be a mediator to whom they must talk that they can see, when God will listen and answer if pleased.

How Received by Them

After my arrival at Abbeokuta, not going out for two days, they expecting me through information from Mr. Campbell, the third day the Chief Atambala called upon me, inviting me in turn to call and see him. In a few days after, the king had a popular religious festival in the great public space, where there were assembled many chiefs and elders;

but, on our approach, the old king sent his messenger to escort us to the porch of the piazza upon which he was seated, eagerly grasping me by the hand, bidding me welcome to Abbeokuta and his court; telling me, pointing to Mr. Campbell, that he was acquainted with him, and had heard of me through him.

Native Estimate of Civilized Educated Men

In December, a meeting of the native cotton-traders, chiefs, and others, was held at the residence of the great chief Ogubonna concerning the price of cotton. On the meeting assembling, and finding that we were not present, the chief at once despatched a messenger, requesting our immediate attendance, as "we knew how things ought to be done." On going down, we found a large assemblage waiting, among whom were Messrs. Samuel and Josiah Crowther, H. Robbing, J. C. During, F. Rebeiro, and C. W. Faulkner, civilized native gentlemen; also Mr. J. G. Hughes, an English gentleman. By a motion from myself, seconded by J. Crowther, the chief Ogubonna was chosen chairman, and, upon a motion by Mr. Campbell, seconded by J. G. Hughes, Mr. Robbing was chosen vice-chairman. The meeting went off well, we making many suggestions during the proceedings, which were always received with approbation.

The following from the native minister, being his own writing and composition, will explain itself:

ABBEOKUTA, Igbore, 23rd Dec., 1857

M. R. DELANY, Esq.:

DEAR SIR—A meeting of the Wesleyan Missionary Society will be held at the Wesleyan Chapel, on Monday next, the 26th instant, at ten o'clock, A.M., precisely. You are sincerely and respectfully solicited to be the Chairman on the occasion.

The object of the Meeting is to offer Thanksgiving to Almighty God for the past years' success; and to pray for an outpouring of the Holy Spirit's influence upon the Church, for a further success, &c.

Collection will be made at the close of the above.

Yours respectfully and affectionately,

EDWD. BICKERSTETH

Wesleyan Minister

P.S. An early answer will be much obliged.

I replied in the affirmative to this kind invitation (the copy of reply is now mislaid), when, at the appointed time, a crowded house was assembled.

Influence of Civilization— Native Demonstration

In a simple and comprehensive address made to them (being interpreted by the minister as I proceeded), such was the effect that it not only produced their unanimous applause, but aroused Mr. During (a native civilized merchant, who had never before spoken in public) to his feet, who approved of what I had said, with such an appeal of native eloquence, that when he ceased, sixty bags of cowries (£54 or $270, esti-mating them at 18s, or $4.50 a bag; the then current value of cowries) were paid down on the spot, to aid the spread of civilization through the gospel and education. Many, very many were the thanks given me that day by these, my native kinsmen and women. Several other gentlemen, among them Surgeon Samuel Crowther, the Pastor, Mr. Rebeiro, and Mr. Campbell my colleague, also addressed them.

Official Transactions

Many had been the social, friendly, and official interchanges between us and the king and chiefs during our stay in Abbeokuta, when, on the twenty-seventh, the day after the missionary meeting, the following document was duly executed, with the express understanding that no heterogeneous nor promiscuous "masses" or companies, but select and intelligent people of high moral as well as religious character were to be induced to go out. And I am sure that every good and upright person in that region, whether native or foreign missionary, would exceedingly regret to see a reckless set of religion-spurning, God-defying persons sent there—especially by disinterested white societies in America, which interferingly came forward in a measure which was originated solely by ourselves (and that, too, but a few of us), as our only hope for the regeneration of our race from the curse and corrupting influences of our white American oppressors.

TREATY

This Treaty, made between His Majesty, OKUKENU, Alake; SOMOYE, Ibashorun; SOKENU, OGUBONNA, and ATAMBALA, Chiefs and Balaguns, of Abbeokuta, on the first part; and MARTIN ROBISON DELANY, and ROBERT CAMPBELL, of the Niger Valley Exploring Party, Commissioners from the African race, of the United States and the Canadas in America, on the second part, covenants:

ART. 1. That the King and Chiefs on their part, agree to grant and assign unto the said Commissioners, on behalf of the African race in America, the right and privilege of settling in common with the Egba people, on any part of the territory belonging to Abbeokuta, not otherwise occupied.

ART. 2. That all matters, requiring legal investigation among the settlers, be left to themselves, to be disposed of according to their own custom.

ART. 3. That the Commissioners, on their part, also agree that the settlers shall bring with them, as an equivalent for the privileges above accorded, Intelligence, Education, a Knowledge of the Arts and Sciences, Agriculture, and other Mechanical and Industrial Occupations, which they shall put into immediate operation, by improving the lands, and in other useful vocations.

ART. 4. That the laws of the Egba people shall be strictly respected by the settlers; and, in all matters in which both parties are concerned, an equal number of commissioners, mutually agreed upon, shall be appointed, who shall have power to settle such matters.

As a pledge of our faith, and the sincerity of our hearts, we each of us hereunto affix our hand and seal this Twenty-seventh day of December, ANNO DOMINI, One Thousand Eight Hundred and Fifty-nine.

> His Mark, + OKUKENU, Alake
> His Mark, + SOMOYE, Ibashorum
> His Mark, + SOKENU, Balagun
> His Mark, + OGUBONNA, Balagun
> His Mark, + ATAMBALA, Balagun
> His Mark, + OGUSEYE, Anaba
> His Mark, + NGTABO, Balagun, O. S. O.
> His Mark, + OGUDEMU, Ageoko
>   M. R. DELANY
>   ROBERT CAMPBELL

Witness—SAMUEL CROWTHER, Jun.
Attest—SAMUEL CROWTHER, Sen.

Executive Council, and
Ratification of the Treaty

On the next evening, the 28th, the king, with the executive council of chiefs and elders, met at the palace in Ake, when the treaty was ratified by an unanimous approval. Such general satisfaction ran through the council, that the great chief, his highness Ogubonna, mounting his horse, then at midnight, hastened to the residence of the Surgeon Crowther, aroused his father the missionary and author, and hastily informed him of the action of the council.

Native Confidence;
Hopes in Educated Blacks; Princess Tinuba

On our return from the interior, having previously made the acquaintance of, and had several interviews with, and visits to and from the Princess Tinuba, being a called upon by her, I informed her that during our tour I learned that she had supplied the chief of Ijaye with the means and implements for carrying on the war, which that chief was then waging against Oyo and Ibaddan.

I had previous to that, obtained her fullest confidence as an adviser, a person of integrity, a friend of my race and of Africa. She had previously expressed to a friend of mine, that she had more hope of a regeneration of Africa through me than ever before. She had promised to place the entire management of her extensive business in my hands, as much advantage was taken of her by foreigners. She has attached to her immediate household about sixty persons, and keeps constantly employed about three hundred and sixty persons bringing her in palm-oil and ivory. She had come with a private retinue of six or seven persons, her secretary, a man and several maid-servants, to counsel and give me a written statement of what she desired me to do. Having conversed for some time, after receiving my admonition concerning the part which I had learned she had taken with Arie of Ijaye, she sat some time after, positively negativing the accusation, when, bidding me farewell, and saying that she would "*send* me a letter," retired. In the course of the afternoon, her secretary, "Charles B. Jones," a native, came to the house, and presenting his mistress's compliments, with her final adieu, handed me a written paper, from which I take the following extracts, simply to show the general feeling and frankness of these people, as well as the hopes and confidence they have in our going there:

DR. MARTIN R. DELANEY: Abbeokuta, April 3rd, 1860
        SIR—This is to certify you, that it is with a willing mind I come to you for help: and I trust you will do according to your promise . . . I return you my sincere gratitude for your kind information gave me while at your house, and can assure you that all what you heard is false respecting my sending guns and powder to Arie, the Chief of Ijaye. . . . I beg to say, you must not forget to find the Clerk who will stop at Lagos to ship my cargo. . . . and make agreement with him before you send him here. . . . I need not say much more about the affairs, as you yourself have known my statements. With hopes that you are well, I am, dear Sir,
                                        Your humble servant,
                                        TINUBA
        P.S. You must not forget to send the two guage-rods. I beg you . . . Yours, &c.,—TINUBA

Per Charles B. Jones.

I have preferred to give these extracts just as they were written, without correcting the composition in any way.

Royal Deference to Black Men

The liberality which is here accorded to the people of Abbeokuta may be also accorded to most other places. The king of Illorin sat in his court exposed to our view, because, he said, we were "his people"; a privilege which he never allowed "a strange white man," who was never permitted to look upon his royal black face publicly. He also sent with us an escort of a horseman and five footmen, with sword and spear, as a guard of honor, sending us cowries to pay the expenses. The king of Oyo paid us distinguished honors through his great Arie Kufu, calling me a relative, and sending the chief to inquire after our health. On my leaving Oyo finally, he sent with me a very large escort, at the head of whom was his commander-in-chief Kufu, as a guard of honor, and three native gentlemen, high in rank, as my special carriers. These gentle men complained to the missioners, Mr. and Mrs. Hinderer at Ibaddan, that I was quite mistaken as to their true social position at home. To this I plead guilty, as they were quite right.

Domestic Animals; Fowls, Chickens, Ducks, Muscovy, Turkeys Swine; Common, Guinea

Chickens (and eggs plentifully) the sweetest and tenderest, ducks and turkeys; also Guinea fowls, as well as the fine Muscovy, are abundant.

The swine consist of two distinct classes; the common,

descended from the wild—a long, lean, gaunt, long-eared, long-nosed, sharp-featured, hungry-looking brute, like the American hog; and the Guinea, a short-legged, heavy-bodied, short-nosed, short-eared, fat-jawed, full-headed, jolly-looking animal, closely resembling the Berkshire of English breeding.

Goats, Sheep

The goats are the most beautiful, shiny, plump, active, saucy creatures, the mutton being most excellent flesh; and the sheep, though hairy instead of woolly, in every other particular are like other sheep, and the mutton frequently equaling English mutton in flavor and sweetness. I suspect the common sheep of this country to be of another genus, as there are some very fine woolly sheep in the interior. We intend testing the woolly sheep when we get settled there.

Cattle—Mandingo and Golah

The cattle are of two classes, and merit particular attention. The windward or Mandingo, a tall, long-horned, beautiful animal, the type of the Herefordshire; and the leeward or Golah, a short-legged, short-horned, heavy-bodied, broad-backed ox, the exact conformation of the splendid English Durham beeves.

Horses; Aku, Bornou

The horses are of two distinct classes, and not only merit much attention here, but must be regarded as among the most surprising evidences (as well as the cattle and improved breed of swine) of the high degree of intelligence and heathen civilization attained by the people.

Aku, or Yoruba Horse

The Aku or Yoruba, is a small, well-built, generally sprightly animal, equal in size to the largest American-Indian pony. They are great travelers, and very enduring, and when broke to the shafts or traces will be excellent in harness as family hackneys.

Bornou, or Soudan Horse

The Bornou, a noble horse, from twelve to seventeen hands high, finely proportioned and symmetrically beautiful, and the type of the description of the sire of the great first English blood horse, Godolphin, is exceedingly high-spirited, and fleet in the race or chase. These noble animals abound in all this part of Africa; are bred in Bornou, where great attention is paid to the rearing of them, from whence they are taken by the Ishmaelitish traders, in exchange for their commodities, to Arabia; from thence they are sent to Europe as their own production; just as, a few years since, and probably up to the present day, mules were reared in great numbers in Mexico, purchased by Ohio and Kentucky muleteers, who sold them in the eastern and northern States of America, where for years the people supposed and really believed that they were bred in the western States, from whence they were purported to come. The fine Bornou, known as the Arabian horse, is a native of Africa, and raised in great numbers. Denham and Clapperton, as long ago as thirty-five or forty years, wrote, after visiting that part of Africa, "It is said that Bornou can muster fifteen thousand Shonaas in the field mounted. They are the greatest breeders of cattle in the country, and annually supply Soudan with from two to three thousand horses." These animals are used for riding, and well exercised, as the smallest boys are great riders, every day dashing at fearful speed along the roads and over the plains.

Game; Quadrupeds

Game is also very plentiful. Deer, antelopes, wild hogs, hedge hogs, porcupines, armadillos, squirrels, hares and rabbits, raccoons and opossoms, are among the most common quadruped game.

Wild Fowl

Wild turkey, wild ducks of various kinds, wild pigeons, ocpara (a very fine quail, much larger, fatter and plumper than the American pheasant), and the wild Guinea fowl, are among the most common biped game.

Markets, and Domestic Habits of the People

The markets are also worthy of note, and by their regular establishment and arrangement indicate to a certain extent the self-governing element and organized condition of the people. Every town has its regular market-place or general bazaar, and everything to be had in the town may be found, in more or less quantities, in these market-places. In describing the large cities through which Mr. Campbell my colleague, and I passed, and those through which I passed alone (none of which were under seventy thousand of a population) there were numerous smaller places of various sizes, from very small villages of one hundred to two thousand inhabitants, which were not mentioned in the enumerated towns. Of these market-places I may mention that Illorin has five, the area of the largest comprising about ten acres, and the general market of Abbeokuta comprising more than twelve altogether, whilst that of Ijaye contains fully twenty acres or more, in which, like the markets generally, everything may be obtained. These markets are systematically regulated and orderly arranged, there being parts and places for everything, and "everything in their places," with officially appointed and excellent managing market-masters. The cattle department of the Abbeokuta and Ijaye markets, as well as Illorin are particularly attractive, there being as many as eight hundred sheep at one time in either of the two former, and horses and mules, as well as sheep and goats exhibited in the latter. When approaching the city of Ibaddan, I saw at a brook, where they had been let out of their cages or coops to drink and wash themselves, as many as three thousand pigeons and squabs going to the Ibaddan market.

The following description of the Illorin market, extracted from "Bowen's Central Africa," is truthful as far as it goes, and will give a general idea of markets in the great cities of Africa:

> The most attractive object next to the curious old town itself—and it is always old—is the market. . . . Here the women sit and chat all day, from early morn till nine

o'clock at night, to sell their various merchandise. Some of the sheds however, are occupied by barbers, who shave people's heads and faces; and by leather dressers, who make charms like Jewish phylacteries, and bridle reins, shoes, sandals, &c.; and by dozens and scores of men, who earn an honest living by dressing calabashes, and ornamenting them with various neat engravings.* . . . The principal market hour, and proper time to see all the wonders, is in the evening. . . . As the shades of evening deepen, if the weather allow the market to continue and there is no moon, every woman lights her little lamp, and presently the market presents, to the distant observer, the beautiful appearance of innumerable stars.

The commodities sold in market are too tedious to mention, even if all could be remembered. Besides home productions, there are frequently imported articles from the four quarters of the globe. Various kinds of meat, fowls, sheep, goats, dogs, rats, tortoises, eggs, fish, snails, yams, Indian corn, Guinea corn, sweet potatoes, sugar-cane, ground peas, onions, pepper, various vegetables, palm-nuts, oil, tree-butter, seeds, fruits, firewood, cotton in the seeds, spun cotton, domestic cloth, imported cloth, as calico, shirting, velvets, &c., gun-powder, guns, flints, knives, swords, paper, raw silk, Turkey-red thread, needles, ready-made clothing, as trowsers, caps, breeches shirts without sleeves, baskets, brooms, and no one knows what all.

This description was given by Mr. Bowen in his (in many respects) admirable work, published in 1857, after a missionary residence and tour of seven years, from 1850 to the time of writing, among the people of whom he wrote.

---

*Lagos is an exception to this, the market commencing early in the day, and closing at night.

Native Houses and Cities

The houses are built of unburnt clay which hardens in the sun, covered with a beautiful thatch-long, peculiar grass —exhibiting only the walls to the streets, the doors all opening inside of these walls, which are entered by a gate or large doorway; the streets generally irregular and narrow, but frequently agreeably relieved by wider ones, or large, open spaces or parks shaded with trees; all presenting a scene so romantic and antiquated in appearance, that you cannot resist the association with Babylon, Nineveh, Tyre, and Thebais. The buildings are heavy and substantial for their kind, many of which are very extensive. These towns and cities are all entrenched and walled; extending entirely around them; that of Abbeokuta with the new addition being twenty-seven miles, though the population is less by forty thousand than Ibaddan, which embraces about twenty-three miles.

Conjugal and Filial Affection. Activity of Children

Great affection exists between husband and wife, the women being mostly restricted to household work, trading, and gathering in the fields, and aiding in carrying, whilst the men principally do the digging, planting, chopping, and other hard work. The children are also passionately beloved by their parents, sometimes with too much indulgence. They are very active, and every day some of them of all sizes may be seen dashing along a road or over a plain at fearful speed on horseback. They are great vaulters and ankle-springers, and boys may frequently be seen to spring from the ground whirling twice— turning *two* summersets— before lighting on their feet.

Population of Monrovia and the State

It may not be out of place here to add, that the population of the capital of Liberia is certainly not above three thousand, though they claim for it five thousand. And what has been said of the lack and seeming paucity of public improvement may be much extenuated when it is considered that the entire population of settlers only number at present some 15,000 souls; the native population being 250,000, or 300,000, as now incorporated.

Canine and Feline

As the enquiry has been frequently made of me as to "whether there are really dogs and cats in Africa," and if so, "whether they are like other dogs and cats"; and since a very intelligent American clergyman said to me that he had read it somewhere as a fact in natural history, that dogs in Africa could not bark; I simply here inform the curious enquirer, that there are dogs and cats plentifully in Africa, which "look like other dogs and cats," and assure them that the dogs bark, eat, and *bite*, just like "other dogs."

Slavery

A word about slavery. It is simply preposterous to talk about slavery, as that term is understood, either being legalized or existing in this part of Africa. It is nonsense. The system is a patriarchal one, there being no actual difference, socially, between the slave (called by their protector *son* or *daughter*) and the children of the person with whom they live. Such persons intermarry, and frequently become the heads of state: indeed, generally so, as I do not remember at present a king or chief with whom I became acquainted whose entire members of the household, from the lowest domestic to the highest official, did not sustain this relation to him, they calling him *baba* or "father," and he treating them as children. And where this is not the case, it either arises from some innovation among them or those exceptional cases of despotism to be found in every country. Indeed, the term "slave" is unknown to them, only as it has been introduced among them by whites from Europe and America. So far from abject slavery, not even the old feudal system, as known to exist until comparatively recent in enlightened and Christian Europe, exists in this part of Africa.

Criminals and prisoners of war are *legally sold* into slavery among themselves, just as was the custom in almost every civilized country in the world till very lately, when nothing but advanced intelligence and progressive Christianity among the people put a stop to it. There is no place, however, but Illorin, a *bona fide* Mohammedan kingdom, where we ever witnessed any exhibition of these facts.

How Slaves Are Obtained

Slaves are abducted by marauding, kidnapping, depraved natives, who, like the organized bands and gangs of robbers in Europe and America, go through the country thieving and stealing helpless women and children, and men who may be overpowered by numbers. Whole villages in this way sometimes fall victims to these human monsters, especially when the strong young men are out in the fields at work, the old of both sexes in such cases being put to death, whilst the young are hurried through some private way down to the slave factories usually kept by Europeans (generally Portuguese and Spaniards) and Americans, on some secluded part of the coast. And in no instances are the parents and relatives known to sell their own children or people into slavery, except, indeed, in cases of base depravity, and except such miserable despots as the kings of Dahomi and Ashantee; neither are the heads of countries known to sell their own people; but like the marauding kidnapper, obtain them by war on others.

DISEASES OF THIS PART OF AFRICA, TREATMENT, HYGIENE, ALIMENT

IX

Diseases, Face of the Country, Spring Water

THE diseases in this part of Africa are still more simple than those of Liberia; and even the *native fever*, for known causes, generally is much less severe. In Liberia, and all that part of Africa, the entire country (except the cleared farms in the republic and the limited rice-fields of the natives) is a dense, heavy-wooded, *primitive* forest, rank with the growth and putrified vegetation of a thousand ages. But the entire Aku country, throughout the second plateau, presents a very different phase. Here, one is struck with the beautiful clear country which continually spreads out in every direction around; and (except the thickets or forests left as defences, ambuscades, and arbors of rest, rugged hilltops, and gullies), there is nothing but recent timber to be found growing on the lands. Timber in Africa is reproduced very speedily; hence may be found in some parts designedly left very heavy timber; but the greatest unbroken forest through which we passed at any one time, of this description, never exceeded, I think, ten miles. All the spring (shallow wells generally) and other living water, as perennial streams, is both good-tasted, and if the constant use of running stream water be a fair test, I would decide as wholesome. There are some good springs in Africa, and good water doubtless may every-where be obtained by digging suitable wells.

To Keep Water Cool. Kind of Vessels

Drinking water in the tropics should always be kept in large vessels of crockery ware (usually termed "stone" and "earthen ware") and smaller bottle or decanter-shaped jugs or vessels for table convenience. If earthen or crockery ware cannot be obtained for table use, by all means use glass bottles—the more globular, or ballon-shaped, the better.

Cool Water

To make and keep water cool in any crockery or glass vessel, wrap around it a cloth or any kind, but especially *woolen* —flannel or blanket being the best—which keep simply *wet*, and the water in the vessel, by *evaporation* from the *cloth*, can be made or kept almost ice cool.

To Keep the Cloth Wet. Apparatus

A most simple method by which the cloth may be kept wet, and evaporation thereby kept up, is to have a large vessel, with the water in for common use, so placed that a small vessel with water can be suspended over it in such a manner that a *drip* can be kept constantly on the cloth. The cloth being first saturated, it will readily be seen that a very small drip is required to keep up the dampness. The drip may be arranged, where convenient, with a small *faucet* so as to regulate the drop, or the more primitive method of a little *spiggot* or *sharpened stick* put into a hole made in the vessel, so regulated as to keep up a sufficient dripping to keep the cloth of sufficient dampness. Simple as this may appear to the reader, it is an important sanitary measure, besides adding greatly to the immediate comfort of the traveler or resident in those regions.

Atmosphere

The atmosphere in this region of the continent is much purer than that of Liberia and the region round about; and, although incorporated with odors, these are pleasant and seem familiar to the sense, and not obnoxious with the rich rank fragrance so sensibly experienced in that country. There is little, comparatively, of the decayed vegetation, which sends up malaria from the surface in Liberia; and the immense fields and plains of grass not under cultivation at the time, are burnt down during the dry season, thereby bringing to bear, though probably unawares to them, a sanitary process throughout that extensive country at least once every year.

Kinds of Disease

Intermittent fever, as described in section VI., page 280 on Liberia, though generally of a mild type, *diarrhoea, dysentery* (neither of which is difficult to subdue by a little rational treatment), *opthalmia*, and *umbilical hernia*, and sometimes, but not frequently, *inguinal hernia*, are the principal diseases. The opthalmia I suspected as originating from taint, probably having been primarily carried from the coast, as it was not so frequently met with as to warrant the idea of its being either a contagion or the effects of poisonous sands or winds, as supposed to exist. The hernia is caused by the absence of proper *umbilical attention* and *abdominal support* to the child after *parturition*. Umbilical hernia is fearfully common all through Africa, I having frequently seen persons, especially females, with the hernial tumor as large as their own head, and those of little children fully as large as the head of an infant a month old.

Guinea Worm

A singular disease affects some persons, though I have never seen this upon a native, and believe it to be peculiar to the region round about Liberia. The person whose case I examined had formerly resided in Liberia, where, doubtless, the disease commenced, but for the last three years previously had resided at Ijaye, in the capacity of cook, for the American Baptist Missionaries, Revs. A. D. Phillips and J. R. Stone and lady, and then resided at Abbeokuta. This is a peculiar ulceration of the leg, immediately above the anklebone, where they say it usually commences; the edges of the ulcer, and the cuticle quite up to the edge, and all the surrounding parts, having a healthy appearance, as though a portion of the flesh had been recently torn out, leaving the cavity as it then was. The most peculiar feature of this singular disease is a *white fiber*, which, coming out from the integuments of the muscles of the leg above, hangs suspended in the cavity (ulcer) the lower end loose, and somewhat inclined to coil (and when *straightened* out, resuming again the serpentine curves, of course from the *elasticity* with *motion*), is supposed to be a *worm*; hence its name—*Guinea worm*. The fibre seems in color and texture to be in a normal condition; indeed, there appear to be little or no pathological symptoms about the parts at all, except a slight appearance of *vermillion* inflammation over the surface of the ulcer, which is more apparent sometimes than others.

What Is Guinea Worm?

I have examined closely this fibre, and from its appearance, color, size, and texture, especially as it is sensibly felt high up in the leg near the tuberosity of the tibia, when pulled by the dangling end, my own impression is that the so-called "Guinea worm" is nothing more than the *external saphenus* or *communis tibiae* (nerve) exposed in a peculiar manner, probably by a disease, which, by a curious pathological process, absorbs away the muscular parts, leaving the bare nerve detached at its lower extremity, suspended loose in this unnatural space. I have never seen but this one case of Guinea worm, but had frequent opportunities of examining it; indeed, the patient consulted me concerning it, and by the advice and consent of the very clever native gentleman, Samuel Crowther, Esq., who received his professional education at the Royal College of Surgeons, Lincoln's Inn Fields, London, insisted on my taking the case, which I declined, partly for the want of time to do justice to the patient, and aside from courtesy and equity to the surgeon who had the case in hand, mainly because I *knew nothing about it*—the best reason of all. The patient was an American quadroon, black nearly in complexion, of one-fourth white blood, from North Carolina. This, of course was a black quadroon.

I should add, that the fiber at times entirely *disappears*

from the cavity (by *contraction*, of course), when again it is seen suspended as before. This is one reason why it is believed to be a *worm*, and supposed to *creep* up and down in the flesh.

Treatment of Diseases—Diarrhoea

The treatment of fever in this part of Africa should be the same as that in Liberia, given on page 280. The best remedy which I have found for diarrhoea is:

℞. Pulv. Rad. Rhei. ʒj.; Syr. Simp. ℥jv.; Spts. Terebinth. ʒj.; Tinct. Opii., gtt. x. M. ft.
Pulverized rhubarb, one drachm, (or one-eighth of an ounce); simple syrup, four ounces (or eight large table-spoonfuls); laudanum, ten drops; spirits of turpentine, one spoonful. Mix this well together to take.

Dysentery

For dysentery the recipe is:

℞. Pulv. Rad. Rhei. Pulv. C. Catech. a. a., ʒj.;
Syr. Simp. f. ℥jv.; Spts. Terebinth. Spis.
Aminon. Arroinat., a. a. f. ʒj.; Tinct. Opii. gtt.
x.M.ft.
Pulverized rhubarb and pulverized gum catechu, each, one-eighth of an ounce; simple syrup, eight large table-spoonfuls; spirits of turpentine and aromatic spirits of ammonia, of each one teaspoonful; laudanum, ten drops. Mix this well together to take. Of this take one teaspoonful (if very bad, a dessert spoonful) every three hours, or four

times a day (always beginning at least one hour before breakfast), till the symptoms cease.

Fever Antidote

During the presence of febrile symptoms, in the absence of all diarrhoea and dysenteric symptoms, even when the person is not complaining, an excellent simple antidote to be taken at discretion, not oftener than once every hour during the day, is:

℞. Syr. Simp., ℥ jv.; Spts. Ammon. Arromat. ℨ jss. M. ft.
Simple syrup, eight large tablespoonfuls; aromatic spirits of ammonia, one and a-half teaspoonfuls. Mix this well together. Take a teaspoonful of this preparation in a little cold water, or a glass of lemonade if preferred, and the condition of the bowels will admit, as often as thought advisable under the circumstances.

I have thus thought proper to simplify this treatment, that it may be in the reach of every person going to the tropics, as I am certain that there has been a great deficiency in the treatment and discovery of remedies in diseases of that continent especially. These prescriptions, as compounded, are entirely new, originating with the writer, who has only to add that he is in hopes that they prove as advantageous and successful in other hands as they have been in his.

Regimen

Persons laboring under fever should eat moderately of such food as best agrees with their appetite; but frequently, if required or desired, that the system may be well supported. When there is *diarrhoea* or *dysentery* present, there should be no solid food taken, but the patient or ailing person should be confined strictly to a thin milk porridge of fine Guinea-corn flour, which is always obtainable in Africa, crumbled crackers or soda biscuits, light (leavened) wheat bread if to be had, or well-done rice boiled to a pulp. The soda-biscuit as a porridge with milk rather aggravates the bowels of most persons; therefore, whenever it is found to have this effect, its use should be immediately abandoned. In many instances, where there is either diarrhoea or dysentery present, without other prominent symptoms, I have found the mere use of cooked milk (merely "scalded," as women usually term it—being heated to the boiling point without permitting it to boil), taken as food alone, to be the only remedy required.

Hygiene—Eating

The laws of health should be particularly observed in going to Africa. In respect to eating, there need be no material change of food, but each individual observing those nourishments which best agree with him or her. When there is little inclination to eat, eat but little; and when there is none, eat nothing. I am certain that a large percentage of the mortality which occurs may be attributed to too free and too frequent indulgence in eating, as was the case with the Lewis family of five at Clay-Ashland, in Liberia—all of whom died from that cause; as well as others that might be mentioned.

Coffee, Air Fruits—

So soon as you have taken your bath and put your morning wrapper, even before dressing, you may eat one or more sweet oranges, then take a cup of coffee, creamed and sweetened, or not, to your taste. Make your toilet, and walk out and take the cool air, always taking your umbrella or parasol, because no foreigner, until by a long residence more or less acclimated, can expose himself with impunity to a tropical sun. If preferred coffee should always be taken with cream or milk and sugar, because it is then less irritating to the stomach. One of the symptoms of native fever is said to be *nervous irritability of the stomach*; hence, all exciting causes to irritation of that part should be avoided as much as possible. Such fruits as best agree with each individual should be most indulged in; indeed, all others for the time should be dispensed with; and when it can be done without any apparent risk to the person, a little fruit of some kind might be taken every day by each new comer. Except oranges, taken as directed above, all fruits should be eaten *after*, and *not* before breakfast. The fruits of the country have been described in another place.

Drinks

Let your habits be strictly temperate, and for human nature's sake, abstain from the erroneous idea that some sort of malt or spirituous drink is necessary. This is not the case; and I am certain that much of the disease and dire mortality charged against Africa, as a "land of pestilence and death," should be charged against the Christian lands which produce and *send bad spirits* to destroy those who go to Africa. Whenever wine, brandy, whisky, gin, rum, or pure alcohol are required as a medical remedy, no one will object to its use; but, in all cases in which they are used as a beverage in Africa, I have no hesitation in pronouncing them deleterious to the system. The best British porter and ale may, in convalescence from fever, be used to advantage as a tonic, because of the bitter and farinoceous substances they contain—not otherwise is it beneficial to the system in Africa. Water, lemonade, effervescent drinks—a teaspoonful of super-carbonate of soda, to a glass of lemonade—all may be drunk in common, when thirsty, with pleasure to the drinker as well as profit. Pure ginger-beer is very beneficial.

Bathing

Bathing should be strictly observed by every person at least once every day. Each family should be provided with a large sponge, or one for each room if not for each person, and free application of water to the entire person, from head to foot, should be made every morning.

Early Rising—Breezes

Every person should rise early in Africa, as the air is then coolest, freshest, and purest; besides the effect upon the senses, the sight and song of the numerous birds to be seen and heard, produce a healthful influence upon the mental and physical system. The land and sea-breezes blow regularly and constantly from half-past three o'clock P.M. till half-past ten o'clock A.M., when there is a cessation of' about five hours till half-past three again.

Never Sultry

The evenings and mornings are always cool and pleasant, *never sultry* and oppressive with heat, as frequently in temperate climates during summer and autumn. This wise and beneficent arrangement of Divine Providence makes this country beautifully, in fact, delightfully pleasant; and I have no doubt but in a very few years, so soon as scientific black men, her own sons, who alone must be more interested in her development than any other take the matter in hand, and produce works upon the diseases, remedies, treatment, and sanitary measures of Africa, there will be no more contingency in going to Africa than any other known foreign country. I am certain, even now, that the native fever of Africa is not more trying upon the system, when properly treated, than the native fever of Canada, the Western and Southern States and Territories of the United States of America.

Dress, Avoid Getting Wet

Dress should be regulated according to the feeling, with sometimes more and sometimes less clothing. But I think it advisable that adults should wear flannel (thin) next to their person always when first going to Africa. It gradually absorbs the moisture, and retaining a proper degree of heat, thus prevents any sudden change of temperature from affecting the system. Avoid getting wet at first, and should this accidentally happen, take a thoroughly good bath, rub the skin dry, and put on dry clothes, and for two or three hours that day, keep out of the sun; but if at night, go to bed. But when it so happens that you are out from home and cannot change clothing, continue to exercise until the clothes dry on your person. It is the abstraction of heat from the system by evaporation of water from the clothing, which does the mischief in such cases. I have frequently been wet to saturation in Africa, and nothing ever occurred from it, by pursuing the course here laid down. Always sleep in clean clothes.

Sanitary Measures

I am sure I need inform no one, however ignorant, that all measures of cleanliness of person, places, and things about the residences, contribute largely to health in Africa, as in other countries.

Ventilation of Houses

All dwellings should be *freely ventilated* during the *night* as well as day, and it is a great mistake to suppose, as in Liberia (where every settler sleeps with every part of his house closely shut—doors, windows, and all) that it is deletereous to have the house ventilated during the evening, although they go out to night meetings, visit each other in the evening, and frequently sit on their porches and piazzas till a late hour in the night, conversing, without any injurious effects whatever. Dr. Roberts, and I think Dr. McGill and a few other gentlemen, informed me that their sleeping apartments were exceptions to the custom generally in Liberia. This stifling custom to save themselves does not prevail among the natives of Africa anywhere, nor among the foreigners anywhere in the Yoruba country, that I am aware of, and I am under the impression that it was the result of fear or precaution, not against the night air, but against the imaginary (and sometimes real) creeping things—as insects and reptiles—which might find their way into the houses at night.

Test of Night Air

While in Liberia, I have traversed rivers in an open boat at night, slept beyond the Kavalla Falls in open native houses, and at the residence of Rev. Alexander Crummel, Mount Vaughan, Cape Palmas, I slept every evening while there with both window and door as ventilators. The window was out and the door inside. In Abbeokuta, Ijaye, Oyo, and Ogbomoso, we slept every night with ventilated doors and windows, when we slept at all in a house. But in Illorin we always slept out of doors by preference, and only retired to repose in-doors (which were always open) when it was too cool to sleep out, as our bedding consisted only of a native mat on the ground, and a calico sheet spread over us. And I should here make acknowledgments to my young colleague, Mr. Campbell, for the use of his large Scotch shawl when I was unwell, and indeed almost during our entire travel—it being to me a great accommodation, a comfort and convenience which I did not possess.

Test of Exposure

I have started two and three hours before daybreak, laying on my bed in an open canoe, ascending the Ogun river, at different times during the six days' journey up to

Abbeokuta; Mr. Campbell and myself have frequently slept out in open courts and public market-places, without shed or piazza covering; and when journeying from Oyo to Ibaddan, for three successive evenings I lay in the midst of a wilderness or forest, on a single native mat without covering, the entire night; and many times during our travels we arose at midnight to commence our journey, and neither of us ever experienced any serious inconvenience from it.

Improved Window and Door Ventilation

That houses in Africa may be properly ventilated during the night without annoyance, or, what is equally as bad, if not worse, the continual fear and imagination of the approach of venomous insects, creeping things, and reptiles, the residents should adapt them to the place and circumstances, without that rigid imitation of European and American order of building. Every house should be well ventilated with windows on opposite sides of the rooms, when and wherever this is practicable, and the same may be said of doors. And where the room will not admit of opposite windows, or windows at least on two sides of a room, whether opposite or otherwise, a chimney or ventilating flue should be constructed on the opposite side to the window—which window should always be to the windward, so as to have a continual draught or current of fresh air. Persons, however, should always avoid sitting in a *draught*, though a free circulation of air should be allowed in each room of every house.

Instead of window-sashes with glass, as in common use, I would suggest that the windows have a sash of four, or but two (if preferred) panels, to each window (two upper and two lower, or one upper and one lower—or one lower and two upper, which would make a neat and handsome window), each panel or space for panes being neatly constructed with a sieve-work, such as is now used as screens during summer season in the lower part of parlor windows. To prevent too great oxydization or too rapid decay of so delicate a structure as the wire must be, it should be made of brass, copper, or some composition which would not readily corrode. Inside or outside doors of the same material, made to close and open like the Venetian jalousies now in use in civilized countries, would be found very convenient, and add much to the comfort and health of dwellings as a sanitary measure. The frames of the panels or sashes should be constructed of maple, cherry, walnut, or mahogany, according to the means of the builder and elegance of the building—as these articles seasoned are not only more neat and durable, but, from their solidity, are less liable to warp or shrink. This would afford such a beautiful and safe protection to every dwelling against the intrusion of all and every living thing, even the smallest insect—while a full and free circulation of fresh air would be allowed—that a residence in Africa would become attractive and desirable, instead of, as now (from imagination), objectionable.

Sanitary Effects of Ants—Termites, and Drivers

A word about ants in Africa—so much talked of, and so much dreaded—will legitimately be in place here, regarding them as a sanitary means, provided by Divine Providence. The *termites*, bug-a-bug or white double ant, shaped like two ovals somewhat flattened, joined together by a cylinder somewhat smaller in the middle, with a head at one end of one of the ovals, is an herbivorous insect, and much abused as the reputed destroyers of books, papers, and all linen or muslin clothing. They feed mainly on such vegetable matter as is most subject to decay—as soft wood, and many other such, when void of vitality—and there is living herbage upon which they feed, and thereby prove a blessing to a country with a superabundance of rank vegetable matter. It is often asserted that they destroy whole buildings, yet I have never seen a person who knew of such a disaster by them, although they may attack and do as much mischief in such cases at times as the wood-worms of America; and, in regard to clothing, though doubtless there have been instances of their attack upon and destruction of clothing, yet I will venture to assert that there is no one piece of clothing attacked and destroyed by these creatures, to ten thousand by the moths which get into the factories and houses in civilized countries, where woolen goods are kept. In all my travels in Africa, I never had anything attacked by the termite; but during my stay of seven months in Great Britain, I had a suit of woolen clothes completely eaten up by moths in Liverpool.

Drivers

Drivers, as every person already knows, are black ants, whose reputation is as bad for attacking living animals, and even human beings, as the termites' for attacking clothing. This creature, like its white cousin, is also an instrument in the hands of Providence as a sanitary means, and to the reverse of the other is carnivorous, feeding upon all flesh whether fresh or putrified. Like the white, for the purpose of destroying the superabundance of vegetable, certainly these black ants were designed by Providence to destroy the excess of animal life which in the nature of things would be brought forth, with little or no destruction without them; and although much is said about their attacking persons, I will venture the opinion that there is not one of these attacks a person to every ten thousand musquitoes in America, as it is only by chance, and *not by search after it*, that drivers attack persons.

How They Travel

They usually go in search of food in narrow rows, say from half an inch to a hand's breadth, as swiftly as a running stream of water, and may in their search enter a house in their course—if nothing attract them around it—when, in such cases, they spread over the floor, walls, and ceiling; and finding no insect or creeping thing to destroy, they gather again on the floor, and leave the premises in the regular order in which they entered. Should they encounter a person when on these excursions, though in bed, does he but lie still and not disturb them, the good-hearted negro insects will even pass over the person without harm or molestation; but, if disturbed, they will retaliate by a sting as readily as a bee when the hive is disturbed, though their sting, so far from being either dangerous or severe, is simply like the severe sting of a musquito. An aged missionary gentleman, of twenty-five years' experience, informed me that an entire myriad (this term is given to a multitude of drivers, as their number can never be less than ten thousand—and I am sure that I have seen as many millions together) passed over him one night in bed, without one stinging him. Indeed, both the black and white ants are quite harmless as to personal injury, and very beneficial in a sanitary point.

How to Drive Them Out of the Houses

There is much more in the imagination than the reality about these things; and one important fact I must not omit, that, however great the number of drivers, a simple *light set in the middle of the floor* will clear the room of them in ten minutes. In this case they do not form in column, but go out in hasty confusion, each effecting as quick retreat and safe escape for himself as possible, forming their line of march outside of the house, where they meet from all quarters of their points of escape.

How to Destroy Them

Chloride of sodium or common salt (fine), slightly damped, will entirely destroy the termites; and *acetum* or vinegar, or *acetic acid* either, will destroy or chase off the drivers. These means are simple, and within the reach of every person, but, aside from this, both classes or races of these creatures disappear before the approach of civilization. In a word, moths, mice, roaches, and musquitoes are much greater domestic annoyances, and certainly much more destructive in America and Europe than the bug-a-bug or driver is in Africa.

Their Pugnacious and Martial Character

I cannot endorse the statement from personal knowledge of the desperate hostility which the drivers manifest towards the termites, as given by Dr. Livingstone, who, calling them "black rascals," says "they stand deliberately and watch for the whites, which, on coming out of their holes, they instantly seize, putting them to death." Perhaps the whites were *kidnappers*, in which case they served the white *rascals* right. Though I have never seen an encounter, it is nevertheless true, that the blacks do subdue the whites whenever they meet. In fact, they go, as do no other creatures known to natural science, in immense incalculable numbers—and I do not think that I exaggerate if I say that I have more than once seen more than six hogsheads of them traveling together, had they been measured—and along the entire line of march, stationed on each side of the columns, there are warriors or soldiers to guard them, who stand sentry, closely packed side by side with their heads towards the column, which passes on as rapidly as a flowing stream of water. I have traced a column for more than a mile, whose greatest breadth was more than a yard, and the least not less than a foot. It is inconceivable the distance these creatures travel in a short time. Should anything disturb the lines, the soldiers sally out a few feet in pursuit of the cause, quickly returning to their post when meeting no foe. The guards are much larger than the common drivers, being about the length of a barley-corn, and armed with a pair of curved horns, like those of the large American black beetle, called "pinching bug." There are no bed-bugs here.

Cesspools

One important fact, never referred to by travellers as such, is that the health of large towns in Africa will certainly be improved by the erection of *cesspools*, whereas now they have none. With the exception of the residences of missionaries and other civilized people, there is no such thing in Africa. Every family, as in civilized countries, should have such conveniences. Our senses are great and good faculties—seeing, hearing, tasting, smelling, and feeling—God has so created them, and designed them for such purposes; therefore, they should neither be perverted nor marred when this can be avoided. Hence, we should beautify, when required and make pleasing to the sight; modify and make pleasant to the hearing; *cleanse* and *purify* to make *agreeable* to the smelling; improve and make good to the taste; and never violate the feelings whenever any or all of these are at our will or control.

Wild Beasts and Reptiles

A single remark about these. The wild beasts are driven back before the march of civilization, I having seen none, save one leopard; and but four serpents during my entire travels, one three and a half feet long (a water snake); one fourteen inches long; and another ten inches long; the two last being killed by natives—and a tame one around the neck of a charmer at Oyo. During the time I never saw a centipede, and but two tarantulas.

T o deny or overlook the fact, the all-important fact, that the missionary influence had done much good in Africa, would be simply to do injustice, a gross injustice to a good cause.

Protestant Missionaries

The advent of the Protestant Missionaries into Africa, has doubtless been effective of much good, though it may reasonably be expected that many have had their short comings. By Protestant, I mean all other Christian denominations than the Roman Catholic. I would not be regarded either a bigot or partialist so far as the rights of humanity are concerned, but facts are tenable in all cases, and whilst I readily admit that a Protestant monarch granted the first letters-patent to steal Africans from their homes to be enslaved by a Protestant people, and subsequently a *bona-fide* Protestant nation has been among the most cruel oppressors of the African race, my numerous friends among whom are many Roman Catholics—black as well as white—must bear the test of truth, as I shall apply it in the case of the Missionaries, as my object in visiting my father-land, was to enquire into and learn every fact, which should have a bearing on this, the grandest prospect for the regeneration of a people, that ever was presented in the history of the world.

Influence of Roman Catholic Religion in Favor of Slavery

In my entire travels in Africa, either alone or after meeting with Mr. Campbell at Abbeokuta, I have neither seen nor heard of any Roman Catholic Missionaries; but the most surprising and startling fact is, that every slave-trading point on the coast at present (which ports are mainly situated South and East) where the traffic is carried on, are either Roman Catholic trading-ports, or native agencies protected by Roman Catholics; as Canot, formerly at Grand Cape Mount, Pedro Blanco, and Domingo at Wydah in Dahomi. And still more, it is a remarkable and very suggestive reality that at all of those places where the Jesuits or Roman Catholic Missionaries once were stationed, the slave-trade is not only still carried on in its worst form as far as practicables, but slaves are held in Africa by these white foreigners at the old Portuguese settlements along the Southern and Eastern coasts, of Loango and Mozambique for instance; and although some three years have elapsed since the King of Portugal proclaimed, or pretended to proclaim "Liberty to all the people throughout his dominions," yet I will venture an opinion, that not one in every hundred of native Africans thus held in bondage on their own soil, are aware of any such "Proclamation." Dr. Livingstone tells us that he came across many ruins of Roman Catholic Missionary Stations in his travels—especially those in Loando de St. Paul, a city of some eighteen or twenty thousand of a population—all deserted, and the buildings appropriated to other uses, as store-houses, and the like. Does not this seem as though slavery were the legitimate successor of Roman Catholicism, or slave-traders and holders of the Roman Catholic religion and Missionaries? It certainly has that appearance to me; and a fact still more glaring is, that the only professing Christian government which in the light of the present period of human elevation and national reform, has attempted such a thing, is that of Roman Catholic Spain, (still persisting in holding Cuba for the wealth accruing from African Slaves stolen from their native land) which recently expelled every Protestant Missionary from the African Island of Fernando Po, that they might command it unmolested by Christian influence, as an export mart for the African Slave-Trade. To these facts I call the attention of the Christian world, that no one may murmur when the day of retribution in Africa comes—which come it must—and is fast hastening, when slave-traders must flee.

Influence of Protestant Religion against Slavery, and in Favor of Civilization

Wherever the Protestant Missionaries are found, or have been, there are visible evidences of a purer and higher civilization, by the high estimate set upon the Christian religion by the natives, the deference paid to the missionaries themselves, and the idea which generally obtains among them, that all missionaries are opposed to slavery, and the faith they have in the moral integrity of these militant ambassadors of the Living God. Wherever there are missionaries, there are schools both Sabbath and secular, and the arts and sciences, and manners and customs, more or less of civilized life, are imparted. I have not as yet visited a missionary station in any part of Africa, where there were not some, and frequently many natives, both adult and children, who could speak, read, and write English, as well as read their own language; as all of them, whether Episcopalian, Wesleyan, Baptist, or Presbyterian, in the Yoruba country, have Crowther's editions of religious and secular books in the schools and churches, and all have native agents, interpreters, teachers (assistants) and catechists or readers in the mission. These facts prove indisputably great progress; and I here take much pleasure in recording them in testimony of those faithful laborers in that distant vineyard of our heavenly Father in my fatherland. Both male and female missionaries, all seemed much devoted to their work, and anxiously desirous of doing more. Indeed, the very fact of there being as many native missionaries as there are now to be found holding responsible positions, as elders, deacons, preachers, and priests, among whom there are many finely educated, and several of them authors of works, not only in their own but the English language, as Revs. Crowther, King, Taylor, and Samuel Crowther, Esq., surgeon, all show that there is an advancement for these people beyond the point to which missionary duty can carry them.

Kindness of Missionaries and Personal Acknowledgments

I am indebted to the Missionaries generally, wherever met with, whether in Liberia or Central Africa, for their uniform kindness and hospitality, among whom may be named: Rev. J. M. Harden and excellent wife, (a refined highly educated native Ibo lady at Lagos), Revs. H. Townsend, C. H. Gollmer, J. King, E. Bickersteth and ladies in Abbeokuta; A.

D. Phillips, J. A. Stone and lady, Ijaye; T. A. Reid, and Mr. Mekin, Oyo; and Rev. D. Hinderer and lady; Ibaddan. I am indebted to the Baptist Missionaries for the use of their Mission House and furniture during our residence at Abbeokuta: Rev. John Roberts and lady, Miss Killpatrick, Reverend Bishop Burns and lady, Rev. Mr. Tyler, Rev. Mr. Gipson, Rev. Edward W. Blyden and others, Rev. Mr. Hoffman and lady, and Rev. Mr. Messenger and lady, all of Liberia, I am indebted for marks of personal kindness and attention when indisposed among them, and my kind friends, the Reverend Alexander Crumell and lady, whose guest I was during several weeks near the Cape, and who spared no pains to render my stay not only a comfortable, but a desirable one.

Hints to Those to Whom They Apply

I would suggest for the benefit of missionaries in general, and those to whom it applies in particular, that there are other measures and ways by which civilization may be imparted than preaching and praying—temporal as well as spiritual means. If all persons who settle among the natives would, as far as it is in their power and comes within their province induce, by making it a rule of their house or family, every native servant to sit on a stool or chair; eat at a table instead of on the ground; eat with a knife and fork (or *begin* with a spoon) instead of with their fingers; eat in the house instead of going out in the yard, garden, or somewhere else under a tree or shed; and sleep on a bed, instead of on a bare mat on the ground; and have them to wear some sort of a garment to cover the entire person above the knees, should it be but a single shirt or chemise, instead of a loose native cloth thrown around them, to be dropped at pleasure, at any moment exposing the entire upper part of the person—or as in Liberia, where that part of the person is entirely uncovered—I am certain that it would go far toward impressing them with some of the habits of civilized life, as being adapted to them as well as the "white man," whom they so faithfully serve with a will. I know that some may say, this is difficult to do. It certainly could not have been with those who never tried it. Let each henceforth resolve for himself like the son of Nun, "As for me and my house, we will serve the Lord."

Changing Names

I would also suggest that I cannot see the utility of the custom on the part of Missionaries in *changing* the names of native children, and even adults, so soon as they go into their families to live, as though their own were not good enough for them. These native names are generally much more significant, and euphonious than the Saxon, Gaelic, or Celtic. Thus, Adenigi means, "Crowns have their shadow." This was the name of a servant boy of ours, whose father was a native cotton trader, it is to be hoped that this custom among Missionaries and other Christian settlers, of changing the names of the natives, will be stopped, thereby relieving them of the impression, that to embrace the Christian faith, implies a loss of name, and so far loss of identity.

XI | WHAT AFRICA NOW REQUIRES

What Missionary Labor Has Done

F ROM the foregoing, it is very evident that missionary duty has reached its *ultimatum*. By this, I mean that the native has received all that the missionary was sent to teach, and is now really ready for more than he can or may receive. He sees and knows that the white man, who first carried him the Gospel, which he has learned to a great extent to believe a reality, is of an entirely different race to himself; and has learned to look upon everything which he has, knows and does, which has not yet been imparted to him (especially when he is told by the missionaries, which frequently must be the case, to relieve themselves of the endless teasing enquiries which persons in their position are subject to concerning all and every temporal and secular matter, law, government, commerce, military, and other matters foreign to the teachings of the gospel; that these things he is not sent to teach, but simply the gospel) as peculiarly adapted and belonging to the white man. Of course, there are exceptions to this. Hence, having reached what he conceives to be the *maximum* of the black man's or African's attainments, there must be a re-action in some direction, and if not progressive it will be retrogressive.

How It Was Done

The missionary has informed him that the white man's country is great. He builds and resides in great houses; lives in great towns and cities, with great churches and palaver-houses (public and legislative halls); rides in great carriages; manufactures great and beautiful things; has great ships, which go to sea, to all parts of the world, instead of little canoes such as he has paddling up and down the rivers and on the coast; that the wisdom, power, strength, courage, and wealth of the white man and his country are as much greater than him and his, as the big ships are larger and stronger than the little frail canoes; all of which he is made sensible of, either by the exhibition of pictures or the reality.

The Result, If Not Timely Aided by Legitimate Means

He at once comes to a stand. "Of what use is the white man's religion and 'book knowledge' to me, since it does not give me the knowledge and wisdom nor the wealth and power of the white man, as all these things belong only to him? "Our young men and women learn their book, and talk on paper (write), and talk to God like white man (worship), but God no hear 'em like He hear white man! Dis religion no use to black man." And so the African *reasonably* reasons when he sees that despite his having yielded up old-established customs, the laws of his fathers, and almost his entire social authority, and the rule of his household to the care and guardianship of the missionary, for the sake of acquiring his knowledge and power—when, after having learned all that his children can, he is doomed to see them sink right back into their old habits, the country continue in the same condition, without the beautiful improvements of the white man—and if a change take place at all, he is doomed to witness what he never expected to see and dies regretting—himself and people entangled in the meshes of the government of a people foreign in kith, kin, and sympathy, when he and his are entirely shoved aside and compelled to take subordinate and inferior positions, if not, indeed, reduced to menialism and bondage. I am justified in asserting that this state of things has brought missionary efforts to their *maximum* and native progress to a pause.

Missionary Aid, Christianity and Law or Government Must Harmonize, to Be Effective of Good

Religion has done its work, and now requires temporal and secular aid to give it another impulse. The improved arts of civilized life must now be brought to bear, and go hand in hand in aid of the missionary efforts which are purely religious in character and teaching. I would not have the standard of religion lowered a single stratum of the common breeze of heaven. No, let it rather be raised, if, indeed, higher it can be. Christianity certainly is the most advanced civilization that man ever attained to, and wherever propagated in its purity, to be effective, law and government must be brought in harmony with it—otherwise it becomes corrupted, and a corresponding degeneracy ensues, placing its votaries even in a worse condition than the primitive. This was exemplified by the Author of our faith, who, so soon as he began to teach, commenced by admonishing the people to a modification of their laws—or rather himself to condemn them. But it is very evident that the social must keep pace with the religious, and the political with the social relations of society, to carry out the great measures of the higher civilization.

Like Seeks Like

Of what avail, then, is advanced intelligence to the African without improved social relations—acquirements and refinement without an opportunity of a practical application of them—society in which they are appreciated? It requires not the most astute reformer and political philosopher to see.

Natives Desire Higher Social Relations

The native sees at once that all the higher social relations are the legitimate result and requirements of a higher intelligence, and naturally enough expects, that when he has attained it, to enjoy the same privileges and blessings. But how sadly mistaken—what dire disappointment!

Native Doubts Respecting the Eventual Good Effects of Missionary Labor

The habits, manners, and customs of his people, and the social relations all around him are the same; improvements of towns, cities, roads, and methods of travel are the same; implements of husbandry and industry are the same; the methods of conveyance and price of produce (with comparative trifling variation) are the same. All seem dark and gloomy for the future, and he has his doubts and fears as to whether or not he has committed a fatal error in leaving his native social relations for those of foreigners whom he cannot hope to emulate, and who, he thinks, will not assimilate themselves to him.

The Proper Element as Progressive Missionary Agencies

It is clear, then, that essential to the success of civilization, is the establishment of all those social relations and organizations, without which enlightened communities cannot exist. To be successful, these must be carried out by proper agencies, and these agencies must be a *new element* introduced into their midst, possessing all the attainments, socially and politically, morally and religiously, adequate to so important an end. This element must be *homogenous* in all the *natural* characteristics, claims, sentiments, and sympathies the *descendants of Africa* being the only element that can effect it. To this end, then, a part of the most enlightened of that race in America design to carry out these most desirable measures by the establishment of social and industrial settlements among them, in order at once to introduce, in an effective manner, all the well-regulated pursuits of civilized life.

Precaution against Error in the First Steps

That no mis-step be taken and fatal error committed at the commencement, we have determined that the persons to compose this new element to be introduced into Africa, shall be well and most carefully selected in regard to moral integrity, intelligence, acquired attainments, fitness, adaptation, and as far as practicable, religious sentiments and professions. We are serious in this; and so far as we are concerned as an individual, it shall be restricted to the letter, and we will most strenuously oppose and set our face against any attempt from any quarter to infringe upon this arrangement and design. Africa is our fatherland and we its legitimate descendants, and we will never agree nor consent to see this the first voluntary step that has ever been taken for her regeneration by her own descendants—blasted by a disinterested or renegade set, whose only object might be in the one case to get rid of a portion of the colored population, and in the other, make money, though it be done upon the destruction of every hope entertained and measure introduced for the accomplishment of this great and prospectively glorious undertaking. We cannot and will not permit or agree that the result of years of labor and anxiety shall be blasted at one reckless blow, by those who have never spent a day in the cause of our race, or know nothing about our wants and requirements. The descendants of Africa in North America will doubtless, by the census of 1860, reach five millions; those of Africa may number two hundred millions. I have outgrown, long since, the boundaries of North America, and with them have also outgrown the boundaries of their claims. I, therefore, cannot consent to sacrifice the prospects of two hundred millions, that a fraction of five millions may be benefitted, especially since the measures adopted for the many must necessarily benefit the few.

National Character Essential to the Successful Regeneration of Africa

Africa, to become regenerated, must have a national character, and her position among the existing nations of the earth will depend mainly upon the high standard she may gain compared with them in all her relations, morally, religiously, socially, politically, and commercially.

I have determined to leave to my children the inheritance of a country, the possession of territorial domain, the blessings of a national education, and the indisputable right of self-government; that they may not succeed to the servility and degradation bequeathed to us by our fathers. If we have not been born to fortunes, we should impart the seeds which shall germinate and give birth to fortunes for them.

TO DIRECT
LEGITIMATE
COMMERCE

First Steps in Political Economy

A s the first great national step in political economy, the selection and security of a location to direct and command commerce legitimately carried on, as an export and import metropolis, is essentially necessary. The facilities for a metropolis should be adequate—a rich, fertile, and productive country surrounding it, with some great staple (which the world requires as a commodity) of exportation. A convenient harbor as an outlet and inlet, and natural facilities for improvement, are among the necessary requirements for such a location.

The Basis of a Great Nation—
National Wealth

The basis of great nationality depends upon three elementary principles: first, territory; second, population; third, a great staple production either natural or artificial, or both, as a permanent source of wealth; and Africa comprises these to an almost unlimited extent. The continent is five thousand miles from Cape Bon (north) to the Cape of Good Hope (south), and four thousand at its greatest breadth, from Cape

Guardifui (east) to Cape de Verde (west), with an average breadth of two thousand five hundred miles, any three thousand of which within the tropics north and south, including the entire longitude, will produce the staple cotton, also sugar cane, coffee, rice, and all the tropical staples, with two hundred millions of *natives* as an industrial element to work this immense domain. The world is challenged to produce the semblance of a parallel to this. It has no rival in fact.

Advantageous Location

Lagos, at the mouth of the Ogun river in the Bight of Benin, Gulf of Guinea, 6 deg. 31 min. west coast of Africa, 120 miles north-west of the Nun (one of the mouths of the great river Niger) is the place of our location. This was once the greatest slave-trading post on the west coast of Africa, and in possession of the Portuguese—the slavers entering Ako Bay, at the mouth of the Ogun river, lying quite inland, covered behind the island till a favorable opportunity ensued to escape with their cargoes of human beings for America. Wydah, the great slave-port of Dahomi, is but 70 or 80 miles west of Lagos. This city is most favorably located at the mouth of a river which during eight months in the year is a great thoroughfare for native produce, which is now brought down and carried up by native canoes and boats, and quite navigable up to Aro the port of Abbeokuta, a distance of eighty or a hundred miles, for light-draught steamers, such as at no distant day we shall have there. Ako Bay is an arm of the gulf, extending quite inland for three and a half miles, where it spreads out into a great sea, extending north ten to fifteen miles, taking a curve east and south, passing on in a narrow strip for two or three hundred miles, till it joins the Niger at the mouth of the Nun. It is the real harbor of Lagos, and navigable for light-draught vessels, as the Baltimore clippers and all other such slavers, formerly put into it; and Her Majesty's war-steamer Medusa has been in, and H. M.'s cruiser Brun lies continually in the bay opposite the Consulate.

Metropolis

This is the great outlet of the rich valley of the Niger by land, and the only point of the ocean upon which the intelligent and advanced Yorubas are settled. The commerce of this part is very great, being now estimated at ten million pounds sterling. Besides all the rich products, as enumerated in another section, palm oil★ and ivory are among the great staple products of this rich country. But as every nation, to be potent must have some great source of wealth—which if not natural must be artificial—so Africa has that without which the workshops of Great Britain would become deserted, and the general commerce of the world materially reduced; and Lagos must not only become the outlet and point at which all this commodity must centre, but the great metropolis of this quarter of the world.

Trade of Lagos

The trade of this port now amounts to more than two millions of pounds sterling, or ten millions of dollars, there having been at times as many as sixty vessels in the roadstead.

★Nine-tenths of all the Palm Oil of commerce goes from this point.

The merchants and business men of Lagos are principally native black gentlemen, there being but ten white houses in the place—English, German, French, Portuguese, and Sardinian—and all of the clerks are native blacks.

Harbor Improvements

Buoys in the roadstead, lighthouses (two) and wharf improvements at the city in the bay, with steam-tugs or tenders to tow vessels over the Ogun bar-mouth or inlet, are all that we require to make Lagos a desirable seaport, with one of the safest harbors in the world for light-draught vessels.

The fish in these waters are very fine, and Ako is one of the finest natural oyster bays in the world. The shell-fish are generally of good site, frequently large, and finely flavored.

Religious and Philanthropic means

As a religious means, such a position must most largely contribute, by not only giving security to the Missionary cause, but by the actual infusion of a religious social element permanently among the natives of the country; and as a philanthropic, by a permanent check to the slave-trade, and also by its reflex influence on American slavery—not only thus far cutting off the supply, but, also by superseding slavery in the growth and supply of those articles which comprise its great staple and source of wealth—thereby tendering slave labor *unprofitable and worthless*, as the succeeding section will show.

Stopping the Slave Trade

As to the possibility of putting a stop to the slave-trade, I have only to say, that we do not leave America and go to Africa to be passive spectators of such a policy as traffic in the flesh and blood of our kindred, nor any other species of the human race—more we might say—that we will not live there and permit it. "*Self-preservation* is the first law of nature," and we go to Africa to be *self-sustaining*; otherwise we have no business there, or anywhere else, in my opinion. We will bide our time; *but the Slave-trade shall not continue!*

Means of Doing It

Another important point of attention: that is, the slave-trade ceases in Africa, wherever enlightened Christian civilization gains an influence. And as to the strength and power necessary, we have only to add, that Liberia, with a coast frontier of seven hundred miles, and a sparse population, which at the present only numbers fifteen thousand settlers, has been effective in putting a stop to that infamous traffic along her entire coast. And I here record with pleasure, and state what I know to be the fact, and but simple justice to as noble-hearted antagonists to slavery as live, that the Liberians are uncompromising in their opposition to oppression and the enslavement of their race, or any other part of the human family. I speak of them as a nation or people and ignore entirely their Iscariots, if any there be. What they have accomplished with less means, we, by the help of Providence, may reasonably expect to effect with more—what they did with little, we may do with much. And I speak with confidence when I assert, that if we in this new position but do and act as we are fondly looked to and expected—as I most fondly hope and pray God that, by a prudent, discretionate and well-directed course, dependant upon Him, we may, nay, I am certain we will do—I am sure that there is nothing that may be required to aid in the prosecution and accomplishment of this important and long-desired end, that may not be obtained from the greatest and most potent Christian people and nation that ever graced the world. There is no aid that might be wanted, which may not be obtained through a responsible, just, and equitable negotiation.

Subsidizing the King of Dahomi

There is some talk by Christians and philanthropists in Great Britain of subsidizing the King of Dahomi. I hope for the sake of humanity, our race, and the cause of progressive civilization, this most injurious measure of compensation for wrong, never will be resorted to nor attempted.

To make such an offering just at a time when we are about to establish a policy of self-regeneration in Africa, which may, by example and precept, effectually check forever the nefarious system, and reform the character of these people, would be to offer inducements to that monster to continue, and a license to other petty chiefs to commence the traffic in human beings, to get a reward of subsidy.

Natural Elements to Produce Cotton

COTTON grows profusely in all this part of Africa, and is not only produced naturally, but extensively cultivated throughout the Yoruba country. The soil, climate, and the people are the three natural elements combined to produce this indispensible commodity, and with these three natural agencies, no other part of the world can compete.

Africans the Only Reliable Producers

In India there is a difficulty and great expense and outlay of capital required to obtain it. In Australia it is an experiment; and though it may eventually be obtained, it must also involve an immense outlay of capital, and a long time before an adequate supply can be had, as it must be admitted, however reluctantly by those desirous it should be otherwise, that the African, as has been justly said by a Manchester merchant, has in all ages, in all parts of the world, been sought to raise cotton wherever it has been produced.

Serious Contingencies and Uncertainty in American Cotton Supply

In America there are several serious contingencies which must always render a supply of cotton from that quarter problematical and doubtful, and always expensive and subject to sudden, unexpected and unjust advances in prices. In the first place, the land is purchased at large prices; secondly, the people to work it; thirdly, the expense of supporting the people, with the contingencies of sickness and death; fourthly, the uncertainty of climate and contingencies of frost, and a backward season and consequent late or unmatured crop; fifthly, insubordination on the part of the slaves, which is not improbable at any time; sixthly, suspension of friendly relations between the United States and Great Britain; and lastly, a rupture between the American States themselves, which I think no one will be disposed now to consider impossible. All, or any of these circumstances combined, render it impossible for America to compete with Africa in the growth and sale of cotton, for the following reasons:

Superior Advantages of Africa over All Other Countries in the Production of Cotton

Firstly, landed tenure in Africa is free, the occupant selecting as much as he can cultivate, holding it so long as he uses it, but cannot convey it to another; secondly, the people all being free, can be hired at a price less than the *interest* of the capital invested in land and people to work it—they finding their own food, which is the custom of the country; thirdly, there are no contingencies of frost or irregular weather to mar or blight the crop; and fourthly, we have two regular crops a year, or rather one continuous crop, as while the trees are full of pods of ripe cotton, they are at the same time blooming with fresh flowers. And African cotton is planted only every seven years, whilst the American is replanted every season. Lastly, the average product per acre on the best Mississippi and Louisiana cotton plantations in America, is three hundred and fifty pounds; the average per acre in Africa, a hundred per cent more, or seven hundred pounds. As the African soil produces two crops a year to one in America, then we in Africa produce fourteen hundred pounds to three hundred and fifty in America; the cost of labor a hand being one dollar or four shillings a day to produce it; whilst in Africa at present it is nine hundred per cent less, being only ten cents or five pence a day for adult labor. At this price the native lives better on the abundance of produce in the country, and has more money left at the end of a week than the European or free American laborer at one dollar a day.

Cotton, as before stated, is the great commodity of the world, entering intimately into, being incorporated with almost every kind of fabric of wearing apparel. All kinds of woollen goods—cloths, flannels, alpacas, merinoes, and even silks, linen, nankin, ginghams, calicoes, muslins, cordages, ship-sails, carpeting, hats, hose, gloves, threads, waddings, paddings, tickings, every description of book and newspaper, writing paper, candle wicks, and what not, all depend upon the article cotton.

Importance of the African Race in the Social and Political Relations of the World

By this it will be seen and admitted that the African occupies a much more important place in the social and political element of the world than that which has heretofore been assigned him—holding the balance of commercial power, the source of the wealth of nations in his hands. This is indisputably true—undeniable, that cotton cannot be produced without negro labor and skill in raising it.

The African Race Sustains Great Britain

Great Britain alone has directly engaged in the manufacture of pure fabrics from the raw material, five millions of persons; two-thirds more of the population depend upon this commodity indirectly for a livelihood. The population (I include in this calculation Ireland) being estimated at 30,000,000, we have then 25,000,000 of people, or five-sixths of the population of this great nation, depending upon the article cotton alone for subsistence, and the black man is the producer of the raw material, and the source from whence it comes. What an important fact to impart to the heretofore despised and underrated negro face, to say nothing of all the other great nations of Europe, as France, for instance, with her extensive manufactures of muslin delaines—which simply mean *cotton and wool*—more or less engaged in the manufacture and consumption of cotton.

The Negro Race Sustains the Whites— Able to Sustain Themselves

If the negro race—as slaves—can produce cotton as an *exotic* in foreign climes to enrich white men who oppress them, they can, they must, they will, they shall, produce it as an *indigene* in their own-loved native Africa to enrich themselves, and regenerate their race; if a faithful reliance upon the beneficence and promise of God, and an humble submission to his will, as the feeble instruments in his hands through which the work is commenced, shall be available to this end.

Home Trade

The Liberians must as a policy as much as possible patronise home manufactured, and home produced articles. Instead of using foreign, they should prefer their own sugar, molasses, and coffee, which is equal to that produced in any other country, and if not, it is the only way to encourage the farmers and manufacturers to improve them. The coffee of Liberia, is equal to any in the world, and I have drunk some of the native article, superior in strength and flavor to Java or Mocca, and I rather solicit competition in judgment of the article of coffee. And singular as it may appear, they are even supplied from abroad with spices and condiments, although their own country as also all Africa, is prolific in the production of all other articles, as allspice, ginger, pepper black and red, mustard and everything else.

Coast Trade

They must also turn their attention to supplying the Coast settlements with sugar and molasses, and everything else of their own production which may be in demand. Lagos and the Missionary stations in the interior, now consume much of these articles, the greater part of which—sugar and molasses—are imported from England and America. This trade they might secure in a short time without successful competition, because many of the Liberia merchants now own vessels, and the firm of Johnson, Turpin and Dunbar, own a fine little coasting steamer, and soon they will be able to undersell the foreigners; whilst at present their trade of these articles in America is a mere *favor* through the benevolence of some good hearted gentlemen, personal *friends* of theirs, who receive and dispose of them—sugar and molasses—at a price much above the market value, to encourage them. This can only last while these friends continue, when it must then cease. To succeed as a state or nation, we must become self-reliant, and thereby able to create our own ways and means; and a trade created *in* Africa *by* civilized Africans, would be a national rock of "everlasting ages."

Domestic Trade, Corn Meal, Guinea Corn and Yam Flour

The domestic trade among the natives in the interior of our part of Africa—Yoruba—is very great. Corn meal, Guinea corn flour very fine, and a fine flour made of yams is plentiful in every market, and cooked food can always be had in great abundance from the women at refreshment stands kept in every town and along the highway every few miles when traveling.

Candy

Molasses candy or "taffy," is carried about and sold by young girls, made from the syrup of sugar cane, which does not differ in appearance and flavor from that of civilized countries.

Soap

Hard and soft soap are for sale in every market for domestic uses, made from lye by percolation or dripping of water through ashes in large earthen vessels or "hoppers."

Coloring and Dying. Making Indigo

Coloring and dying is carried on very generally, every woman seeming to understand it as almost a domestic necessity; also the manufacturing of indigo, the favorite and most common color of the country. Red comes next to this which is mostly obtained of camwood, another domestic employment of the women. Yellow is the next favorite color. Hence, blue, red, and yellow may be designated as the colors of Yoruba or Central Africa.

Weaving and Cloth Manufacturing; Leather

The manufactory of cotton cloth is carried on quite extensively among them; and in a ride of an hour through the city of Illorin we counted one hundred and fifty-seven looms in operation in several different establishments. Beautiful and excellent leather is also manufactured, from which is made sandals, shoes, boots, bridles, saddles, harness-caparisons for horses, and other ornaments and uses. They all wear clothes of their own manufacture. The inhabitants of Abbeokuta are called Egbas, and those of all the other parts of Yoruba are called Yorubas—all speaking the Egba language.

A Fixed Policy for the Blacks, as a Fundamental Necessity

Our policy must be—and I hazard nothing in promulging it; nay, without this design and feeling, there would be a great deficiency of self-respect, pride of race, and love of country, and we might never expect to challenge the respect of nations—*Africa for the African race and black men to rule them*. By black men I mean, men of African descent who claim an identity with the race.

Internal Medium of Communication. Navigable Rivers

So contrary to old geographical notions, Africa abounds with handsome navigable rivers, which during six or eight months in the year, would carry steamers suitably built. Of such are the Gallinos, St. Paul, Junk, and Kavalla of Liberia;

the Ogun, Ossa, the great Niger and others of and contiguous to Yoruba; the Gambia, Senegambia, Orange, Zambisi and others of other parts. The Kavalla is a beautiful stream which for one hundred miles is scarcely inferior to the Hudson of New York, in any particular; and all of them equal the rivers of the Southern States of America generally which pour out by steamers the rich wealth of the planting States into the Mississippi. With such prospects as these; with such a people as the Yorubas and other of the best type, as a constituent industrial, social, and political element upon which to establish a national edifice, what is there to prevent success? Nothing in the world.

Native Government

The Governments in this part are generally Patriarchial, the Kings being elective from ancient Royal families by the Council of Elders, which consists of men chosen for life by the people, for their age, wisdom, experience, and service among them. They are a deliberative body, and all cases of great importance; of state, life and death, must be brought before them. The King as well as either of themselves, is subject to trial and punishment for misdemeanor in office, before the Council of Elders.

Lagos is the place of the family residence of that excellent gentleman, Aji, or the Rev. Samuel Crowther, the native Missionary; and also his son-in-law Rev. T. B. Macaulay, who has an excellent school, assisted by his wife an educated native lady.

"Princes shall come out of Egypt; Ethiopia shall soon stretch out her hands unto God."—Ps. lxviii. 31. With the fullest reliance upon this blessed promise, I humbly go forward in—I may repeat—the grandest prospect for the regeneration of a people that ever was presented in the history of the world. The disease has long since been known; we have found and shall apply the remedy. I am indebted to Rev. H. H. Garnet, an eminent black clergyman and scholar, for the construction, that "soon," in the Scriptural passage quoted, "has reference to the period ensuing *from the time of beginning*." With faith in the promise, and hope from this version, surely there is nothing to doubt or fear.

SUCCESS IN GREAT BRITAIN

Departure from Africa and Arrival in England

MR. Campbell and myself left Lagos on the 10th of April, per the British Royal Mail steam-ship Athenian, commander Lowrie, arriving in Liverpool May 12th, and in London on the 16th, having spent four days in the former place.

First Meeting

On Thursday, the 17th, by a note of invitation, we met a number of noblemen and gentlemen, interested in the progress of African Regeneration, in the parlour of Dr. Hodgkin, F. R.G.S., among whom were the Lord Alfred S. Churchill, Chairman; Right Hon. Lord Calthorpe; Hon. Mr. Ashley, brother of the Earl of Shaftesbury; Colonel Walker; Charles Buxton, Esq., M.P.; Rev. J. Baldwin Brown, A.B.; Rev. Samuel Minton, M.A.; Dr. Hodgkin, and others. By request of the noble chairman, I made a statement of our Mission to Africa, imparting to the first of their knowledge, our true position as independent of all other societies and organizations then in existence. Mr. Campbell also made some remarks.

Origin of the African Aid Society

Many subsequent meetings were held in various places, private and public, several of which were presided over by the Lord Alfred S. Churchill and Rt. Hon. Lord Calthorpe, at which I and Mr. Campbell both spoke; when in June an invitation was received by each of us from the "Committee of the National Club," to attend a "Company," on "Wednesday evening, June 27th, 1860, when information will be given on the Condition and Prospects of the African Race." The invitation (being the same as sent to all other persons) went on to state that, "Among others, Dr. Delany, of Canada West, and R. Campbell Esq., of Philadelphia, gentlemen of color, lately returned from an exploring tour in Central Africa, will take part in the proceedings."

This was the first great effective move in aid of our cause, though all other previous meetings were preliminary to it. At this, as at previous meetings, a full and thorough statement was made of our mission, several gentlemen taking part in the discussion.

Subsequently the following note was received—Mr. Campbell receiving a similar one—with the accompanying circular, referred to as the "enclosed paper":—

African Aid Society, 7, Adams Street, Strand, W. C.,

July 14th, 1860

DEAR SIR—The Provisional Committee of the above-named Society will feel obliged if you will kindly attend a meeting to be held at the Caledonian Hotel, Robert Street, Adelphi Terrace, on Thursday next, July 19th, to consider the enclosed paper, and to decide on a further course of action. Lord Alfred Churchill, M.P., will take the chair at half-past two o'clock.

I am, dear Sir, yours faithfully,

Dr. Delany.   WILLIAM CARDWELL, Hon. Sec.

At a meeting held at 7, Adams Street, on July 6th, 1860 (arising out of the proceedings of a *soiree*, which took place at the National Club, on the 27th of the previous month, when the subject of the "Condition and Prospects of the African Race" was discussed) present, Lord Alfred Churchill, M.P. in the chair; Lord Calthorpe; Sir C. E. Eardley, Bart; Joseph Ferguson, Esq., late M.P. for Carlisle; Rev. Mesac Thomas, Secretary of the Colonial Church and School Society; Rev. J. Davis; Rev. Samuel Minton, Minister of Percy Chapel; J. Lyons Macleod, Esq., late H. B. M.'s Consul at Mozambique; Rev. J. Baldwin Brown, Claylands Chapel; and Rev. W. Cardall, the following resolutions were unanimously passed:—

> I. That it is desirable to form a Society, to be designated the African Aid Society.' II. That the noblemen now present be a Provisional Committee of such Society, with power to add to their number; and that Lord Alfred Churchill, M.P., be requested to be Chairman. III. That Sir C. E. Eardley, Bart., J. Lyons Macleod, Esq., the Rev. S. Minton, and the Rev. J. Baldwin Brown, be a Sub-Committee to prepare a draft statement of the proposed objects of the Society, and rules for its government.

At a subsequent meeting of the Committee, on a report of the Sub-Committee, the statement of objects and rules was adopted, which is given above.

What Black Men Want

The contents of this paper had been fully and fairly discussed at a previous meeting to which myself and colleague were honored with an invitation, when I then and there, fully, openly, and candidly stated to the noblemen and gentlemen present what was desired and what we did not; that we desired to be dealt with as men, and not children. That we did not desire gratuities as such in the apportioning of their benevolence—nothing eleemosynary but means *loaned* to our people upon their *personal obligations, to be paid in produce or otherwise.* That we did not approve of *restriction* as to *where* such persons went (so that it was to some country where the population was mainly colored, as that was our policy) letting each choose and decide *for himself,* that which was *best for him.*

Primary Objects of the African Aid Society

To these sentiments the noblemen and gentlemen all cordially and heartily agreed, establishing their society, as we understand it, expressly to aid the *voluntary* emigration of colored people from America in general, and our movement as originated by colored people in particular. Indeed I here now say, as I did then and there, that I would give nothing for it, were it not a self-reliant project originating with ourselves. The following completes the doings of the gentlemen in London. I should have remarked, that at many of these meetings, especially that at White Hall on the 27th day of June, and that of the 19th July, and the preliminary ones above referred to, the respected president of our Council, Wm. Howard Day, Esq., M.A., was present. For some of the important preliminary meetings, he and Rev. D'Arcy Irvine kindly made arrangements.

AFRICAN AID SOCIETY

7,★ ADAMS STREET, STRAND, W. C., LONDON

PRESIDENT

VICE-PRESIDENTS

•The Right Hon. Lord
 Calthorpe.

The Rt. Rev, the Bishop
of Sierra Leone.

COUNCIL

•The Lord Alfred Churchill,
 M.P., F.R.G.S., Chairman
 of the Executive Com-
 mittee

Ashley, Hon. Wm., St.
James's Palace.

Bagnall, Thomas, Esq., J.P.,
Great Barr, near Birm-
ingham

Brown, Rev. J. Baldwin,
B.A., 150, Albany Street.

Dunlop, Hy., Esq., Craigton,
Glasgow.

•Eardley, Sir C. E., Bart.,
 F.R.G.S. Bedwell Park.

Ferguson, Joseph, Esq., late
P.M. for Carlisle.

•Seymour, H. Danby, Esq.,
 M.P., F.R.G.S.

Bullock, Edward, Esq.,
Handsworth, near Birm-
ingham

•Cardall, Rev. Wm., M.A.,
 Sec., of the Evangelical
 Alliance.

Clegg, Thomas, Esq.,
Manchester.

•Davis, Rev. James, Sec. of
 the Evangelical Alliance.

Shaw, Dr. Norton, Sec. of
the Royal Geographical
Society.

Snopp, Rev. C. B., Perry
Bar, near Birmingham.

★Now 8 Adolphi Terrace, Strand.

Fowler, R. N., Esq., F.R.G.S., 50, Cornhill.

La Trobe, C. J., Esq., F.R.G.S., late Governor of Victoria

La Trobe, Rev. P., Sec. of the Moravian Missions.

Lecke, Rear-Admiral Sir H. J., K.C.B., M.P.

•M'Arthur, Wm., Esq., Brixton-rise

Macleod, J. Lyons, Esq., F.R.G.S. late H.B.M.'s Consul at Mozambique. Society.

•Minton, Rev. Samuel, M.A., Minister of Percy Chapel

Richardson, Jonathan, Esq M.P.

Sykes. Col. W. H. r.i'., Vice President of the Royal Geographical Society.

•Thomas, Rev. Mesac, M.A. Sec. of the Colonial Church and School Society

Thompson, Geo., Esq., Drixton.

Tidman, Rev. Dr., Sec. Of the London Missionary Society.

Trestrail, Rev. Fred., Sec. of the Baptist Missionary Society.

Wingfield, R. W., Esq., J.P., Birmingham.

William Cardall and J. Lyons Macleod, *Hon. Secretaries*

Those marked thus (•) constitute the Executive Committee.

STATEMENT OF OBJECTS AND RULES

I. That the name of the Society be the "African Aid Society."

II. That its chief objects shall be to develop the material resources of Africa, Madagascar, and the adjacent Islands; and to promote the Christian civilization of the African races; as by these means the Society believes that the annihilation of the Slave Trade will ultimately be accomplished.

III. That for the attainment of these objects it will strive to employ the following and other suitable means:—

1. Encourage the production of cotton, silk, indigo, sugar, palm oil, &c., by the introduction of skilled labor, African or European, into those parts of the earth which are inhabited by the African race.
2. Assist, by loans or otherwise, Africans willing to emigrate from Canada and other parts to our West Indian Colonies, Liberia, Natal, and Africa generally, or to any countries that may offer a suitable field of labor.
3. Form Industrial Missions in harmony, where practicable, with the agency already established for the extension of Christianity in Africa.
4. Supply (as occasion may require) suitable Mechanical and Agricultural Implements for the use of the same.
5. Procure samples of every kind of native produce, for the purpose of submitting the same to the mercantile and manufacturing communities of this country, with a view to the promotion of legitimate commerce.
6. Encourage and assist exploring expeditions into the interior of Africa and Madagascar.

IV. That Subscribers of not less than Half a Guinea annually be Members of this Society, during the continuance of their subscriptions; that the subscriptions be payable in advance, and be considered due at the commencement of each year; that Donors of Ten Guineas and Collectors of Twenty Guineas be Life Members.

V. That the management of the Society be vested in a Patron, Vice-Patrons, President, Vice-Presidents, and a Council consisting of not less than Twenty Members.

VI. That a general Meeting of the Members of the Society be held in London in the spring of each year, when the financial statement shall be presented, and the Council elected for the year ensuing, who shall appoint an Executive Committee to conduct the business of the Society.

VII. That the Honorary and Corresponding Members may be nominated by the Council.

VIII. That any funded property of the Society be invested in the names of three Trustees, to be chosen by the Council, and that all orders for payments on account of the Society be signed by two Members of the Executive Committee and the Secretary.

IX. That the accounts of the Society be audited annually by a professional auditor, to be chosen by the General Meeting.

X. That the Council shall have power to appoint such officers and assistants as they shall deem necessary for the efficient conduct of the affairs of the Society, subject to the approval of the next Annual Meeting.

XXI. That the Council shall have power to convene Special General Meetings of the Members of the Society when necessary.

XII. That no alteration shall be effected in the constitution of the Society, except at the Annual Meeting, or at a Special General Meeting convened for the purpose on the requisition of Twenty Members.

In furtherance of the objects of this Society, the Executive Committee, with the generous aid of friends to this movement, have already assisted Dr. Delany and Professor Campbell (two colored gentlemen from America) with funds to enable them to continue their labors and to lay before the colored people of America the reports of the Pioneer Exploration Expedition into Abbeokuta, in West Africa, from which they have lately returned.

A correspondence has already been opened with Jamaica, Lagos in West Africa, Natal, the United States of America, and "The Fugitive-Aid Society"—which for the last *ten years* has been receiving and instructing fugitive Africans in agricultural and other pursuits on the Elgin settlement—at Buxton, Canada West.

The assistance of all friends to Christianity, Freedom, and lawful Commerce, as opposed to the Slave Trade and Slavery, is earnestly solicited.

"COTTON IS KING! IN AMERICA"
"COTTON IS BREAD! IN ENGLAND"

The free colored people of America are said to be looking forward to their ultimate removal from the United States, and are anxiously seeking for locations suitable for their final settlement in Africa or other intertropical regions; where they may obtain that freedom which is the inherent right of man, and by their industry acquire adequate independence.

The African Aid Society has been formed to assist this

movement, and to annihilate the slave trade, by encouraging the development of the resources of those countries inhabited by the African races generally, as well as to cause African free labor to supersede African slavery and degradation.

In Canada West no less than 45,000 colored persons, flying from slavery, have now taken refuge; willing to meet the rigors of the climate, so that they are assured of personal freedom under the aegis of the British flag. From the enactments lately made in some States of the Union, for the purpose of compelling all the free people of color either to leave the country or to be again reduced to a state of slavery, a considerable addition will, no doubt, shortly be made to the number of those who have already found their way to Canada; while, from physical causes, Canada can be looked upon by the colored only as a "City of Refuge."

Great Britain has for half a century been employing physical force for the suppression of the slave trade, which after the expenditure of upwards of forty millions sterling, and the noble sacrifice of the lives of some of the best and bravest of her sons, still exists. It is but just to state that the exportation of slaves from Africa has been reduced from 150,000 to 50,000 per annum, by the persevering effort of those who are opposed to a traffic disgraceful to Christianity.

Is the ultimate object of those who are opposed to this traffic its suppression or its annihilation? The annihilation of the slave trade and slavery in Africa was unquestionably the aim of the philanthropists who originated this great movement.

The experience of half a century has proved that physical force cannot destroy the traffic while there is a demand for slave labor. Diplomacy must be baffled in its well-intentioned efforts to oppose this traffic while the profits for carrying each slave from the continent of Africa to the island of Cuba amount to the enormous return of fourteen hundred percent.

It is a well-attested fact, that the same quality of cotton may be obtained from Africa for twenty millions of money for which Great Britain pays the slaveholders in America thirty millions per annum. If cotton can be sold in the Liverpool market at anything less than 4¾d. per lb., the slaveholders in America will cease to grow what, under altered circumstances, would be unprofitable. Cotton of middling quality (which is in the greatest demand) may be obtained in West and Eastern Africa at 4d. per lb.; and, already, cotton from Western Africa (Liberia) has been sent to Liverpool, there re-shipped, and sold at Boston, in the United States, at a less cost than cotton of a similar quality could be supplied from the Southern States of the Union.

The Executive Committee feel assured that the peaceful means adopted by this society for the Christian civilization of the African races require only the advocacy of *Christian Ministers* and the *Press* generally to be responded to by the people of Great Britain.

The horrors of the slave trade, as perpetrated on the continent of Africa and during the middle passage, can only be put an end to by the establishment of a lawful and a lucrative, a powerful and a permanent, trade between this country and Africa; which will have the effect of destroying the slave trade, spreading the Gospel of Christ, and civilizing the African races. For this purpose the support of the mercantile class is earnestly solicited for a movement which —commenced by the colored people of America flying from oppression—bids fair to open new cotton fields for the supply of British industry, and new markets for our commerce, realizing the sublime promise of Scripture, "Cast thy bread upon the waters, and after many days it shall return unto thee."

Alarmists point to the sparks in the cotton fields of America, while thoughtful men reflect that the commercial prosperity of this great country hangs upon a thread of cotton, which a blight of the plant, an insurrection among the slaves, an untimely frost, or an increased demand in the Northern States of the Union, might destroy; bringing to Lancashire first, and then to the whole kingdom, a return of the Irish famine of 1847, which reduced the population of that portion of the kingdom from eight to six millions.

The Southern States of the American Union are following the example of the infatuated Louis the Fourteenth of France. As he drove into exile thousands of his subjects engaged in manufactures and trade, who sought refuge in England and laid the foundation of our manufacturing supremacy, so are the Slave States now driving from their confines thousands of freed colored men. Where are the exiles to go? The Free States are too crowded, and Canada too cold for them. Can we not offer them an asylum in Jamaica and other colonies? They are the cream, the best of their race; for it is by long-continued industry and economy that they have been enabled to purchase their freedom, and joyfully will they seize the hand of deliverance which Great Britain holds out to them. We only want additional labor; give us that, and we shall very soon cultivate our own cotton.—*Slavery Doomed.*

FUGITIVE-AID SOCIETY IN CANADA

At a meeting held in the Town Hall, Manchester, on the 8th of August inst., the following remarks were made by Thomas Clegg, Esq., who presided on the occasion.

The Chairman said that they held but one opinion as to the horrors and evils of slavery; and he thought that most of them believed that one of the great benefits which would result from Africans trained in Canada being sent to Africa, would be that they could there, for the advantage of themselves and their country, grow cotton, sugar, and fifty other articles, which we much needed. During his first year's operations in getting cotton from Africa, all his efforts only purchased 235 lbs.; but in 1858, he got 219,615 lbs.; and he saw from one of the London papers of the previous day, that not less than 3,447 bales, or 417,087 lbs., were received from the West Coast during 1860. This rapid increase, in the early history of the movement, showed that Africa was the place that could grow cotton, and that Africans were the men who ought to grow it. (Hear, hear.) There was no part of Africa, of which he had heard, where cotton did not grow wild; there was no part of the world, except India, perhaps, in which cotton was cultivated, where it was not sought to obtain Africans as cultivators. Wild African cotton was worth from 1½ d. to 2¼ d. a pound more than the wild produce of India; cultivated cotton from the West Coast was worth, on an average, as much as New Orleans possibly could be. (Hear, hear.) He would undertake that good African cotton could be laid down free in Liverpool at 4¼d. per pound; that it should be equal to New Orleans; and at this moment such cotton was worth probably 6¼ d. per pound. (Hear, hear.) He looked upon this question as affecting not only the success of missions, but as affecting also the eternal welfare of the Africans and the temporal welfare of our people.

HEATHEN AND SLAVE-TRADE HORRORS

At Lagos, communication between the town and the shipping had been suspended for ten days, in consequence of the high surf at the entrance of the river and along the beach, and great difficulty was experienced in getting off the mails. The war in the interior, between the chiefs of Ibadan and Ijaye, continued with unabated fury; the former district is said to contain 100,000 inhabitants, and the latter 50,000. Abbeokuta had taken side with Ijaye, but at the last battle, which took place on the 5th of June, his people are reported to have suffered severely. The King of Dahomey was about to make an immense sacrifice of human life to the memory of the late King, his father. The *West African Herald*, of the 13th ult., referring to this intention, says: His Majesty Badahung, King of Dahomey, is about to make the 'Grand Custom' in honor of the late King Gezo. Determined to surpass all former monarchs in the magnitude of the ceremonies to be performed on this occasion, Badahung has made the most extensive preparations for the celebration of the Grand Custom. A great pit has been dug which is to contain human blood enough to float a canoe. Two thousand persons will be sacrificed on this occasion. The expedition to Abbeokuta is postponed, but the King has sent his army to make some excursions at the expense of some weaker tribes, and has succeeded in capturing many unfortunate creatures. The young people among these prisoners will be sold into slavery, and the old persons will be killed at the Grand Custom. Would to God this might meet the eyes of some of those philanthropic Englishmen who have some feeling for Africa! Oh! for some man of eloquence and influence to point out to the people of England the comparative uselessness of their expensive squadron out here, and the enormous benefits that must result to this country, and ultimately to England herself, morally and materially, if she would extend her establishments on this coast! Take away two-thirds of your squadron, and spend one-half its cost in creating more stations on shore, and greatly strengthening your old stations.—*The Times*, August 13, 1860.

The following extract from the *Times*, August 11, 1860, shows that noble hearts across the Atlantic are ready to respond to our call:—

A NOBLE LADY—Miss Cornelia Barbour, a daughter of the Hon. James Barbour, of Virginia, formerly Governor of that State, and a Member of President J. Q. Adams' Cabinet, has resolved to emancipate her numerous slaves, and locate them in a Free State, where they can enjoy liberty and (if they will) acquire property.—*New York Tribune*.

☞*Contributions to the Funds of this Society may be paid to the Chairman, the Hon. Secretary, or to the Society's account at the London and Westminster Bank, I, St. James's square. P.O. Orders to be made payable to the Honorary Secretaries at Charing-cross.*—AUGUST, 1860.

The subjoined paper has been issued by the African Aid Society London, England, which I give for the benefit of those desirous of going out under its auspices, as it will be seen that the Society is determined on guarding well against aiding such persons as are objectionable to us, and likely to be detrimental to our scheme:

AFRICAN AID SOCIETY
PAPER FOR INTENDING SETTLERS IN AFRICA

1. Are you desirous to leave   and go to the Land of your Forefathers. 2. Name. 3. Age. 4. Married or Single. 5. What Children (state ages:) Boys   , aged   years;   Girls   , aged   years. 6. How many of these will you take with you? 7. Of what church are you a member? 8. How long have you been so? 9. Can

you read and write? 10. Will you strive to spread the truths of the Gospel among the natives? 11. What work are you now doing? 12. What other work can you do well? 13. Have you worked on a plantation? 14. What did you do there? 15. Will you, in the event of the African Aid Society sending you and your family to Africa, repay to it the sum of   Dollars, as part of the cost of your passage and settlement there,   as soon as possible, that the same money may assist others to go there also?

N.B.—It is expected that persons desiring to settle in Africa, under the auspices of this society, should obtain Certificates from their Minister, and if possible from their Employer, or other competent person, as to their respectability, habits, and character. These certificates should be attached to this paper.

I have every confidence in the sincerity of the Christian gentlemen who compose the African Aid Society, and for the information of those who are unacquainted with the names of those noblemen and gentlemen, would state that the Lord Alfred Churchill is the learned Oriental traveler and Christian philanthropist, brother to His Grace the Duke of Marlborough and son-in-law of Right Hon. Lord Calthorpe; Right Hon. Lord Calthorpe is the great Christian nobleman who does so much for Churches in Great Britain, and member of Her Majesty's Privy Council; Sir Culling Eardley Eardley is time great promoter of the Evangelical Alliance; George Thompson, Esq., is the distinguished traveler and faithful friend of the slave, known in America as a Garrisonian Abolitionist; and J. Lyons Macleod, Esq., the indefatigable British Consul who so praiseworthily exerted himself, and brought the whole of his official power to bear against the slave-trade on the Mozambique Channel. There are other gentlemen of great distinction, whose positions are not explained in the council list, and a want of knowledge prevents my explaining.

Before leaving England for Scotland, I received while at Brighton, the following letter, which indicates somewhat the importance of our project, and shows, in a measure, the superiority of the people in our part of Africa, and what may be expected of them compared with some in other parts; and how the Portuguese influence has ruined them. I may add, that the writer, Mr. Clarence, is a gentleman of respectability, brother-in-law to Edmund Fry, Esq., the distinguished Secretary of the London Peace Society. Mr. Clarence has resided in that part of Africa for twenty-five years, and was then on a visit to his relatives:

DR. DELANY: Brighton, August 28, 1860
MY DEAR SIR—I am sorry that I am obliged to leave Brighton before you deliver your lectures, and as we may not meet again, I thought I would write you a few lines just to revive the subject that was passing our minds yesterday. I cannot but think, if it were practicable for a few thousands, or even hundreds, of your West Coast men to come round to the East Coast, that is, to Port Natal, an immense amount of good would be derived therefrom; not only in assisting to abolish the barbarous customs of our natives in showing them that labor is honorable for man, but that the English population would appreciate their services and that they would be able to get good wages. What we want is constant and reliable laborers; not those who come by fits and starts, just to work for a month and then be off. They must select their masters, and then make an engagement for twelve months; or it might be after a month on approval. Good laborers could get fifteen shillings per month, and as their services increased in value they would get twenty shillings, and their allowance of food, which is always abundant.

I have thought that some might work their passage down to the Cape of Good Hope in some of Her Majesty's Men-of-War, and from there they might work their passage in some of the coasting vessels that are continually plying backwards and forwards. My farm is only five miles from the Port. Should any ever come from your representations, direct them to me, and should I not require them myself I will give them such information as may lead them to find good masters. I have always said that Natal is the key to the civilization of South Africa; but, however, there are sometimes two keys to a door, and yours on the West, though a little north of the Line, may be the other; and, by God's blessing, I trust that the nations of the East and West may, before long, meet in Central Africa, not in hostile array, as African nations always have done, but in the bonds of Christian fellowship. Wishing you every success in your enterprize.

Believe me, dear Sir, yours most sincerely,

RALPH CLARENCE

NOTE—Mr. Clarence is requesting to be sent some of our industrious natives from Western Africa, as he informed me that those in the East think it disreputable to work. The term "master" is simply English; it means employer. The "fifteen" and "twenty" referred to, means shillings sterling.

Commercial Relations

I have only to add, as a finality of my doings and mission in Great Britain, that in Scotland I fully succeeded in establishing commercial relations for traffic in all kinds of native African produce, especially cotton, which businesses are to be done directly and immediately between us and them, without the intervention or agencies of any society or association whatever. The only agencies in the case are to be the producers, sellers, and buyers—the Scottish house dealing with us as men, and not children. These arrangements are made to facilitate, and give us the assurance of the best encouragement to prosecute vigorously commercial enterprises—especially, as before stated, the cotton culture—the great source of wealth to any people and all civilized nations.

Business Integrity

The British people have the fullest confidence in our integrity to carry out these enterprises successfully, and now only await our advent there, and commencement to do anything necessary we may desire, or that the circumstances justify. Each individual is regarded as a man in these new relations, and, as such, expected to make his own contracts according to business custom, discharging in like manner his individual obligations. It must here be expressly understood that there are to be nothing but *business relations* between us, their entire confidence and dependence being in the self-reliant, independent transactions of black men themselves. We are expected, and will be looked for, to create our own ways and means among ourselves as other men do.

Public Endorsement

As an earnest of the estimate set upon our adventure, I subjoin the names of a number of the leading commercial British journals—the two first being English, and all the others Scottish, in the midst of manufacturing districts, and all speaking favorably of the project:

The Leeds Mercury, the Newcastle Daily Chronicle, the Glasgow Herald, the Glasgow Examiner, the Scottish Guardian, the North British Daily Mail, the Glasgow Morning Journal, the Mercantile Advertiser, and others. (For absence of these notices, see author's prefatory note.)

FROM THE DAILY CHRONICLE

Newcastle-on-Tyne, Monday, September 17th, 1860

DANGER AND SAFETY.— . . . The cotton of the United States affords employment to upwards of three millions of people in England, and a famine of cotton would be far worse than a famine of bread; the deficiency of the latter could be supplied; but the destruction of the cotton crop in America would be an evil of unparalleled magnitude, and against which we have no present protection . . . From the district of Lagos on the Gold coast, near the kingdom of Dahomey, there comes amongst us Dr. Delany with promises of a deeply interesting exposition of the prospects of Africa, and the probabilities of the civilization and elevation of the black races. He is a *bona fide* descendant of one of the elite families of Central Africa, a highly educated gentleman, whose presence at the International Statistical Congress was noticed by Lord Broughham, and whose remarks in the sanitary section of the Congress upon epidemics were characterized by a great knowledge of the topic combined with genuine modesty. He is a physician of African blood, educated in America, who has revisted the lands of his ancestry, and proposes a most reasonable and feasible plan to destroy the slave trade, by creating a *cordon*, or fringe of native civilization, through which the kidnappers could not penetrate from without, and through which no slaves could be transported from within. Dr. Delany is one of the Commissioners sent out by the convention of the colored people of Canada and the United States. He has recently returned from the Yoruba country, adjoining the territory of the King of Dahomey, and desires to elicit a favorable consideration for the African Aid Society. His explorations have been productive of the most promising results, his fellow blacks having everywhere received him with distinguished honors. His anecdotes are interesting, and his lectures are illustrated by specimens of native produce and manufactures highly curious. Of his lectures at Brighton and other places we have read lengthy reports, which represent the influence these addresses have produced, and which speak in eulogistic terms of Dr. Delany's matter and manner. The subject is one of vast importance to England, and we trust that we may witness ere long a proper appreciation of it.

FROM THE GLASGOW HERALD

All this betokens a considerable degree of intelligence. The towns had their market-places; in one of these, that of Ijaye Dr. Delany saw many thousands of persons assembled, and carrying on a busy traffic. What a field might thus, in the course of time, be opened for European commerce.

FROM THE LEEDS MERCURY (ENGLAND)

*Published by E. Baines, Esq., M.P., and Sons,
December 8th, 1860*

ELEVATION OF THE COLORED RACE, AND OPENING OUT OF THE RESOURCES OF AFRICA.—An important movement for opening out the resources of a vast portion of the continent of Africa has been made by some of the most intelligent colored people of the United States and Canada. Having formed a society with this object in view, among others, Dr. Delany and Professor Campbell were commissioned to go out and explore a considerable portion of Western Africa, near to the mouths of the Niger, and not far from the equator. A report of this expedition is in progress by Dr. Delany, who is himself so fully convinced of the advantages which the rich resources of that part of Africa offer, that he has concluded to remove his family there immediately. A meeting of the Leeds Anti-Slavery Committee was held on Wednesday night, Wm. Scholefield, Esq., in the chair, when valuable information was communicated by Dr. Delany and William Howard Day, Esq., M.A., from Canada, who is connected with this movement.

The following summary of their remarks will be found of deep interest:—

Wm. Howard Day, M.A., having been called upon, pointed out the necessity for an active anti-slavery organization in this country, as was so well expressed by the Chairman, to keep the heart of the English people warm upon the subject of human bondage . . . By the production of cotton slavery began to be a power. So that as the cotton interest increased the testimony of the Church decreased. Cotton now is three-fifths of the production of the South. So that the Hon. Amasa Walker, formerly Republican Secretary of State for the State of Massachusetts, at the meeting held in London, August 1, 1859, and presided over by Lord Brougham, really expressed the whole truth when he said—"While cotton is fourteen cents per pound slavery will never end." Now we propose to break the back of this monopoly in America by raising in Africa—in the African's own home—as well as in the West Indies, cotton of the same quality as the American, and at a cheaper rate. It had been demonstrated by Mr. Clegg, of Manchester, that cotton of superior quality could be laid down at Liverpool cheaper from Africa than America. We have sent my friend, Dr. Delany, to see what Africa is, and he will tell you the results—so very favorable—of his exploration. Then we feel that we have in Canada the colored men to pioneer the way—men reared among the cotton of the United States, and who have found an asylum among us. The bone and sinew is in Africa—we wish to give it direction. We wish thereby to save to England millions of pounds by the difference in price between the two cottons; we wish to ward off the blow to England which must be felt by four millions of people interested in the article to he produced if an untimely frost or an insurrection should take place—and, above all, to lift up Africa by means of her own children. After speaking of the

organization among the colored people, which sent out
Dr. Delany and of which Mr. Day is president, he said
one of the means to secure these ends was the establishment of a press upon a proper footing in Canada among
the fugitive slaves; and to collect for that is now his especial work. It would aid powerfully, it was hoped, in
another way. Already American prejudice has rolled in
upon the borders of Canada—so that schoolhouse doors
are closed in the faces of colored children, and colored
men denied a place upon juries merely because of their
color. It was with difficulty that last year even in Canada
they were able to secure the freedom of a kidnapped little
boy who was being dragged through the province to be
sold in the slave-mart of St. Louis. In view of all these
points, hastily presented, he asked the good will and
active aid of all the friends of liberty.

Dr. M. R. Delany, whose name has become so celebrated in connection with the Statistical Congress, was
invited to state what he had contemplated in going to
Africa, and if he would kindly do so, what he had discovered there. Dr. Delany first dwelt upon the expectation
which had been raised in his mind when a young man,
and in the minds of the colored people of the United
States, by the beginning of the anti-slavery work there by
William Lloyd Garrison and his coadjutors. They had
found, however, that all the anti-slavery people were not
of the stamp of Mr. Garrison, who, he was proud to say,
believed in giving to colored men just the same rights and
privileges as to others, and that Mr. Garrison's idea had
not, by the professed friends of the black man, been
reduced to practice. And finding that self-reliance was the
best dependence, he and others had struck out a path for
themselves. After speaking of the convention of colored
people, which he and others called in 1854, to consider
this subject of self-help, and of the general organization
which began then, and in which Mr. Day succeeded him

as president, he said he went to Africa to find a locality suitable for a select emigration of colored people; if possible, a large cotton-growing region, and with a situation accessible by civilization. All this he had found, with, in addition, a well-disposed and industrious people. The facts which Dr. Delany grouped together as to the climate and soil; as to productions and trade; as to the readiness of the people to take hold of these higher ideas; and as to the anxiety of the people to have him and his party return, were new and thrilling. An interesting conversation ensued on the points brought forward, and the following minute, moved by Mr. Wilson Armistead, and seconded by the Rev. Dr. Brewer, was unanimously passed:—

That the thanks of this meeting be tendered to Dr. Delany and Wm. Howard Day, Esq., for the valuable information received from them, with an ardent desire that their plans for the elevation of their race may be crowned with success, and it is the opinion of this meeting that they be made materially to hasten the extinction of the slave-trade and slavery.

Character of Commercial Relations

The commercial relations entered into in Scotland are with the first business men in the United Kingdom, among whom are Henry Dunlop, Esq., Ex-Lord Provost of Glasgow, one of the largest proprietors in Scotland; Andrew Stevenson, Esq., one of the greatest cotton dealers; and Messrs. Crum, Graham & Co., 111 Virginia Place, Glasgow, one of the heaviest firms in that part of the old world, which is the house with which I have negotiated for an immediate, active and practical prosecution of our enterprise, and whose agency in Europe for any or all of our produce, may be fully relied on.

I speak from personal acquaintance with these extensively-known, high-standing gentlemen.

Reliable Arrangements

One of the most important parts of such an adventure as this, is to have reliable Foreign Agencies, and these have been fully secured; as whilst these gentlemen, as should all business men, deal with us only on business terms, yet they have entered into the matter as much as Christians and philanthropists, to see truth and right prevail whereby humanity may be elevated, as for anything else; because they are already wealthy, and had they been seeking after wealth, they certainly could and would have sought some more certainly immediate means.

I left Scotland December 3rd, and sailed from Liverpool the 13th via Londonderry, arriving at Portland the 25th, the epoch of the Christian Era, and in Chatham the 29th.

XVI THE TIME TO GO TO AFRICA

Caution against Danger

THE best time for going to Africa is during "the rainy season," which commences about the middle or last of April, ending near or about the first of November. By going during this period, it will be observed that you have no sudden transition from cold to heat, as would be the case did you leave in cold weather for that country. But the most favorable time to avoid the *heavy surf* at Lagos, is from the first of October to the first of April, when the surges in the roadstead are comparatively small and not imminently dangerous. And I here advise and caution all persons intending to land there, not to venture over the heavy-rolling surf of the bar in one of those native canoes.

Safety in Landing

Yet persons can land with safety at any season of the year; but for this there must be a proper boat. Any person going there at present ought not to land if the surf is high, without *Captain Davies' large sail-boat*, which is as safe as a tug, and rides the sea like a swan. Send him word to send his *largest boat at the best hour for landing.* The Captain is a native merchant, and most obliging gentleman.

A Tender

So soon as we get a Tender (called in America, steam-tug and tow-boat), which will be one of the first things done so soon as we get to Lagos, landing will be as safe at any and all times there as in the harbor at New York or Liverpool. For the information of many intelligent persons who are not aware of it, I would state that a pilot or tender has to take vessels into both of these great seaports on account of shoal water.★

Rainy Season

The rainy season usually thought by foreigners to be "wet, muddy, and disagreeable weather," so far from this, is the most agreeable season of the year. Instead of steady rains for several days incessantly, as is common during "rainy weather" in the temperate zones, there is seldom or never rain during a whole day. But every day to a certainty during this season it rains, sometimes by showers at intervals, and sometimes a heavy rain for one, two, or three hours at a time—but seldom so long as three hours—when it clears up beautifully, leaving an almost cloudless sky. The rains usually come up very suddenly, and as quickly cease when done.

★I have received information from London, that an iron steam Tender has already been sent out to Lagos by an English house.

Drizzling Rain, Sudden Showers

There is seldom or never such a thing in this part of Africa as a "drizzling" or mizzling rain, all suddenly coming on and as suddenly passing off; and should one be out and see indications of an approaching rain, they must hurry to a near shelter, so suddenly does the shower come on.

Tornadoes

Tornadoes are sudden gusts or violent storms of wind and rain, which are more or less feared, but which may always be known from other storms on their aproach, by the blackness of the clouds above, with the *segment of a circle of lighter cloud* just beneath the dark, and above the horizon.

Summer

The entire *wet* season may be justly termed the *summer* instead of "winter," as the old writers have it; and it is observable that at the commencement of Spring in the temperate zones (March) vegetation starts forth in Africa with renewed vigor.

Winter

Winter is during the *dry* season, and not the "wet," for the above reason; and it is also worthy of remark, that during autumn in the temperate zone (from October to the last of November) the foliage in Africa begins to fade and fall from the trees in large quantities.

Harmattans

It is during this season that the *harmattans* prevail, (from two to three weeks in December) which consist of a *dry cold* and *not* a "dry hot" wind as we have been taught; when furniture and wooden-ware *dries* and *cracks* for want of moisture, and the thermometer frequently rates as low as 54 deg. Fahr. in the evening and early in the morning; when blankets on the bed will not be out of place, and an evening and morning fire may add to your comfort.

XVII CONCLUDING SUGGESTIONS

Native Mariners

IT may not be generally known as a fact, which is of no little importance in the industrial economy of Africa, that vessels of every class, of all foreign nations, are manned and managed by native Africans, so soon as they enter African waters.

The Krumen are the watermen or marines generally of Africa, going in companies of greater or less numbers, with one in the lead called "headman," who, hiring all the others, makes contracts with a vessel, which is met outside of the roadsteads or harbors, to supply a certain number of men to manage it during her coasting voyage. They usually bring with them the recommendations of all the commanders whose vessels they have managed on the coast. These are generally carried in the hat to prevent getting wet, and sometimes in calabashes, stopped up like a bottle, or in a tin can or case, (when such can be obtained,) suspended by a string like a great square medal around the neck.

So expert have these people become in marine affairs, that, with the exception of navigation, a vessel at sea might be managed entirely by many of those companies of Krumen. Everything that is to be done as the common work of seamen, is done by them during their engagement on the coasting vessels. The agility with which they scale the shrouds and rigging, mounting frequently to the very pinnacle of the main-mast head, or going out to the extreme end of the yard arms, is truly surprising. In these feats, they are far more dextrous than the white civilians.

The Fever—Stages Of

In cases of real intermittent fever—fever and ague or chills and fever—there are usually three distinct stages when the attack comes on—on what is usually termed *fever day*: the *cold* or shivering stage, the *hot* or burning stage, succeeded by the *sweating*.

Cold Stage

So soon as there are symptoms of a chill, a cup of quite hot ginger or cinnamon tea—not too strong—may be taken, the person keeping out of the sun, and, if inclined, going to bed and covering warmly. He should always undress, putting on a night-shirt or gown, for the convenience of changing when required. A hot cup of tea, of any kind, is better than nothing, when neither cinnamon nor ginger is convenient.

Kneading or Friction-Bath. Hot Stage

During the hot stage, the person must be kept as cool as possible, and when the fever is at its height—and, indeed, it is well to commence long before this—the entire person, from head to foot, should be continually bathed by a free application of cold water, used *plentifully* and *frequently changed* during the application, with a large sponge, napkin, or cloth of some kind.

Lime–Bath

An excellent addition to the water is the juice of limes or lemons, and *less* of the first (lime) than the last is required, because of the superior strength of the one to the other.

Soda

Soda may also be used in the bath as an adjuvant to the water—not with the lime juice, of course, because they would effervesce or disagree. When lime or lemon juice is used, care should be taken, in the use of it, that it be not too strong: say, use two lemons, or one and a half limes if large, to a pail of water—as it will produce irritation on all of the tender parts of the person, and even over the general surface. A lime bath once or twice a week, in the absence of all fever, is said to be an excellent hygeian or prophylactic treatment. But, by all means, don't neglect the cold water application during the hot stage.

Sweating Stage

So soon as the sweating commences, the patient must have sufficient covering to prevent taking cold, which is then very readily done, in consequence of the general relaxation of the system and open state of the pores. When the sweating ceases, the shirt or gown must be immediately taken off, the entire person sponged off in clear lukewarm or air-cold water, fresh clean clothes put on, the sheets and wet bed-clothes removed by clean ones supplying their places; and in no case must a person ever be permitted to keep on the same clothes after the sweating stage, as the *virus* or fever-poison is expelled through the medium of the sweat and pores, and consequently absorbed by the clothing. The clothes should be changed *every day*, whether there be perspiration or not.

All the stages

Either of these symptoms is to be treated as advised, independently of the other in the order of arrangement.

Fatigue-Clothes—Caution

Persons should be careful not to sleep in sweaty clothes, especially those in which they have traveled; and they should be cautious not to sleep in the same clothes worn on any day, as before but slightly alluded to. Clean, unsoiled night-clothes should be put on every evening, and those which may be worn again should be well aired and sunned during the day.

Colonization—an Error in Philanthropy

The Colonization Society has committed a great error in its philanthropic arrangements of providing for *six months' passiveness* after going to Africa. The *provisions, for those who require them*, I do not object to, but the *passiveness* is fatally injurious.

Activity Conducive to Health

Instead of going to Africa and quietly sitting down in utter idleness, in anticipation *waiting in anxious expectation for the fever to come*—in which cases the person becomes much more susceptible—did they go directly about some active employment, to keep both mind and body properly exercised, I am certain that there would not be one-fourth of the mortality that there is even now, which is comparatively little.

Evidences of the Fact

This will account for the reason that, among the numerous travelers and explorers who visit such countries, there is so much less, nay, so seldom any mortality from disease, compared with the missionaries, whose lives are rather easy and inactive, except the really energetic ones, who generally are they who survive. And I have the testimony of my friends Professor Crummell of Liberia College, late of Mount Vaughn High School, a most industrious, persevering gentleman, and W. Spencer Anderson, Esq., the largest sugar and coffee grower in Liberia, also a most energetic industrious gentleman—who corroborate my opinion on this important subject. Indeed, the people generally seem to have been long conscious of this fact, since among them they have an adage: "The *more* work, the *less* fever." But no one should infer that it meant that they should exercise without regard to care and judgment, with all the precautions and observations on health laid down in the preceding pages. I return of course, to Africa, with my family.

CLASSICS *in* BLACK STUDIES SERIES

Martin R. Delany, *The Condition,
Elevation, Emigration, and Destiny of the
Colored People of the United States
Official Report of the Niger Valley Exploring Party*

Anna E. Dickinson, *What Answer?*

Frederick Douglass,
My Bondage and My Freedom

W. E. B. Du Bois, *Darkwater*

W. E. B. Du Bois, *The Negro*

T. G. Steward, *Buffalo Soldiers:
The Colored Regulars in the United States Army*

Booker T. Washington and Others,
The Negro Problem

Ida B. Wells-Barnett, *On Lynchings*